Non-Demo e Arab Spring

"Reflective, objective, and expertly written, this is an important contribution to the literature on post-Arab Spring comparative authoritarianism. Essential reading for scholars and practitioners alike."

—Christopher M. Davidson, *Henry Jackson Society, UK*

"Due-Gundersen provides a timely analysis of non-democratic legitimacy within the context of the Arab Spring. Case studies of Bahrain, Egypt, Jordan, and Tunisia highlight how regimes employ combinations of socioeconomic and political agents to justify the continuation of nondemocratic rule. His creative use of discourse analysis makes a major contribution to our understanding of why authoritarianism remains the dominate form of governance in North Africa and the Middle East."

—Ronald Bruce St John, *Independent Scholar, USA*

"Theoretically nuanced and full of fascinating detail reflecting his intimate knowledge of the area, Due-Gundersen deftly analyses the contrasting strategies of authoritarian governments to cultivate legitimacy for their regimes during the Arab Spring. This book is an important contribution to debates on the politics of authoritarian stability and democratization in the Middle East and North Africa."

—Francis Owtram, *University of Exeter, UK*

"In the wake of the Arab Spring, now a decade ago, a large number of books have been written to explain the resilience of dictatorships in the region. Defending Dictatorship by Nicolai DueGundersen will undoubtedly emerge as one of the most astute and insightful, relying on a careful analysis of what rulers in the Middle East themselves have put forward in defense of their governments and their actions. Detailed, and relying in part on a number of social scientific earlier research, it will prove invaluable to those trying to understand why authoritarian regimes in the region have been so successful at resisting real political reforms."

—Dirk Vandewalle, *Dartmouth College, USA*

"Impressively researched and engagingly written, Defending Dictatorship offers a rich and compelling analysis of the ways in which regimes in the Middle East – monarchies and republics alike – sought to maintain legitimacy during the Arab Spring. Due-Gundersen uses case studies to draw out and examine the range of responses that break new ground in the study of contemporary Jordan, Bahrain, Egypt, and Tunisia. The result is a volume that is as accessible and readable as it is timely and relevant."

—Kristian Coates Ulrichsen, *Rice University's Baker Institute for Public Policy, USA*

"At a time of widespread political crises and the resurgence of authoritarian rule, critical analysis of the inner workings of such forms of political organisation and their discursive justification are of paramount importance. Nicolai Due-Gundersen's timely book Defending Dictatorship offers a powerful analysis of the ways in which rulers across the Middle East sought to ensure their survival in the face of popular protest. Wide in scope yet rich in empirical detail, this is a must read for anyone wanting to understand the ongoing survival of authoritarian regimes."

—Simon Mabon, *Lancaster University, UK*

Nicolai Due-Gundersen

Non-Democratic Legitimacy During the Arab Spring

Defending Dictatorship

palgrave
macmillan

Nicolai Due-Gundersen
Geneva, Switzerland

https://doi.org/10.1007/978-3-031-11882-1

This Palgrave Macmillan imprint is published by the registered company Springer Nature Switzerland AG
The registered company address is: Gewerbestrasse 11, 6330 Cham, Switzerland
(www.springernature.com/mycopy)

Contents

1 Introduction 1

1.1 Analyzing the Defense of Dictatorship 1

1.2 Defending Tradition or Buying off the Masses? 5

References 7

2 A Historical Overview of MENA Politics Leading Up to the Arab Spring 9

2.1 Introduction 9

2.2 Legitimizing Dictatorship: Religion, Regimes and Resources 10

2.3 Historical Context 19

References 31

3 Case Studies 37

3.1 Introduction 37

3.2 The Hashemite Kingdom of Jordan 38

3.3 The Kingdom of Bahrain 55

3.4 Mubarak's Egypt 71

3.5 Ben Ali's Tunisia 86

3.6 Understanding MENA Monarchies 93

3.6.1 Bahrain's Sectarianism and Jordan's Tribalism 98

3.7 Conclusion 100

References 102

4 The Speeches Defending Dictatorship During the Arab Spring 111
4.1 Introduction 111
4.2 Speeches of Legitimacy During the Arab Spring 112
4.2.1 The Hashemite Kingdom of Jordan's Abdullah II 112
4.2.2 The Kingdom of Bahrain's Hamad Bin Isa Al-Khalifa 120
4.2.3 Egypt's President Mubarak 128
4.2.4 Tunisia's President Ben Ali 133
References 143

5 Tyranny and the Constitution: Formalizing Dictatorship During the Arab Spring 147
5.1 Introduction 147
5.2 Constitutions, Speeches and the Arab Spring 148
5.2.1 Constitution of the Hashemite Kingdom of Jordan 148
5.2.2 Constitution of the Kingdom of Bahrain 156
5.2.3 Constitution of the Arab Republic of Egypt 164
5.2.4 Constitution of the Republic of Tunisia 169
References 184

6 Conclusion 189
References 195

Appendices 197

Bibliography 215

Index 239

CHAPTER 1

Introduction

1.1 Analyzing the Defense of Dictatorship

I had not expected praise of Crown Prince Muhammad bin Salman when I first snuck into Saudi Arabia. "I do believe [MBS] is changing this country", one Saudi citizen insisted on my trip to Riyadh. "He is closer to the younger generation and is bringing the change that youth want. A generation ago, my parents would be closed-minded, using religion as an excuse. My uncle would say, women shouldn't work as it's against Islam. Or my parents would say their children shouldn't study abroad as it's against Islam. That's changing" (Due-Gundersen, 2020). I had applied for and received an online tourist visa within minutes of completing the application, despite appearances on Al Jazeera and publications criticizing the Middle East monarchies. As Covid began sweeping across the Middle East and looming across Europe, I was tempted to cancel my trip. After email exchanges with colleagues, I stuck to my plan. "You'll be fine", assured one contact working as an energy analyst in Qatar and Riyadh. "Just don't get political".

Of course, the same day I was exposed to praise of MBS had to be the same day I was arrested. An enthusiastic tour of ruins ended with a bulky Jeep pulling over. I ignored the car and kept taking photos of what I thought was an ancient structure. The car door opened. A uniformed figure emerged.

"Excuse me, are you taking photos?".

N. Due-Gundersen, *Non-Democratic Legitimacy During the Arab Spring*,
https://doi.org/10.1007/978-3-031-11882-1_1

After a friendly chat with several officers at the local station, I was released. The building that had caught my camera's eye was not a tourist attraction but for the Saudi police, conveniently designed to blend in with the historic setting of old Riyadh. In exchange for my misunderstanding, the police got my fingerprint and my signature. The printed form bore the Saudi emblem, its accusations all in Arabic.

I gripped the proffered pen. "What exactly am I signing?" I had to ask.

One officer smiled warmly. "It's just to acknowledge that you took prohibited photos. And you promise not to do so again".

A stroke of the pen and I could leave. When I returned to London and talked again to my contacts, I realized I was lucky.

"It could have been worse", said a high-ranking analyst in Washington D.C. "If the officers were in a bad mood, they could have jailed you". He smiled. "And remember, you used a tourist visa to enter Saudi Arabia for journalism. You'd have been in trouble if they'd looked up your social media presence".

My wife also confirmed that being a Westerner gave me a huge privilege. If my passport had been Egyptian or Syrian, it's unlikely I would have left that station.

Saudi Arabia wants tourism. And it wants the Arab Spring to be forgotten. Having lived across the Middle East, I am more than aware of what I should and should not discuss in the streets of Riyadh, Kuwait or Cairo. Yet, if regimes want to deny political freedoms, other privileges must be granted to maintain their powerbase.

It was my first arrest in the Hashemite Kingdom of Jordan that encouraged me to think about who benefitted from dictatorship, how regimes maintain support, like a steady flow of oxygen feeding struggling lungs. One night outside a mall, we argued with a plainclothes police officer, mistaking him for a rude passenger shouting at our cab driver. After he grabbed my arm, my wife intervened. Only when he demanded her ID card did we realize who he was.

"We're being arrested", my wife sobbed. Another officer, clearly uniformed, escorted us to the station.

"You are in our country as a guest", a senior officer warned. "We will not take any action this time but next time, there will be consequences".

My wife called her boss, a Jordanian with connections or *wasta* in Arabic. It was because of his privilege that we could file a formal complaint. He arrived, called his cousin. The mood at the station changed so quickly.

Suddenly, the senior officer was scared. He politely gave me his card. "Call me if you need anything. Now, there will be an investigation".

I never did call his number. I didn't have to. The next time we drove past that mall, the police van that was usually parked by the entrance was gone. I never saw any of those officers again.

When you begin to live in the Middle East and marry a local, when you cease to be tourist and start to become family, you realize that regimes oversee two nations. The official nation is one diversifying from oil wealth, following Visions 2030 and 2040, the mirage for tourists and business. Beneath lies the true nation, established by force, run by oil or aid, with loyalty through patronage. It is this reality that was challenged by the Arab Spring. And as protestors took to the streets with their slogans, regimes talked back.

"I have understood everyone", insisted Tunisia's Ben Ali. "The unemployed, the needy, the politician and those demanding more freedoms" (Ben Ali, 2011). Ben Ali's pleas were contrasted by Mubarak's clueless confidence when protestors swarmed Cairo's Tahrir Square. "I am addressing the youth of Egypt today in Tahrir Square and across the country. I am addressing you all from the heart, a father's dialogue with his sons and daughters" (British Broadcasting Corporation, 2011).

Both presidents' pleas were met with disdain. They each resigned within a day or less of their final speeches. However, their kingly counterparts remained on their thrones.

"Let us speak frankly", insisted Jordan's Abdullah II, "about some slogans raised by a limited number of protestors—'overthrow the regime'. Every individual in this society is part of the regime [and] empty slogans and attempts to incite chaos and *fitna* (sedition) are rejected by Jordanians" (Royal Hashemite Court, 2012).

If Jordan's Abdullah II had the confidence to discuss protest slogans calling for his overthrow, Bahrain's King Hamad bin Isa al-Khalifa was more empowered after Saudi and regional intervention. The once reform-minded autocrat saw unrest as part of a wider conspiracy. "[The] Government of Bahrain was not in a position to provide evidence of links between Iran and specific events in our country this year (2011). But this propaganda, an objective fact to be observed by all who have eyes and ears and comprehend Arabic, not only directly challenges the stability and sovereignty of our country, but also poses a threat to the security and stability of [the Gulf countries]. We hope that the Iranian leadership will reflect and abandon this policy of enmity and discord" (Bahrain

Independent Commission of Inquiry, 2011). Appealing to fellow Sunni monarchs and feeding the fear of Shia'a intervention had mobilized the Peninsula Shield Force, the Gulf's military arm into action. Bahrain was a lynchpin in the Gulf, too strategic to see revolution. With demonstrations suppressed, Hamad's next response was to buy off protestors. "In addition to retrials and reinstatement [from job dismissals], affected persons have access to a range of remedies, including the newly established Victims Compensation Fund" (ibid.). The Victims Compensation Fund was a direct response to the Arab Spring and came atop other welfare increases, a pattern followed by many oil states during unrest.

Did surviving monarchs choose their words more carefully than dead presidents (Ben Ali and Mubarak both passed within months of each other)? While countering the Arab Spring required more than sweet talk, the series of protests that began in 2010 and is still discussed in 2022 saw many regimes forced to defend dictatorship. This required not only crackdowns but political persuasion.

Linguist John Searle understood the weight of words. For him, any act of speaking (or speech act) by a president or king was an intentional political act to convey messages and, more importantly, issue instructions (called essential conditions) (Searle, 1965, pp. 1–2). Searle's understanding of political persuasion includes acknowledging that a legitimate speech act must be given through rules that are mutually accepted by speaker and listeners (such as in a specific language) but also includes filtering speeches through the speaker's issuance of promises and threats, again linked to the speaker's desire for their instructions to be obeyed (ibid., pp. 3, 10–11). Many promises were certainly made during the Arab Spring. "[W]e'll see the peaceful transition of power", Mubarak insisted in his final address. In addition, Mubarak hastily promised constitutional reforms. "[N]ational dialogue has focused on the setting up of a constitutional committee that will look into the required amendments of the constitution and the needed legislative reforms" (British Broadcast Corporation, 2011). Libya's Muammar Gaddafi made no such promises but issued plenty of threats in the final televised address before his demise. "I'm calling on the millions to purify Libya inch by inch, house by house, home by home, street by street, person by person, until the country is clean of dirt and impurities" (Warden, 2011).

Searle's Speech Acts is an analytical framework that parallels the themes explored in this book of promises made, threats issued and more importantly political persuasion. Hence, each analyzed speech is filtered through

Searle's Speech Acts to understand the legitimacy of promises and threats under what Searle calls preparatory conditions or the specific political and historical context of each regime when the speech is given (Searle, 1965, p. 15). Such analysis is then measured against the reactions of citizens. Did citizens stop protesting? Did they continue to accept non-democratic rule? Ultimately, this understanding of political persuasion seeks to answer one question: can regimes defend dictatorship?

1.2 Defending Tradition or Buying off the Masses?

It was my second visit to Kuwait. This time, I was spending a month in the country rather than three rapid days. My wife was visiting the Kuwaiti branch of her employer and we were spending time with Arab expats who'd been living in Kuwait for years. The evening sun was bright as we sped past a Ferrari dealer and reached the highway. Palatial houses dotted both sides.

"Over here we have the usual hotels", my wife's colleague beamed. "Hilton, Blue Radisson". He pointed casually to an adjacent compound, tucked in by a generous driveway. "This belongs to the royals. One of the palaces for the ruling Al-Sabah family".

My jaw dropped in disbelief. The palace was on a street lined with buildings visited by the public. Its security consisted of a simple barrier and guard station, staffed by a single officer.

"Oil money", my wife chimed in, noticing my expression. "We have none of that in Jordan".

She was right. Jordan's Abdullah II might have championed himself as a man of the people, but his family's palaces were far away from them. In Aqaba by the Red Sea, Hashemite property was on the other side of the city, away from his citizens. Security was high. Indeed, when I worked for a Jordanian NGO, we participated in a conference that saw the appearance of two royal family members. On stage, the Prince and Princess freely moved toward the podium for their respective speeches. However, at the conference's end, security swarmed the couple, with the Prince being ushered out more hurriedly than the Princess. As I tried to push through journalists and snap my own photos of the Prince, the couple got separated. "Everyone wants a photo of the Prince!" I quipped to a colleague I thought was nearby. I turned around to confirm. The Princess looked back at me in shock. We were three feet apart. To this day, I'm not sure what offended her: my undiplomatic comment or the fact that I'd gotten so physically close.

Despite a 1985 assassination attempt on then-ruling Jaber al-Ahmad al-Sabah, Kuwait is not Jordan (United Press International, 1985). Resources keep people comfortable. And comfortable citizens have no reason to attack their rulers. Perhaps, this is why a royal palace in a busy street is normal in Kuwait but shunned in Jordan. Perhaps, this is why a Jordanian Princess did not like a stranger cutting through her security detail, and why our conferences with such esteemed speakers needed military officers (which I was instructed to omit from our promotional photos from the event).

Political analysts Yom and Gause have referred to the phenomenon of "resilient royals" during the Arab Spring. Why is it that kings kept thrones while republicans lost their right to rule? "Arab kingships enjoy traditional religious and tribal legitimacy, which induces exceptionally loyal support from citizens" (Yom & Gause, 2012, p. 75). Indeed, Yom and Gause outline that the "stability of monarchies during the Arab Spring has so strikingly defied theoretical explanations that many analysts [...] now contend that inherent cultural and institutional forces make such regimes *more* durable than their republican counterparts" (ibid., p. 77). In other words, it's no surprise that monarchy survived the Arab Spring as they embody historical traditionalism, an accepted form of family rule that became a socio-political norm. Perhaps, equally important, monarchs did not seize power through coups but were part of what is presented as a natural succession. In an ironic ode to succession, many coups that have occurred in Arab monarchies have been a family affair, with son replacing father and thus maintaining the uninterrupted rule of the same royal family (BBC, 2016). Republics, on the other hand, have often been the result of coups replacing traditional monarchies. In other words, these eventual presidents-for-life became new (and sometimes young) rulers with no links to religion or traditionalism. Instead, these "successors" in Egypt, Libya and Yemen hailed from a military background and gained popular support through the demonization of West-leaning monarchies and by establishing ruling bargains or socio-economic benefits such as employment, subsidies and welfare in exchange for citizens forfeiting political involvement and representation (Kartveit & Jumbert, 2014, p. 9). While Arab oil monarchs also utilize the ruling bargain, it is their links to traditionalism and religion that has allowed them to survive the Arab Spring, so much so that Yom and

Gause agreed that the "Arab Spring might as well be called the Arab *Republics'* Spring" (Yom & Gause, 2012, p. 74).

From this perspective, non-democratic legitimacy during the Arab Spring was maintained through emphasizing either traditionalism or welfare. Hence, this book will also examine select speeches (and relevant constitutions) to determine whether surviving monarchies drew heavily on traditionalism in their attempts at political persuasion. Were tradition and faith key elements in monarchies defending dictatorship? Did republics rely more than monarchies on a ruling bargain? Analysis of speeches and constitutions explore these assumptions and address these key questions: What factors did Arab leaders draw on in speeches defending their rule in response to the Arab Spring? Do these factors support a socio-economic ruling bargain and religion as a source of political legitimacy (referred to henceforth as Religious Legitimacy)?

References

Bahrain Independent Commission of Inquiry. (2011). *Speech of HM King Hamad bin Isa Al Khalifa on 23rd November.* Available at: http://www.bici.org.bh/indexc971.html?news=speech-of-hm-king-hamad-bin-isa-al-khalifa-on-23rd-november (accessed 12 January 2022).

BBC. (2016, September 28). *Oman Country Profile.* Available at: http://www.bbc.co.uk/news/world-middle-east-14654150 (accessed 7 January 2022).

Ben Ali, Z. (2011). *The Last Official Address by Tunisian President Zine el-Abidine Ben Ali* (T. Badran, Trans.). Available at: https://msmunatunagb.wikispaces.com/file/view/The+Last+Official+Address+of+Ben+Ali.pdf (accessed 20 November 2017. Inaccessible since 2021, saved as a pdf by author).

British Broadcasting Corporation. (2011). *Egypt Unrest: Full Text of Hosni Mubarak's Speech.* Available at: http://www.bbc.co.uk/news/world-middle-east-12427091 (accessed 12 October 2021).

Due-Gundersen, N. (2020, June 15). Playing Tourist: Impressions of Riyadh, Saudi Arabia During the Coronavirus. *International Policy Digest.* Available at: https://intpolicydigest.org/playing-tourist-impressions-of-riyadh-saudi-arabia-during-the-coronavirus/ (accessed 20 January 2022).

Kartveit, K., & Jumbert, M. G. (2014). *Civil-Military Relations in the Middle East: A Literature Review* (Chr. Michelsen Institute Working Paper 5).

RHC JO. (2012). *His Majesty King Abdullah II Remarks During a Gathering with National Public Figures at the Royal Hashemite Court on 23 October 2012* [video]. Available at: https://www.youtube.com/watch?v=Bf60Ft2B6HQ (accessed 14 February 2022).

Searle, J. (1965). What Is a Speech Act? In M. Black (Ed.), *Philosophy in America* (pp. 221–239). Allen and Unwin.

United Press International. (1985, May). *Car Bomber Fails in Attempt to Kill Leader of Kuwait.* Available at: https://www.nytimes.com/1985/05/26/world/car-bomber-fails-in-attempt-to-kill-leader-of-kuwait.html (accessed 23 January 2022).

Warden, P. (2011). *Gadhafi's Speech Transcript.* Available at: https://petewarden.com/2011/02/26/gadhafis-speech-transcript/ (accessed 12 January 2022).

Yom, S. L., & Gause, F. G., III. (2012). Resilient Royals: How Arab Monarchies Hang On. *Journal of Democracy, 23*(4), 74–88.

CHAPTER 2

A Historical Overview of MENA Politics Leading Up to the Arab Spring

2.1 Introduction

The imam's eyes burned into mine. "Why do you want to convert to Islam?".

I stood across from him, with our lawyer beside me. He was dressed in religious garb rather than a suit, taking the guise of a fellow religious scholar. That way, it was more likely my conversion would be granted. "I want to choose the right path to peace", I replied in decent Arabic. We were at Jordan's Supreme Court, and before I'd been allowed to see the imam for conversion, a court officer had asked the same question. My answer had satisfied both him and curious onlookers. A passer-by stopped to shake my hand.

"Good", the officer smiled. "Tell the imam what you told me".

The imam did not seem fully convinced. "This is not for marriage?".

"No".

After confirming with me that I believed Jesus was "only a man", he relented. "Nicolai, you are now Muslim. So, study the Quran well".

Religion is inescapable in the Middle East, forming a part of daily life and of politics. My conversion included the filling out of legal documents by the same court officer. "What was your previous religion?".

"Christian", I replied.

He frowned. That answer was apparently not good enough. "Which branch of Christianity?".

I shrugged, having never thought of it before.

N. Due-Gundersen, *Non-Democratic Legitimacy During the Arab Spring*,
https://doi.org/10.1007/978-3-031-11882-1_2

The officer's pen hovered above the form, moving down with purpose. He ticked a box. "Roman Catholic", he decided for me.

I left Jordan's Supreme Court as a Muslim and with a specific branch of Christianity as my former faith. It was unthinkable for the court officer to imagine that anyone would not follow a specific branch of any religion, a reminder of the Middle East's sectarianism that can be manipulated by rulers during times of crisis or challenge to their regimes.

This chapter considers how religion can be merged with utilitarian (and hence non-democratic) forms of political legitimacy, before considering the historical context of regimes across the Middle East and North Africa, how these regimes defended dictatorship through religious claims and ruling bargains.

2.2 Legitimizing Dictatorship: Religion, Regimes and Resources

Fabienne Peter's Political Legitimacy presents a framework that considers democratic and non-democratic means of rule. Peter's overview of Political Legitimacy is most relevant to dictatorship, as Peter does not assume that democracy is the exclusive or most significant source of legitimacy and also questions the political limits of democratic decision-making (Peter, 2016).

Peter's theory presents three separate sources of Political Legitimacy, including Consent, Beneficial Consequences and Public Reason/ Democratic Approval. Consent is perhaps the most obvious criterion. Peter traces the evolution of consent from the seventeenth century onward as "[...] the main source of political legitimacy" (ibid.). However, Peter does so within the context of European history and the gradual "[...] replacement of natural law and divine authority theories of legitimacy" (ibid.). It should be noted that this aspect of Political Legitimacy does not fully apply to the political evolution of the Arab world and the history in the MENA (the Middle East and North Africa) region of Islam and Islamic law. At the same time, Peter is willing to explore degrees of consent in her theory. Peter is willing to consider that consent may be the most impractical source of Political Legitimacy, as "[...] those governed [can] consent [only] under certain ideal conditions". Peter also brings attention to the fact that objections to the feasibility of consent "[...] are about as old as consent theory itself" (ibid.). Given the fact "[...] that actual states have almost always arisen from acts of violence", consent as a true indication of legitimacy is "[…] at best, wishful thinking" (ibid.).

The lack of pragmatic implementation regarding consent leads Peter to her second source of Political Legitimacy: Beneficial Consequences. This type of legitimacy is regarded by Peter as far more utilitarian than consent. What makes this particular source so interesting to the ruling bargain is its framework under a social contract, while still existing as "[…] a distinctively political—not moral […] source of legitimacy" (ibid.). At the same time, Peter outlines to what extent this utilitarian alternative may be moral yet still pragmatic (or whether it is more pragmatic than moral). Philosopher Jeremy Bentham, Peter argues, rejects the social contract outright. Under Bentham's definition, the state can monopolize power through binding rather than social contracts; however, "[…] legitimacy depends on whether a law contributes to the happiness of the citizens" (ibid.; Burns, 2005, p. 47). This definition derived through Bentham allows the state to present a skewed social contract between the ruler and the ruled, provided that the state's actions and monopoly contribute to the vague "happiness" of subjects. Without objectively defining happiness, Peter's Beneficial Consequences can certainly be linked to the MENA rentier states and the heretofore tangible benefits of political acquiescence in exchange, for example oil welfare.

The utilitarian image of Beneficial Consequences is complemented by notions of paternalism in Peter's explication. Analyzing Beneficial Consequences through the work of Raz (2009, p. 134), the simplest definition of political authority is "[…] a right to rule", in which the social contract is simplified into de facto legitimacy. Hence, if a law is "[…] issued by someone who has a right to rule, then its recipients are bound to obey" (ibid.). Peter expands on this directive by arguing that governments do not need to justify their form of rule so long as positive results of their political administration can be presented to their subjects (Peter, 2016). In other words, this understanding of Political Legitimacy argues that "[…] legitimacy based on beneficial consequences is compatible with everyone having reasons to obey the directives of a legitimate authority" (ibid.). This form of de facto recognition in exchange for benefits allows Peter's second source of Political Legitimacy to bolster the ruling bargains of Arab states. Further, the "[…] paternalistic ring" of such politics connects with non-democratic legitimacy, conjuring images of Arab rulers such as Mubarak holding an unequal "[…] dialogue with his sons and daughters" (ibid.; British Broadcasting Corporation, 2011).

Public Reason/Democratic Approval, Peter's final source is also relevant to Arab politics. However, Peter's explanation of Democratic Approval does not necessarily mean a pure democracy, or a definition of democracy espoused by the West for so-called "developing" nations. Nonetheless, Democratic Approval is strongly linked to consent theory. Peter draws heavily from John Rawls' *Political Liberalism* to discuss the appropriate political format in which to merge public reasoning and democratic approval (Peter, 2016). As explained by Rossi (2014, p. 1), Rawls regarded the social contract between the ruler and the ruled as contingent upon "[...] the rise of public justification as the dominant account of political authority" (ibid.). Rossi expounds this trend by quoting Rawls' view of political authority being expedient "[...] only when [...] exercised in accordance with a constitution, the essentials of which all citizens as free and equal may be expected to endorse" (ibid., p. 11). Peter herself agrees that Public Reason/Democratic Approval is best symbolized by a publicly approved constitution. For under a constitution, "[...] legitimate authority is created by appropriately constrained collective decision-making procedures" (Peter, 2016).

However, Peter does place limits on the role of democratic processes in her overall explanation of Political Legitimacy. First, Peter argues that a publicly approved constitution allows the masses to "[...] accept a democratic decision even if they disagree substantively with it" (ibid.). This insinuation implies limits to democracy between the ruler and the ruled, allowing flexibility in a government's actions that do not necessarily need public approval if following supposedly constrained democratic formalities.

Further, Peter even considers the plain fact that within "[...] contemporary political philosophy, not everyone agrees that democracy is necessary for political legitimacy" (ibid.). Peter's argument may be separated into two distinct views. First, there is her view of pure proceduralist conceptions of democratic legitimacy. This bureaucratic account of democracy places emphasis on "[...] pure proceduralism" rather than the outcome of such proceduralism (ibid.). Peter cites Christiano (2003, p. 1), who defines the proceduralist view of understanding political outcomes "[...] as essentially evaluable solely in terms of the procedure that brought them about" (ibid.). In other words, "[...] [w]hatever the results of the discussions, deliberation, and decision making ..., they are legitimate" (Peter, 2009, p. 146).

The proceduralist approach to democratic decision-making can certainly be linked to Gulf and other Arab monarchies and their parliaments. More specifically, an approach that considers democratic formalities more important than the democratic nature (or lack thereof) of political results can be linked to the perceived nature of the Arab *majlis* or parliament, which is often regarded as a "[...] rubber stamp for [a] ruling family's policies" (Whrey, 2014, p. 322).

Second, widening the non-democratic scope of Political Legitimacy is Peter's overview of what she terms Democratic Instrumentalism. Despite the use of 'democratic" as part of its namesake, this aspect of Peter's Political Legitimacy actually argues "[...] against democracy" by promoting the view that "[i]f democracy does not contribute to better outcomes, it is not necessary for political legitimacy" (Peter, 2016). Expounding on this theory, Peter argues that it is possible for the existence of a political administration that can create "[...] an ideal outcome that can be identified independently of the democratic process" and from which the regime's "[...] legitimacy can be gauged" (ibid.). Peter cites contemporary thinkers such as Arneson (2004, p. 40) who argues that "[s]ystems of governance should be assessed by their consequences". In other words, an individual ruler "[...] has a moral right to exercise political power [...] [if producing] best consequences overall" (ibid.).

Democratic Instrumentalism links back to Peter's source of Beneficial Consequences. Both provide non-democratic forms of legitimacy that focus on the notion of a public good accepted by an apolitical populace. Public benefits return to the notion of a ruling bargain. Both Democratic Instrumentalism and Beneficial Consequences are theoretical buttresses for the ruling bargain. After all, an emir or president can, under Democratic Instrumentalism, minimize democratic processes or even reduce them to superficial formalities, if they provide a palatable outcome to the process such as welfare benefits. Alternatively, the purer ruling bargain linked to Beneficial Consequences can be that the state's ability to provide subsidies and other socio-economic gifts is proof enough of its legitimacy, without the need for democratic bureaucracy.

Returning to the notion of monarchies and traditionalism, it is worth mentioning that Peter draws on Weber's definitions of non-democratic legitimacy. Weber defines the state as "[...] a human community that (successfully) claims the monopoly of the legitimate use of physical force within a given territory" (Weber & Gerth, 2009, p. 78). The birth of states through violence creates a political relation between ruler and subject of domination, in which force and coercion bolster the belief that if "[...] the state is to exist, the dominated must obey the authority claimed by the powers that be" (ibid.). From this description, Weber structures basic legitimacy through tradition or "[…] ancient recognition and habitual orientation", charisma or "[…] the authority of the extraordinary and personal gift of grace" and legality, explained by Weber as "[…] the belief in the validity of legal statute and functional "competence" based on rationally created rules" (ibid., pp. 78–79). These three sources of legitimacy are echoed in Peter's discussion of the state and how obedience to the state should in turn create a faith bestowed on a ruler by their citizens that is rewarded by the ruler with "[…] social regularities that are more stable than those that result from the pursuit of self-interest or from habitual rule-following", foreshadowing Peter's Beneficial Consequences and discussion of the social contract (Peter, 2016).

However, Peter's Political Legitimacy does not consider the role of religion as a service or Beneficial Consequence. Peter's Political Legitimacy does not have a sustained religious context. Only the limited role of Christendom and its influence on consent theory is briefly addressed. It is plausible, however, to start considering religion as one Beneficial Consequence or public good/service provided by MENA states.

Bulliet's *Religion and the State in Islam* can build upon Peter's Political Legitimacy by providing three elements of what may be termed Religious Legitimacy. These are: practice of Islamic law and customs; use of Islamic titles; and custodianship of holy sites (Bulliet, 2013, pp. 4–5, 12, 3). Hence, analysis of non-democratic legitimacy will merge Peter's sources of Political Legitimacy with Bulliet's sources of Religious Legitimacy. This merger will mean that Peter's Political Legitimacy (especially Beneficial Consequences) will remain the primary framework of analysis. However, Bulliet's own sources of Political Legitimacy or Religious Legitimacy will be used to analyze aspects of each case study's speech/constitution that involve or refer to Islam. In these instances, what the author has termed Religious Legitimacy will be given the same weight as Peter's Beneficial Consequences, e.g. religion will be treated as a public good that the state is expected to maintain in order to possess (non-democratic) legitimacy.

Both Peter's Political Legitimacy and Bulliet's Religious Legitimacy can be linked to the Arab Spring and to the four examined case studies. Ben Ali's Tunisia and the Khalifa Kingdom of Bahrain present security as a Beneficial Consequence. In his last public address of January 10th, 2011, Ben Ali insisted that the movement against him was due to "[h]ostile elements in the pay of foreigners […] from outside the country", contrasting this "[…] isolated act of desperation" with promises of justice, employment and educational reform (Ben Ali, 2011). King Hamad bin Issa al-Khalifa's own response to the Arab Spring insisted too that external forces were responsible for "[...] inciting our population to engage in acts of violence, sabotage, and insurrection". King Hamad warned that any such interference with his rule "[...] not only directly challenges the stability and sovereignty of our country, but also poses a threat to the security and stability of the GCC countries" (Bahrain Independent Commission of Inquiry, 2011). The implications of both Ben Ali and King Hamad are clearly hinting at socio-economic and political security, respectively, in turn conjuring images of stability. Stability can indeed be regarded as one of Peter's Beneficial Consequences. In fact, under Beneficial Consequences, Peter goes so far as to quote Milton's belief that authoritarianism "[...] is a legitimate mode of government in dealing with barbarians". Perhaps, Ben Ali and King Hamad would regard the "barbarians" as the external forces they argue are threatening their countries (Peter, 2016).

Mubarak's Egypt and King Abdullah II's Jordan complete the aforementioned case studies with research sites that can be analyzed through Religious Legitimacy as well as social contract theory and paternalism. Both Mubarak and King Abdullah II evoke God "[...] the Most Merciful, the Compassionate" when addressing their respective people, with Mubarak seeing his speech not as his final moment as president but simply "[...] a father's dialogue with his sons and daughters" (Abdullah II, October 2012; British Broadcasting Corporation, 2011).

Peter formulates descriptive and normative definitions of legitimacy. For Peter, descriptive legitimacy is perhaps vaguely defined as "[...] people's beliefs about political authority and, sometimes, political obligations" (ibid.). While perchance a compact definition, the notion of popular belief in not only authority but also obligation links back to the notion of a social contract, under which authority is granted to the state in exchange for the state meeting obligations toward subjects (Bërdufi & Dushi, 2015, p. 392). Such obligations, if broadly defined, can of course be of a non-democratic nature, returning Peter's definition to the skewed ruling bargain of the Arab states (Kamrava, 2013a, 2013b, p. 1). On the other hand, Peter's normative definition of legitimacy reflects an expanded understanding but one that still returns to a broad comprehension of a social contract or ruling bargain. For Peter, "[...] the normative concept of political legitimacy refers to some benchmark of acceptability or justification of political power or authority and—possibly—obligation" (Peter, 2016). Peter continues by categorizing the normative definition of legitimacy as creating a

"[…] moral duty to obey [the state's] commands". At the same time, Peter returns to the typical conditions of a social contract by asserting that "[…] if the conditions for legitimacy are not met, political institutions exercise power unjustifiably and the commands they might produce do then not entail an obligation to obey" (ibid.).

Peter's assertion returns her definition of political legitimacy to the seminal core of social contract theory, especially that of Hobbes' cap on authoritarian rule (Lloyd, 2014). At the same time, Peter's normative definition also connects with the ruling bargain as discussed by creating a moral duty for citizens to obey the state in exchange for an undefined standard for state monopolization of authority. If this benchmark is broadly defined (or undefined), it can be assumed that the justification for the state's authority can be non-democratic and/or a Beneficial Consequence, to use Peter's term, including welfare benefits often seen in Arab Gulf States (Gengler & Lambert, 2016, pp. 322–323).

Peter also balances the significance of the international system with the state as the highest political authority within its borders by introducing the concepts of Political Nationalism and Political Cosmopolitanism. Political Cosmopolitanism discusses how states exist in a system of "[…] both international and global legitimacy" and that, under such a system, states co-exist through "[…] international [stability], and the rules that regulate their behaviour are supposed to preserve a peaceful order of sovereign states" (Peter, 2016).

On the other hand, Peter also discusses the equal importance of Political Nationalism. She describes its significance in legitimation theory as opposed to Political Cosmopolitanism as the "[…] more familiar, contrasting position" that places political legitimacy firmly in the hands of states and their domestic rulers. In Peter's words, it is "[…] the [common] view that only the political institutions of nation states can overcome the legitimacy problem and hence be a source of political legitimacy" because, inter alia, Political Nationalism ensures that "[…] obligations of justice [are tied to] nation states" (ibid.).

However, as expedient as Peter's Political Legitimacy may be, both the aforementioned literature and Peter's own theory do not directly address the role of religion in political legitimacy. Given the significance of religion in the MENA region, it is imperative to understand how religion may be analyzed from a theoretical perspective.

In his paper, *Religion and the State in Islam*, Richard W. Bulliet provides an overview of Islamic history, focusing on how such a history between the earlier Muslim North and the later converts of the Muslim South "[...] sheds light on the crisis of legitimacy in Muslim-majority states like Egypt today" (Bulliet, 2013, p. 3). From a theoretical perspective, Bulliet's chronological tracing of Islamic history provides the context for the three-tier definition of Religious Legitimacy used by this author. These elements are: the preservation of Islamic law and customs; the use of a custodian title as guardian of religious landmarks; and the use of an Islamic ruling title.

Bulliet compares the evolution of Christian laws with those of Islam. In short, the seventeenth century's Peace of Westphalia gradually replaced universal divine law with "[...] fixed boundaries and limited legal jurisdictions", ensuring that "[...] the idea of a universal religious law [...] was abandoned in favor of individual laws for each state [...] with no jurisdiction stretching beyond the newly recognized state borders" (ibid., p. 12). However, no such "[...] parallel legal evolution occurred in the Islamic world. Muslim theorists declared that universal Islamic law limited the tyranny of Muslim rulers, and every ruler had to enforce at least some of those laws [...] to maintain theoretical legitimacy" (ibid.).

Bulliet's focus on a custodian title and religious ruling title examines the use of such titles within the context of political splits away from the supreme title of Caliph, which initially was regarded as bestowing the divine right to rule all Muslim lands (Karateke, 2005, p. 21). This split was most noticeable during the twelfth and thirteenth centuries and the time of the Crusades. Salah al-Din is often cited as the shift away from an all-powerful Caliph. As "[...] the Kurdish general who [...] drove the crusaders from Jerusalem in 1187" (ibid., p. 6), Salah al-Din expected recognition (and perhaps reward) from the Caliph of Baghdad. Reporting of his victory in Jerusalem to the Caliph, Salah al-Din was most disappointed when the Caliph retorted that al-Din's victory was due to the symbolic "[...] troops of the Caliph, under the banners of the Caliph" (ibid., p. 6). In response, Salah al-Din declared himself "[...] the Servitor of the Two Holy Places [...] the two holy places being Mecca and Medina [...] and also [...] the Dome of the Rock and al-Aqsa mosque in Jerusalem" (ibid.). These two titles were known in Arabic as *Khadim al-Haramain* and *al-bait al-muqaddas* respectively, and "[...] became the core political concept of the later centuries of Islam" (ibid.). Perhaps the importance of these titles was augmented by the fact that it meant usurpation by Salah al-Din from a function of the Caliph to an independent status, creating a true split and independent political claim "[...] without reference to the caliphate" (ibid.).

Finally, there is Bulliet's related factor of how rulers use Islamic titles for Religious Legitimacy. To put such usage in historical context, it is worth returning to the Ayyubid dynasty founder Salah al-Din and the expropriation of two core titles previously held by the Caliph. Until the arrival of Salah al-Din, other Islamic titles such as Sultan existed at the (theoretical) pleasure of the Caliph and in a subservient role. Salah al-Din's seizure of Custodianship from the Caliph eroded this relationship, allowing Islamic titles to exist independently of a Caliph (ibid.).[1]

All three of Bulliet's factors for Religious Legitimacy can be linked back to Peter's Beneficial Consequences. As previously discussed, Beneficial Consequences allow political legitimacy to be "[...] grounded on the principle of utility" (Peter, 2016). However, the importance of religion to political legitimacy in the Arab world can be partially accommodated by Peter's admission that faith can affect the "[...] conception of legitimacy [to become] necessarily a moralized one" (ibid.). From the perspective of, for example, morality, which religion is ostensibly grounded in, it is possible to understand both the limitations of Peter's Political Legitimacy when analyzing religion but also how Bulliet's Religious Legitimacy expands upon Peter's theory by complementing Beneficial Consequences with a structured consideration of how faith plays a political role. In turn, this approach allows analysis to more fully investigate the element of religion as a non-democratic factor in political legitimacy.

Bulliet further attempts to discuss the post-Arab Spring era, in which "[...] Muslims everywhere in the world are becoming deeply engaged in visualizing the return of Islam to the political arena" while admitting that the mass "[...] desire to reconnect Islam with governance [despite] [poor] knowledge of what Islamic law is" foreshadows "[...] a long period of confusion, uncertainty, and conflict before the outlines of a new relationship between Islam and the state become clear" (Bulliet, 2013, p. 18). This contemporary context allows Bulliet's three-tier Religious Legitimacy to be applied to the case studies within the same historical context of both the Arab Spring and how Islam has been used as a source of political legitimacy.

[1]See, e.g. the Sultanate of Oman, whose head of state is Sultan Haitham bin Tariq. Source: BBC (2016).

Peter's utilitarian approach will be merged with Bulliet's Religious Legitimacy to ensure discussion of non-democratic factors of political legitimacy as utilitarian, including religion. Peter's sources of Political Legitimacy provide an appropriate utilitarian theoretical context by acknowledging both democratic and non-democratic factors of legitimacy within a domestic context and from a more balanced perspective that leans toward the state, matching the goal of this book to understand non-democratic legitimacy from the perspective of Arab governments. However, a lack of religious context requires a complementary framework to understand the political role of faith. Bulliet's Religious Legitimacy fills this gap. Bulliet's limited framework for Religious Legitimacy provides a three-tier definition within a historical and contemporary context that considers the future of Arab governance post-Arab Spring, allowing for a focused approach that combines theory with a chronological tracing of Islamic history.

2.3 Historical Context

> [T]he tyranny of the masses is the cruellest kind of tyranny. Who can stand against the crushing current and the blind engulfing power? How I love the liberated masses on the march! They are unfettered, with no master, singing and merry after their terrible ordeals! On the other hand, how I fear and apprehend them! I love the masses as much as I love my father. Similarly, I fear them no less than I fear him. In a Bedouin society, where no government system exists, who can deter a father from persecuting any of his children? Yes. How much they love him, and how much they fear him at the same time! That is how I love and fear the masses. Exactly as I love and fear my father. (Gaddafi, 2016)

These are the words of former Libyan leader Muammar Gaddafi. They form the opening paragraph of "Escape to Hell", the first essay of Gaddafi's short story collection, *Escape to Hell and Other Stories.* The work was issued in English in 1999 (London: Blake Publishing). Yet that same year, Libya's UN sanctions were being suspended (BBC, 2003). Libya's neighbor, Egypt saw President Mubarak sworn in for a fourth term in 1999 (New York Times, 2014). Indeed, by the start of the new millennium, it appeared that MENA rulers were presiding over stable (if not liberal) nations. Zine el Abidine Ben Ali's Tunisia enjoyed a strong Tourism sector.

With "affordable luxuries" amid picturesque beaches and its Mediterranean coastline, Tunisia even saw growth predictions of up to 6% in 2001, despite the September 11th Attacks that same year (Glusac, 2009; News, 2002). Hosni Mubarak's Egypt saw strong GDP growth, gaining over 6% from 2005 to 2011 (Ayres & Macey, 2011).

In a 2008 speech, First Lady Suzanne Mubarak boasted that Egypt's lower-income classes also benefitted from such growth. GDP gains allowed "[…] poverty-stricken communities to benefit from an upgraded infrastructure, an improved access to basic health and education services as well as income generating schemes" (Food & Agriculture Organization of the United Nations, 2008). In the Levant, the Hashemite Kingdom of Jordan was consistently represented as an oasis of stability in an unstable region (Schaer, 2021). In the Persian Gulf, Bahrain's Hamad bin Issa al-Khalifa fancied himself a liberal ruler. His tentative years saw him release up to 320 political prisoners in 1999 (UNHCR, 1999). By 2002, Bahrain had transformed into a constitutional monarchy, with Hamad as King. The nation's first parliamentary elections in 27 years were expected shortly thereafter (Darwesh, 2002).

Gaddafi's words, however, would prove both ironic and prophetic. In under a decade since strong GDP growth and shifts toward constitutional kingdoms, a spark was lit in a modest Tunisian town. On the 17th of December 2010, twenty-six-year-old Mohamed Bouazizi became the first flame in what was to be known as the Arab Spring (Ryan, 2011). Gaddafi was right to fear the masses. For Mohammed, a hard-working fruit vendor, harbored the frustrations of millions of Arabs (Fahim, 2011). After having his wares confiscated by officials who harassed him daily, Bouazizi's last words were: "How do you expect me to make a living!" (Uzzel, 2012). Oil wealth, economic reforms and constitutionalism had hidden the socio-economic ills of widespread unemployment and open corruption. With the spark of its first martyr, the Arab Spring had begun (ibid.). From Tunisia, the Arab Spring blossomed across the North African states of Egypt and Libya before spreading to the Levant and the Gulf (Shah, 2011).

A war of words began in state after state. As protests spread and intensified, Arab leaders began to defend their governments and the legitimacy of their rule, in turn revealing their own perceptions of legitimacy. For some, their right to reign was paternalistic. Egypt's Mubarak argued that he was the father of the nation in his speech that served as a "[…] dialogue with his sons and daughters" (British Broadcasting

Corporation, 2011). Others such as King Abdullah of Saudi Arabia pointed to the perennial MENA beacon of Islam and his family's role as custodians of the dominant faith (Nazer, 2013). For Gulf and oil states, blunter perceptions of legitimacy were given, including security against (perceived) external threats. Bahrain's King Hamad insisted that foreign forces were "[...] inciting our population to engage in acts of violence, sabotage and insurrection" (Bahrain Independent Commission of Inquiry, 2011). Last but not least, were government responses that not only played on security fears but openly advertised the tacit ruling bargain of oil states. In the final speech before his death, Muammar Gaddafi insisted that protests would lead to civil war and Libya's degeneration into another Somalia (Warden, 2011). In addition, he angrily reminded the masses of their ruling bargain with the state and his generosity with Libya's resources. "Even the money [from] oil", he thundered, "I ask you to take every month" (ibid.).

This overview of governmental responses to the Arab Spring provides the outline of this book's themes for non-democratic legitimacy, including security, socio-economic benefits (in exchange for an apolitical populous) and religion. However, in order to understand how Arab governments have traditionally perceived their legitimacy and to further comprehend the traditional relations between the ruler and the ruled, it is necessary to trace how governance evolved in the Arab world under the umbrella of Islam and beyond.

Brown (2000, p. 1) notes that Islam's place in Arab politics was unavoidable since its beginnings in the seventh century (ibid., p. 10). For Islam combined belief in the divine with concerns for both daily life and the creation of a "[...] divinely ordained political community" here on Earth (ibid., p. 3). At the same time, the faith of Arabia had the potential to limit interactions between the ruler and the ruled. Belief in the divine necessarily curbed the belief in human actions, and thus "[...] Muslims [...] were fatalists, disinclined to believe that human exertions could shape events significantly" (ibid.). If Islam is compared to the politics of Christendom in Europe, it is possible to make analogies between Muslim rule and the power of the Papacy and Church (ibid., p. 33). However, a key difference that explains Islam's links to the state is the nature of its organization. The Church is often structured around a religious hierarchy (ibid., p. 29). Over time, such hierarchies have often become subservient to governmental structures (ibid., p. 33). Islam, on the other hand, differs markedly from this political pattern because it has never had a rigid or structured hierarchy. Brown explains that "[...] Islam knows no "church" in the sense of a corporate body whose leadership is clearly defined, hierarchical and distinct from the state" (ibid., p. 31). Hence, structured challenge to the state (or equally structured integration of Islam into the state) has been traditionally implausible. Because Islam was not formally organized into a representative council per se, Islam could not directly challenge the state as it did not have the organizational capacity to do so, nor could the state formally absorb representatives of Islam into its own governmental hierarchy. However, this did not mean that Islam was apolitical. Nor did it mean that Arab rulers could ignore the values of Muslim subjects (ibid., p. 32).

Here it is important to note that Islam's lack of hierarchy did not mean lack of popular representation. In Sunni Islam, the Arab world's dominant Muslim branch, there exist the *ulema*. Kechichian (1986, p. 55) outlines their role as religious specialists that straddle Islam's lack of clergy/hierarchy and Islam's need for "[…] theological interpretative skills", in exchange for which *ulema* receive "[…] rights and privileges", including traditional "[…] advisory roles [that] cannot [be], indeed were not ignored by […] political leaderships throughout history" (ibid.).

An expedient understanding of the *ulema* and their political significance can be framed twofold. First and as previously stated, the *ulema* were not historically a distinct socio-political class per se. Rather, they have existed as "[…] a category of religiously inclined persons who study Islamic law with great care and with a well-established methodology of interpretation and precedence" (ibid.). In a sense then, this definition of the *ulema* almost constructs them as a socio-religious community that only "[…] seek[s] to shed light on their capacity to understand, interpret, and compare their findings with others who are similarly inclined" (ibid.). Second, however, it must be recalled that *ulema* have traditionally been accorded political privileges and status by the state. This second aspect of defining the *ulema* is what allows a tracing of Islam's role in state relations between ruler and subjects. Brown (2000, p. 32) elucidates why the *ulema* were traditionally appeased by political rulers. As representatives of Muslims, *ulema* became and continue to be the de facto spokespersons for the masses. Historically, the popular support for the *ulema* has been a power that kings, presidents and emirs have been forced to acknowledge. Failure to do so can and has been fatal, for the "[…] ulama have often led or been intimately involved in movements toppling rulers from power" (ibid.).

Conversely, if the *ulema* can topple political governments, they have also been involved in their creation. The most salient case in point is the founding of the Kingdom of Saudi Arabia. Though named after the ruling

Saud family, Saudi Arabia was not monopolized by the House of Saud. Indeed, Ismail (2012, p. 404) describes the first Saudi state (1744–1818) not as an exclusive monarchy but as a politico-religious "[...] partnership between [*Sheikh*] Ibn 'Abd al-Wahhab and Muhammad ibn Saud, the state's first ruler". Over time, this arrangement expanded into "[...] a wider partnership between the Sunni ulema and the House of Saud, under which the clerics [...] provide the House of Saud with the legitimacy to rule" (ibid.). To this very day, the Saudi *ulema* continue to wield influence and power. The Council of Senior *Ulema* stands as a rare MENA example of an Islamic clerical framework that symbolizes the relationship in the Arab world between religion and governance. The Council's state sanctioned status is given by the House of Saud in return for the body's senior *ulema* providing "[...] tacit approval and, when requested, public sanction for potentially controversial policies" (Global Security, 2016). The privileges of Saudi *ulema* have also extended to include key posts in government, business and even the Armed Forces (ibid.).

An overview of Islam's relationship with the state reveals a historical connection between state and religion out of necessity. Not only was this due to the nature of Islam and its concern with the divine and the worldly but also because of the particular structure that became an established norm governing the ruler and the ruled. Rather than a direct relationship between government and populace, the *ulema* stood as a bridge between the Muslim masses and the political elite. The *ulema* represented Islamic values, tradition and thus embodied the concerns of the people. A government's need for religious legitimacy could thus not be ignored.

Perhaps, this need for religious approval explains why governments in the Arab world share a historic tradition (to varying degrees) of cementing their rule with Islamic titles. Bulliet (2013, pp. 1, 12) describes the history of Islamic titles as one element of a tripartite framework that eventually emerged as a form of religious legitimacy used by Arab governments. The emergence of Islamic titles is arresting, as it can be regarded as a time in history in which Islam did indeed start to become more organized. While lacking a formal hierarchy, the introduction of Islamic titles created a structure of religious authority, thus making Islam more concentrated as a movement that now had the nascent organization to become more political. As Bulliet notes, "[...] titles designated the political and spiritual leaders of the community and reflected the varying notions of how God thought the community of Muslims should be governed" (ibid., p. 4).

The most desired title from Islam's beginning (yet also the least pragmatic) was that of Caliph, ruler of a Caliphate or Islamic State. The desirability of this title arose early on in Islam's history. Due to its swift emergence, Karateke (2005, p. 21) describes being Caliph as "[...] [t]he most powerful and effective claim to normative legitimacy in [...] Islamic political discourse [.] [...] A sitting [C]aliph assumed not only a hereditary right but also indirectly a divine right to rule". As ideal a ruler's dream as it might have seemed, however, widespread disagreement over how to define and appoint a divine ruler was compounded by the parallel emergence of *Imam* as a title that could hold equal merit (Bulliet, 2013, p. 4). As with many historical events, the dispute of how a Caliph was designated often ended up being settled through territorial conquest and military victories (ibid., p. 5; see also the execution of the last Abbasid Caliph in 1258, whose power was by then restricted to the city limits. Source: Boyle, 1961, p. 145). Nonetheless, the Caliph/*Imam* debate prompted an alternatively constructed title: Sultan (Bulliet, 2013, p. 4).

Perhaps it is no coincidence that the word Sultan is derived from the Arabic *Sulta*, meaning power or influence (Bulliet, 2013, p. 5). While Caliph held divine emphasis but temporal complexities, the title of Sultan succeeded in gaining territorial and political emphasis while retaining religious elements (Bartold, 1963, p. 118). Interestingly, the title was originally associated with (and theoretically subservient to) the Caliph. Over time, however, the term Sultan came to be less understood as an office of the Caliph and more interpreted as a politically autonomous post that could be gained through, inter alia, conquest (Bulliet, 2013, p. 5). Under the rule of a Sultan, the foundations were laid for the typical traits of a modern Arab Sheikhdom. Many Sultanates, from infant governments to eventual empires often relied on the personal rule of one man (Ahmed et al., 2009, p. 1). Furthermore, while there could only be one Caliph, it was theoretically possible for there to be several sultans (and thus several Muslim states), all holding defined (but possibly large) territory (Bulliet, 2013, p. 5; Khan, 2007, p. 4). Whether under a Caliph or Sultan, the creation of an Islamic political order (Caliph/*Imam*, Sultan, *Ulema*), often by conquest, evoked connotations of political clout and power. In other words, without a system of checks and balances, the fear of tyranny looms upon the masses. It is for this reason that subjects expected not only the use of Islamic titles by their governments but the incorporation of Islamic law (Bulliet, 2013, p. 12).

Ibrahim (2006, pp. 6–7) expounds on why Islamic law should act as a counterweight to, e.g. personal rule. For "[...] freedom is the object of the divine law. Islam has always expressed the primacy of *'adl*, or justice, which is a close approximation of what the West defines as freedom. Justice entails according to the dictates of Islamic law [s], which emphasize consultation and condemn despotism and tyranny" (ibid., p. 7). It is worth adding that Ibrahim's explanation of Islamic law is not unfamiliar to Western concepts of governance. Indeed, Ibrahim argues that Islamic law or *Shari'a* bears a "[...] striking resemblance to Locke['s] ideals that would be expounded centuries later" (ibid.). This description echoes notions of a social contract between the ruler and the ruled. In the case of *Shari'a*, said contract should not be defined by the state's monopolized authoritarianism. Rather, in return for obedience from its citizens, the state must uphold the universal rights of Islam: "[...] freedom of conscience, freedom of expression, and the sanctity of life and property—as demonstrated very clearly by the Koran, as well as by the teachings of the Prophet Muhammad" (ibid.).

As this chapter has already discussed, the status of Islam among the masses and their de facto representatives (the *ulema*) has rarely been dismissed by governments without fatal consequences. Ibrahim's overview of universal values therefore creates a social contract that Arab governments must comply with. To stay in power, Arab leaders must accept limitations upon that power. However, just as states found ways around the Caliph to gain their own Islamic leadership, more contemporary rulers would find ways around *'adl* or the Islamic concept of justice by tacitly promoting and enforcing an apolitical social contract, the ruling bargain.

Some scholars such as Korany (2013, p. 19) have defined the ruling bargain as both evolving yet static. The basic definition of a ruling bargain is that "[...] citizens surrender their political and social rights to participatory government, are expected to accept the legitimacy of the ruling regime, [...] and in return are rewarded with a variety of [...] socio-economic benefits" (ibid, pp. 19, 1).

However, Korany argues that this definition of the ruling bargain cannot survive alone without being placed within the framework of the three Ms: the Military, the Mosque and the Masses. In an expanded argument, Korany observes that the three Ms were of paramount importance in Egypt's overthrow of Mubarak because the Military, the Mosque and the Masses "[...] were [all] present [to protest against Mubarak] at [Cairo's] Tahrir [Square]" (2014, p. 256). The fact that all three Ms united against Mubarak illustrates the power of each group in preserving the ruling bargain and how such a framework of cooption can evolve over time. Hence, the ruling bargain, while possessing a simple definition, must also adapt to this politico-religious framework during waves of change (ibid.).

In any event, it is worth noting that the ruling bargain as a MENA norm can be regarded as contemporary. Not until the 1950s, when Caliphs and Islamic States had been partially replaced with Arab republics and presidents did this skewed social contract emerge (Kamrava, 2013a, 2013b, p. 2). Nonetheless, the apolitical nature of the ruling bargain and even its modern origins are contrasted by how political rule may be comprehended under Islam and what Brown terms Political Quietism. Brown skillfully defines Political Quietism and illustrates its Islamic legitimacy by quoting a specific *hadith* or saying of the Prophet Muhammad (Brown, 2001, p. 67). In the *hadith*, it is claimed that the Prophet was asked whether Muslims should combat authoritarian rulers. "No", Muhammad replied. "[N]ot so long as [these rulers] say their prayers" (ibid.). The subsequent religious context created by this *hadith* cannot be overlooked by the ruler or the ruled, as it birthed a Political Quietism with both "[…] a theological and cultural basis" that have become perennial due to their mutual and cohesive nature (ibid.).

Emphasizing the notion of Political Quietism as a public good has been the historic use of religion and religious terms or practices by Muslim leaders. Their historical utility can be linked to both Political Quietism and state rule. Ayoob (2004, p. 9) argues that Muslim jurists created a two-tier framework to validate "[…] the legitimacy of [a government's] temporal rule". This minimal definition of politico-religious legitimacy decreed that any ruler that can maintain his Muslim territories or *Dar al-Islam* and does not prevent his subjects from practicing their faith is a legitimate head of state. As such, tyranny was actually permissible under a ruler that passed the two-tier test. Furthermore, the Prophet's *hadith* and Islamic juridical practice meant that power-hungry but pious rulers could sleep at night, safe in the knowledge that "[…] rebellion was forbidden" (ibid.). Indeed, Muslim jurists gave unlawful rebellion its own term, calling it *fitna* and arguing that such dissension was "[…] worse than tyranny since it could threaten the integrity of the *umma* (community of believers)". Inevitable chaos and political conflict would most certainly ensue (ibid.). Thus, a form of stable but Islamic tyranny was ensured from at least "[…] the eighth to the eighteenth centuries", with the ruling bargain able to build upon rather than raze the Political Quietism accepted by the Muslim masses (ibid.).

Modern rulers tried to maintain the framework of Political Quietism right up to the Arab Spring. Under Hosni Mubarak, the Egyptian government tried to take advantage of Political Quietism and its links to emerging religious trends (al-Anani & Mali, 2013, pp. 57, 61). In particular, Mubarak paid close attention to the Salafist movement, which began intensifying its media presence and gained increasing support from 2003 onward. No doubt, Mubarak appreciated the growing popularity of a Muslim branch that "[...] reshaped the religious sphere in Egypt to become more conservative and less progressive in terms of political and religious views" (ibid.). The Political Quietism of Salafist Egyptians prompted the regime to give "[...] more space and venues for the Salafis to spread their views and expand their social network". Further, Mubarak even "[...] employed the political quietism of Salafis to counter-balance [his opposition]" (ibid.).

The ruling bargain can thus be understood as a more recent phenomenon created as a skewed social contract between the ruler and the ruled. However, a brief examination of Political Quietism and its origins in Islam illustrate how the ruling bargain did not appear out of context with definitions of Islamic legitimacy, however loosely defined. So long as a king, president or brotherly leader maintains his territory (under Islamic customs) and preserves the practice of faith, the masses must accept his social contract. To not do so would be unlawful rebellion and encourage *fitna*, dissent that bred anarchy thought to be worse than the stable clutches of tyrannical governance. Nonetheless, this is not to say that unrest never occurred until the Arab Spring. In fact, the Arab world has been subject to a history of contention between protest and acceptance that outlines the limits of *fitna*. Such a history may somewhat explain why Arab leaders did not react strongly to initial protests that would blossom into the Arab Spring.

As is often the case in history, ideology does not always win against pragmatism. Bulliet (2013, p. 13) outlines the consequences of secularized rule under Islamic theory. Bulliet claims that un-Islamic and thus illegitimate rule should "[...] engender the arousal among Muslim populations of a sort of [...] instinctual inclination to see in religion a corrective force against this political imbalance. Thus, as tyranny increased, oppositional movements should have emerged bent on using religion and appeals to Islamic law to [...] limit tyranny and introduce more equitable governance" (ibid.). Yet, it must be remembered that should a populace take to the streets against their regime, this action would likely violate the tacit and apolitical ruling bargain that became increasingly common and dominant in the contemporary MENA region. Indeed, Brown (2000, p. 68) traces the importance of the ruling bargain over religion all the way back to the Ottoman era. One tale of the time describes the poor relations between local subjects and their ruler. Wishing to remove the tyrannical governor, the villagers send a representative to the "[…] Ottoman capital" and request the governor's dismissal. However, "[w]hen the governor got wind of the plan, he summoned the group to his house […] pointed out a chest and told them to open it. It was filled […] with coins and precious metals". The governor then said, "When I arrived […] I brought with me that trunk empty. Now it is almost full. My successor will arrive with his empty trunk" (ibid.). Resistance to his rule promptly folded, illustrating how the ideology of political freedom, at least in this case, could not win against the pragmatics of financial leverage (ibid.).

At the same time, the very distance created by Political Quietism and the subsequent inability to identify with the state can encourage resistance to its governance. Resistance, according to Brown, is often tied to dignity. It is dignity and honor that caused Algerian tribes to confront Tunisian tax collectors with the sword before opening their purses in the nineteenth century. "[I]f we pay without difficulty one year, [the governor] may well be tempted to increase the levy the following year", explained a tribal leader. "In any case, it would be shameful for mountaineers to pay at the first demand" (Brown, 2000, pp. 69–70). The act of militarily confronting Tunisian tax collectors before meeting payment balances recognizing the legitimacy of the state's right to rule with the dignity of its subjects, and it is dignity that was at the heart of the Arab Spring (Fukuyama, 2012, available online). As Francis Fukuyama put it, "[i]t's hard power that often makes the headlines. But never underestimate the strength of the simple desire for respect" (ibid.).

Finally, the tradition of half-hearted resistance to government can be complemented by financial considerations and the political implications of government repression. Brown (2012, p. 73) again illustrates how perennial dictatorships and empires survived through, inter alia, cost-effectiveness. In other words, dissidents and combative rebels were not targeted in an "inch by inch, house by house" manner. Rather, it was more common for rulers to ration resources by "[…] awaiting a propitious time when rebel areas could be brought back into the system without undue cost in manpower or money" (ibid.). Guriev and Treisman (2015, p. 6) broaden this model by assessing why repression can be more dangerous than cooption, propaganda and the ruling bargain, even if the government appears to be under threat. Indeed, if the ruling bargain remains reasonably strong, perhaps bolstered by censorship and propaganda, the illusion of strength and competence becomes pervasive. Hence, using violence "[...] signals to the general public that the regime is incompetent and vulnerable". Violence, in other words, breaks the mirage (ibid.).

By examining the facets of Islamic legitimacy, Political Quietism and financial considerations, it is possible to compose a picture of how mass opposition to tyrants may have been minimized. Without painting with too broad a brush, it is not inaccurate to argue that the Muslim belief in divinity and fatalism, coupled with distance from government allowed rulers to impose their will upon the masses, provided they also upheld Islamic traditions. At the same time, financial and political implications made governments reluctant to resort to mass repression. Nonetheless, propaganda, censorship and ruling bargains could not prevent covert expression by subjects of their own political will. From a religious point of view, "[...] that is precisely what happened. Starting with the Muslim Brotherhood in Egypt in the 1930s, movements and parties supporting the concept of Islamic government became increasingly vociferous and popular" (Bulliet, 2013, p. 13).

It is certainly possible to link Islamist will to the Arab Spring, especially when analyzing elections held in Tunisia and Egypt shortly after their respective leaders fell (Haqqani, 2012). However, it is also possible to consider the broader repercussions of tyranny, regardless of how much Islamic legitimacy a government may claim to have. For the Arab Spring was not born purely out of Islamist interests, it was provoked by the human drive for dignity. A drive that, for the Muslim masses, should have been enshrined in constitutions and Islamic law (Pin, 2016, p. 3). Indeed, what is most heartbreaking is that the context of dignity can be found in the early years of many governments that found themselves at the mercy of the Arab Spring's masses. Upon seizing power in 1987, Tunisia's Ben Ali promised that he would "[...] see that the law is correctly enforced in a way that will proscribe any kind of iniquity or injustice" (Ben Ali, 2015). Gaddafi's 1969 coup against the Libyan monarchy saw the twenty-seven-year-old officer declare that henceforth the state would be a body of "[...] freedom, the path of unity and social justice, guaranteeing equality to all her citizens" (Gaddafi, 2015). Perhaps, such promises of dignity forgotten for decades led to the popular expression for such social justice. Dignity is one of the most basic human needs, on par with food and water.

As Pin (2016, p. 3) explains "[the] Arabs who occupied the roads of Cairo, Tunis, Damascus, Amman, and many other cities did not call simply for the enforcement of *human rights* or *Islamic law*. In Egypt, the most populated Arab country, the early rallying cry of the 2011 revolution was "Bread, Freedom, Social Justice, and Human Dignity", and it was later enshrined in the 2012 and 2014 constitutions' Preambles" (ibid.).

Nonetheless, an overview of Islamic titles, laws and legitimacy illustrates that, from an Arab government's perspective, a framework and thus culture of political legitimacy did exist. In keeping with this theme, it is worth exploring how states and governments have traditionally wielded political legitimacy and how this tradition has been regarded. From a historical perspective, it is possible to trace the ruling bargain of today's oil sheikhs back to Western philosophy and the social contract theory. Commonly linked to Hobbes, Locke and Rousseau, the social contract theory was introduced to explain the human transition from stateless groups to organized political communities (Steele, 1993, p. 1). This transition necessitated a centralized administrator, birthing the basic definition of the social contract. Bërdufi and Dushi (2015, p. 392) summarize the social contract as "[...] a way by which people, in order to escape the state of nature, an insecure state of unavoidable war, implicitly agreed to give away some of their individual freedoms to a political ruler, a State, in order for the State to better protect some more important needs and rights to them" (ibid.).

All three philosophers argue that a social contract exists between the ruler and the ruled, and that the authority of the state is accepted in exchange for, inter alia, benefits, whether they be security or representation. The notion of benefits is central to the ruling bargain and further expanded upon by contemporary scholars of social contract theory. Within this context, Fabienne Peter's Political Legitimacy presents a framework that considers democratic and non-democratic means of rule. Peter's overview of Political Legitimacy is most relevant to defending dictatorship, as Peter does not assume that democracy is the exclusive or most significant source of legitimacy and also questions the political limits of democratic decision-making (Peter, 2016).

Finally, the relations of regimes with the (Western) world are worth mentioning within the context of 9/11, expanded upon in Chapter 3. The September 11th Attacks represent a significant shift in MENA-Western relations. It was after 9/11 that the United States especially began to question Arab culture and socio-politics and Arab relations with the world and the West (Fadda-Conrey, 2011, pp. 532–533). Further, the so-called War on Terror, a product of George W. Bush's response to 9/11, gave MENA leaders a chance to tighten the grip on their own people. Dictators like Gaddafi feigned cooperation in the War on Terror and used it as cover to target their own subjects under the pretense of stopping Islamist militants or other terrorist cells (with Western assistance) (Chorin, 2012, pp. 142–143). Indeed, renowned Arab scholar Edward Said emphasized a week after 9/11 that the War on Terror was a vaguely phrased response that risked confirming "[…] America's role in the [Muslim] world" and its "[…] sanctimoniously munificent support […] of numerous repressive Arab regimes" (Said, 2001). Hence, 9/11 serves as an expedient starting point of analysis, as it is after 9/11 that Western interest in Arab politics grew, while simultaneously, certain MENA leaderships took advantage of that interest to strengthen domestic repression.

References

Primary Data

Abdullah II, H. M. (2012a, October). *Remarks by His Majesty King Abdullah II During a Gathering with National Public Figures, Amman, Jordan*. Available at: http://kingabdullah.jo/index.php/en_US/speeches/view/id/507/videoDisplay/0.html (accessed 21 October 2016. Inaccessible since 2021, saved as a pdf by author).

Bahrain Independent Commission of Inquiry. (2011). *Speech of HM King Hamad bin Isa Al Khalifa on 23rd November*. Available at: http://www.bici.org.bh/indexc971.html?news=speech-of-hm-king-hamad-bin-isa-al-khalifa-on-23rd-november (accessed 12 January 2022).

Ben Ali, Z. (2011). *The Last Official Address by Tunisian President Zine el-Abidine Ben Ali* (T. Badran, Trans.). Available at: https://msmunatunagb.wikispaces.com/file/view/The+Last+Official+Address+of+Ben+Ali.pdf (accessed 20 November 2017. Inaccessible since 2021, saved as a pdf by author).

Ben Ali, Z. (2015). *Speech to the Tunisian Parliament by Zine el Abidine Ben Ali on 7 November 1987 After President Bourguiba Was Declared Unfit to Govern*. Available at: http://al-bab.com/albab-orig/albab/arab/docs/tunisia/declaration_07111987.htm (accessed 11 November 2021).

British Broadcasting Corporation. (2011). *Egypt Unrest: Full Text of Hosni Mubarak's Speech*. Available at: http://www.bbc.co.uk/news/world-middle-east-12427091 (accessed 12 October 2021).

Food and Agriculture Organization of the United Nations. (2008). *Keynote Speech of H.E. Mrs Suzanne Mubarak on the Occasion of the World Food Day Ceremony. "World Food Security: the Challenges of Climate Change and Bio-energy"*. FAO. Available at: http://www.fao.org/fileadmin/user_upload/newsroom/docs/mubarak.pdf (accessed 12 October 2021).

Gaddafi, M. (2015). *Communique Number One by Muammar Al Gaddafi, 1969, September 1st.* Available at: http://english.algaddafi.org/4/post/2015/07/communique-number-one-by-muammar-al-gaddafi-1969-september-1st.html (last accessed 11 November 2021).

Warden, P. (2011). *Gadhafi's Speech Transcript.* Available at: https://petewarden.com/2011/02/26/gadhafis-speech-transcript/ (accessed 12 January 2022).

Secondary Data

Academic Reports/Papers

Ahmed, R., Coşgel, M., & Miceli, T. (2009). *Law, State Power and Taxation in Islamic History.* Available at: https://www.academia.edu/21412100/Law_state_power_and_taxation_in_Islamic_history?auto=download (accessed 13 January 2022).

al-Anani, K., & Mali, M. (2013). Pious Way to Politics: The Rise of Political Salafism in Post- Mubarak Egypt. *DOMES: Digest of Middle East Studies, 22*(1), 57–73.

Ayoob, M. (2004). Political Islam: Image and Reality. *World Policy Journal, 21*(3), 1–14.

Bartold, V. V. (1963). Caliph and Sultan. *Islamic Quarterly, 7*(3), 117–135.

Bërdufi, N., & Dushi, D. (2015). Social Contract and the Government's Legitimacy. *Mediterranean Journal of Social Sciences, 6*(6 S1), 392–398.

Boyle, J. A. (1961). The Death of the Last "Abbasid Caliph: A Contemporary Muslim Account." *Journal of Semitic Studies, 6*(2), 145–161.

Bulliet, R. W. (2013). *Religion and the State in Islam: From Medieval Caliphate to the Muslim Brotherhood* (Occasional Paper Series, Paper No. 2). Center for Middle East Series, University of Denver.

Burns, J. H. (2005). Happiness and Utility: Jeremy Bentham's Equation. *Utilitas, 17*(1), 46–61.

Christiano, T. (2003). The Authority of Democracy. *The Journal of Political Philosophy, 11*(2), 1–25.

Fadda-Conrey, C. (2011). Arab American Citizenship in Crisis: Destabilizing Representations of Arabs and Muslims in the US after 9/11. *MFS Modern Fiction Studies, 57*(3), 532–555.

Gengler, J., & Lambert, A. L. (2016). Renegotiating the Ruling Bargain: Selling Fiscal Reform in the GCC. *The Middle East Journal, 70*(2), 321–329.

Guriev, S., & Treisman, D. (2015). *How Modern Dictators Survive: An Informational Theory of the New Authoritarianism*. Available at: https://www.eui.eu/Documents/DepartmentsCentres/Economics/Seminarsevents/Guriev-Micro.pdf (accessed 17 January 2022).

Haqqani, H. (2012). Islamists and the "Arab Spring." *Journal of Democracy, 24*(2), 5–14.

Ibrahim, A. (2006). *Universal Values and Muslim Democracy*. Available at: https://www.journalofdemocracy.org/articles/universal-values-and-muslim-democracy/ (accessed 13 January 2022).

Ismail, R. (2012). The Saudi Ulema and the Shi'a of Saudi Arabia. *Journal of Shi'a Islamic Studies, V*(4), 403–422.

Kamrava, M. (2013a). Introduction. In *The Evolving Ruling Bargain in the Middle East: Summary Report* (p. 1). Georgetown University Center for International and Regional Studies.

Kamrava, M. (2013b). The Rise and Fall of Ruling Bargains in the Middle East. In *The Evolving Ruling Bargain in the Middle East: Summary Report* (pp. 2–3). Georgetown University Center for International and Regional Studies.

Karateke, H. K. (2005). *Legitimizing the Ottoman Sultanate: A Framework for Historical Analysis*. Available at: https://lucian.uchicago.edu/blogs/ottomanturkish/files/2011/01/LEGITIMIZING-THE-OTTOMAN-SULTANATE.pdf (accessed 13 January 2022).

Kechichian, J. A. (1986). The Role of the Ulama in the Politics of an Islamic State: The Case of Saudi Arabia. *International Journal of Middle East Studies, 18*(1), 53–71.

Khan, S. A. (2007). *The "Caliphate Question": British Views and Policy Toward Pan-Islamic Politics and the End of the Ottoman Caliphate*. Available at: https://www.ajis.org/index.php/ajiss/article/download/427/2158 (accessed 13 January 2022).

Korany, B. (2013). Microcosms of the Arab Spring: Sociology of Tahrir Square. In *The Evolving Ruling Bargain in the Middle East: Summary Report* (pp. 19–20). Georgetown University Center for International and Regional Studies.

Korany, B. (2014). A Microcosm of the Arab Spring: Sociology of Tahrir Square. In B. Korany (Ed.), *Beyond the Arab Spring: The Evolving Ruling Bargain in the Middle East* (pp. 249–276). Oxford University Press.

Lloyd, S. A. (2014). *Hobbes's Moral and Political Philosophy*. Available at: http://plato.stanford.edu/entries/hobbes-moral/#StaNatStaWar (accessed 18 January 2022).

Peter, F. (2016). *Political Legitimacy*. Available at: http://plato.stanford.edu/entries/legitimacy/ (accessed 18 January 2022).

Pin, A. (2016). *The Arab Road to Dignity: The Goal of the "Arab Spring"* (Working Paper #408). Kellogg Institute for International Studies.

Rossi, E. (2014). Legitimacy and Consensus in Rawls' Political Liberalism. *Iride: Filosofia e discussione pubblica*, *27*(1), 1–23.

Steele, D. A. (1993). *A Comparison of Hobbes and Locke on Natural Law and Social Contract*. The University of Texas at Austin. Available at: https://apps.dtic.mil/sti/citations/ADA270299 (accessed 18 January 2022).

Uzzel, J. (2012, November 7). Biopolitics of the Self-Immolation of Mohamed Bouazizi. *E-International Relations*. Available at: http://www.e-ir.info/2012/11/07/biopolitics-of-the-self-immolation-of-mohamed-bouazizi/ (accessed 18 January 2022).

Media Reports

Ayres, I., & Macey, J. (2011, February 18). Egypt's Economy and Mubarak's Fall. *Politico*. Available at: http://www.politico.com/story/2011/02/egypts-economy-and-mubaraks-fall-049736 (accessed 12 January 2022).

BBC. (2003, September 12). *UN Lifts Libya Sanctions*. Available at: http://news.bbc.co.uk/1/hi/world/africa/3102342.stm (accessed 10 January 2022).

BBC. (2016, September 28). *Oman Country Profile*. Available at: http://www.bbc.co.uk/news/world-middle-east-14654150 (accessed 7 January 2022).

Darwesh, G. (2002, February 15). Bahrain Becomes a Kingdom. *Arab News*. Available at: http://www.arabnews.com/node/218544 (accessed 12 January 2022).

Fahim, K. (2011, January 21). Slap to a Man's Pride Set Off Tumult in Tunisia. *The New York Times*. Available at: http://www.nytimes.com/2011/01/22/world/africa/22sidi.html?_r=3&pagewanted=2&src=twrhp (accessed 12 January 2022).

Fukuyama, F. (2012, January 12). The Drive for Dignity. *Foreign Policy*. Available at: http://foreignpolicy.com/2012/01/12/the-drive-for-dignity/ (accessed 17 January 2022).

Global Security. (2016). *Council of Senior Ulema*. Available at: http://www.globalsecurity.org/military/world/gulf/sa-ulama.htm (accessed 13 January 2022).

Glusac, E. (2009, November 22). A Night, and Day, in Tunisia at a New Resort. *The New York Times*. Available at: http://query.nytimes.com/gst/fullpage.html?res=9F0DE4D81538F931A15752C1A96F9C8B63 (accessed 12 January 2022).

Nazer, F. (2013). "Saudi Code" Prevents Arab Spring in Kingdom. *Al-Monitor*. Available at: https://www.al-monitor.com/originals/2013/02/saudi-arabia-arab-spring-king-abdullah-saudi-code.html (accessed 09 September 2021).

New York Times. (2014, May 21). Hosni Mubarak's Path from Presidency to Prison and Beyond. Available at: https://www.nytimes.com/interactive/2013/08/21/world/middleeast/Mubarak_timeline.html (accessed 10 January 2022).

News, A. (2002, March 20). Despite 11/9, Tourism Up in Morocco and Tunisia. *Afrol News.* Available at: http://www.afrol.com/News2002/mor004_tun_tourism.htm (accessed 12 January 2022).

Ryan, Y. (2011, January 20). The Tragic Life of a Street Vendor. *Al Jazeera.* Available at: http://www.aljazeera.com/indepth/features/2011/01/201111684242518839.html (accessed 12 January 2022).

Said, E. (2001). *Islam and the West Are Inadequate Banners.* Available at: https://www.theguardian.com/world/2001/sep/16/september11.terrorism3 (accessed 26 January 2022).

Schaer, C. (2021). How Stable is Jordan Really? *DW News.* Available at: https://www.dw.com/en/how-stable-is-jordan-really/a-57106768 (accessed 9 September 2022).

Shah, D. (2011, December 26). *Arab Spring: "It Was the First Time I Felt I Belonged".* BBC. Available at: http://www.bbc.co.uk/news/world-middle-east-16275176 (accessed 12 January 2022).

Printed/Online Books

Arneson, R. J. (2004). Democracy Is Not Intrinsically Just. In K. Dowding, R. E. Goodin, & C. Pateman (Eds.), *Justice and Democracy* (pp. 40–59). Cambridge University Press.

Brown, L. C. (2000) *Religion and State: The Muslim Approach to Politics.* Columbia University Press.

Brown, N. J. (2001). *Constitutions in a Nonconstitutional World: Arab Basic Laws and the Prospects for Accountable Government.* SUNY Series in Middle Eastern Studies. State University of New York Press.

Chorin, E. (2012). *Exit the Colonel: The Hidden History of the Libyan Revolution.* Public Affairs.

Gaddafi, M. (2016). *Other Books by Muammar Al Gaddafi—The Escape to Hell.* Available at: http://algaddafi.org/booksbymuammaralgaddafi/books-by-muammar-al-gaddafi—the-escape-to-hell (accessed 12 January 2022).

Peter, F. (2009). Democratic Legitimacy Without Collective Rationality. In B. de Bruin & C. F. Zurn (Eds.), *New Waves in Political Philosophy* (pp. 143–158). Palgrave Macmillan.

Raz, J. (2009). *Between Authority and Interpretation: On the Theory of Law and Practical Reason.* Oxford University Press.

Weber, M., & Gerth, H. H. (Eds.). (2009). *From Max Weber: Essays in Sociology.* Routledge Classics in Sociology. Routledge.

Whrey, F. (2014). Bahrain's Decade of Discontent. In L. Diamond & M. F. Plattner (Eds.), *Democratization and Authoritarianism in the Arab World* (pp. 315–326, p. 322). Johns Hopkins University Press.

International Organization Reports

UNHCR. (1999). Freedom in the World 1999 – Bahrain. *Refworld*. Available at: https://www.refworld.org/category,COI,FREEHOU,,BHR,5278c8e3b,0.html (accessed 9 September 2022).

CHAPTER 3

Case Studies

3.1 Introduction

A profile of each case study is required to place Religious and Political Legitimacy within the context of each Arab government's ruling style. Such a context will provide a deeper understanding of each leader's rhetorical response to the Arab Spring and domestic unrest, allowing more specific analysis of each case study in the succeeding chapters. Further, this chapter seeks to place each profile within the context of these questions: What are the factors Arab leaders use in discourse justifying their rule within the context of the Arab Spring? To what extent does this discourse support a (socio-economic) ruling bargain and Religious Legitimacy? It is for this reason that case studies in this and subsequent chapters will not be presented according to the chronology of the Arab Spring but rather in the order of how strongly they correspond to or challenge the assumption that monarchs rely on traditionalism while republicans rely more on the ruling bargain. Such restructuring will highlight thematic analysis of each case study, including Religious Legitimacy and a socio-economic ruling bargain. Hence, the order of selected case studies is:

- Jordan, the last stable Levant state and the author's site of residence from 2012 to 2016 and the strongest confirmation of the assumption that monarchs rely on traditionalism.
- Bahrain, the Gulf case study and the strongest example of a socio-economic ruling bargain that contrasts with expectations that

N. Due-Gundersen, *Non-Democratic Legitimacy During the Arab Spring*, https://doi.org/10.1007/978-3-031-11882-1_3

republicans will draw on the ruling bargain due to them being the result of coups rather than established familial rule.

- Egypt, the most populous nation in the Arab world (Central Intelligence Agency) that contrasts with expectations that only monarchies will draw on Religious Legitimacy.
- Tunisia, the origin of the Arab Spring and the weakest conformation of the assumption that republicans justify rule through a socio-economic ruling bargain.

3.2 The Hashemite Kingdom of Jordan

> You know, […] when I reached my 10-year anniversary, I remember sitting down with members of my family and my close friends and saying, "I don't want to do this anymore". […] I was so depressed because of all the forces I was dealing with on the inside. It wasn't the outside—the outside, I understood. It was inside. […] Two steps forward, one step back. […] Institutions I had trusted were just not on board. It was the *mukhabarat* [secret police] […] and the old guard. […] [If there is a revolution,] [my] character is, I won't shoot. I don't think we as [the] Hashemite [ruling family] shoot. If you, as a monarch, have created a situation in which half the population rises up and wants you out, then you've done something wrong. […] The monarchy is going to change. When my son becomes of age and becomes king, the system will be stabilized and … it will be a Western democracy with a constitutional monarchy. [But] even with all the changes I'm doing here, there is still going to be a monarchy. I hope [my successor] works hard, but not with the same pressures. (Goldberg, 2013)

King Abdullah II of Jordan gave a rare glimpse into the political and geostrategic pressures facing the monarch of a nation without the oil wealth of proximate Gulf sultans and sheikhs. In a 2013 interview (later condemned by Abdullah as misinterpreting his statements), he discussed the antiquated notion of monarchy, the social contract between tribe and throne with its "coldly transactional quality" and how it is "not necessarily good to be the king of a Middle Eastern country that is bereft of oil" (Goldberg, 2013; Miller, 2013).

At the same time, the role of religion provides a political advantage not enjoyed by King Abdullah's peers. While republican presidents-for-life may attempt to manipulate Islam and their association with the majority faith

(British Broadcasting Corporation, 2011), King Abdullah and his Hashemite kin share direct descendance from the Prophet Muhammad. This form of Religious Legitimacy may not compensate for the barrenness of Jordan's deserts, yet it provides Abdullah with an intrinsic confidence. "It gives you a sense of calm", he claimed in the same interview. "Obviously there's a tremendous sense of responsibility. It makes you feel very sure of yourself. I'm very comfortable in myself. I inherited this from my father, and he inherited it from his father" (Goldberg, 2013).

As will be revealed in Chapter 4, Religious Legitimacy is a key theme of analysis. To reiterate, we assume that monarchies will draw less on a socio-economic ruling bargain and more on traditionalism and length of rule, with traditionalism including religion. The main analysis of Chapter 4 will show that Jordan's Abdullah II is the strongest example of this assumption, and it is for this reason that Jordan is presented first out of the four case studies. Section 3.6 hence discusses the role of religion while also discussing tribalism or *'asabiyya* as a form of social inclusion/exclusion that may have deepened as a political tactic in response to the Arab Spring (Valbjørn, 2019, p. 127). The prospect of tribalism as a form of political inclusion/exclusion and the parallels between Jordan's *'asabiyya* and Bahrain's sectarianism will be further explored in Sect. 3.6.1.

The legacy of religion was politicized by the history of Hashemite rule and leadership since before Jordan's birth as a nation. For the Hashemite Kingdom of Jordan was the long-term result of Hashemite resistance against the Ottoman Empire in the Great Arab Revolt (1917). This act against the Ottomans was a response of Arab nationalism, resisting Arab cultural and political persecution by imperialists now pursuing a policy of secularization at the expense of its subjects (*The Economist*, 2016). King Abdullah's great, great grandfather, Sharif Hussein bin Ali already enjoyed Religious Legitimacy as the Emir of Mecca (Royal Hashemite Court, 2001a, *The Great Arab Revolt*). By leading Arab armies into successful battle against the Ottomans and ensuring his sons also acted as commanders, Ali built upon his Religious Legitimacy to create a platform for political rule under the Hashemite banner, ensuring that such rule could be dynastic yet legitimate by striving to uphold Arab traditions, customs and faith (ibid.).

Under his son, Abdullah I, Jordan would be birthed as a Hashemite land. However, nationalism would be hindered by British desires to contain any patriotism that could resent British presence and influence in-country (Alshboul & Oudat, 2010, p. 68). Further, nationalism would be constructed through the incorporation of powerful but disparate Bedouin tribes. The deserts of nascent Jordan were populated by rival clans that "loathed central authority" (ibid.). Hence, nationalism would be built on cooption of such tribes into a social contract between the tribes and the monarchy. Jordan's political system therefore ignored the concept of national inclusion and instead promoted a system of regime loyalty "based on the desire to defend both the honour of the tribes and the institution of the monarchy" (ibid., p. 66). At the same time, tribes were also incorporated into the state Arab Legion as a form of regime security that defended the throne while also enforcing law and taxation (Royal Hashemite Court, 2001b, *The Making of Transjordan*). Jordan's nationalism thus ensured the protection of the crown by tribal elites now united in monarchical loyalty in exchange for "rewards or economic security" but excluded "a notion of the Jordanian nation" (Alshboul & Oudat, p. 66).

Tracing the Hashemite lineage and path to power, Islam must not be overlooked. For although the social contract between throne and tribes is socio-economic, religion and Religious Legitimacy was an important starting point in uniting hostile clans. Hashemite lineage to the Prophet Muhammad is a significant factor in explaining support for king (not country) in a culture "whose loyalties are fractured by *'asabiyya* (clannishness)" (Shryock, 1995, p. 346). As explained by Muslim historian Ibn Khaldun, "the Bedouins are [not] […] willing to subordinate themselves to each other, as they are rude, proud, ambitious and eager to be leaders. […] But when there is religion (among them) through prophethood […], then they have some restraining influence among themselves. […] When there is a prophet or a saint among them who calls upon them to fulfill the commands of God, […] they become fully united and acquire superiority and royal authority" (ibid.).

Whether tribal unity was ultimately enforced through shared faith or not, by the time of Emir Abdullah I's grandson, King Hussein (1952–1999), tribalism was an entrenched political culture. This culture was ultimately an "authoritarian bargain that offered [tribes] and key interest groups economic security in exchange for loyalty" (Greenwood, p. 94). Such a patronage system was financed almost solely from external aid, which was then distributed "to key constituencies as patronage, often in the form of subsidies and employment" (Robinson, 1998, p. 391). Atop this rentier distribution network was the framework of political elections and its link to tribalism. Indeed, the social contract between throne and tribe has often encouraged monarchical control of parliament and manipulation of the voting system "by the government to favor tribal gatherings at the expense of political parties" (ibid., p. 397). This latter shift in the 1993 elections may have been a top-down process; however, it built on the cultural fact that even in previous multiple-vote elections it was common for Jordanians to "cast their 'first' vote for a clan member and then cast their 'second' vote on ideological grounds" (ibid.).

Deepening pro-regime elections up to the present day has been the ostensible buying of votes, as claimed by local NGOs given observer status during parliamentary elections (Fahim, 2013). In addition to encouraging a tribal voting pattern through direct and indirect means, a Bedouin Control Law administered influential tribes under a separate legal status (Shryock, 1995, p. 328) until 1976, when this special law was abolished. Such annulment did not reflect a changing attitude within tribal politics. Rather, as Hussein's reliance on the tribes deepened, the customs of the tribes simply "worked [their] way firmly into civil jurisprudence, and today government judges [...] will decide a case involving tribespeople only after the dispute has been settled by customary means" (ibid., p. 328).

On the other hand, the fact that "the state does not officially sanction any of these procedures" is a reminder that tribalism under the Hashemites is permitted within a framework of ruler and subject, with the dominant Hashemite monarchy supported by influential tribes tied to the regime (ibid.). Hence, Hashemite bureaucrats ensure that administration of key sectors, including education, is not bequeathed to loyal tribes but governed by members of the ruling family (ibid., p. 353). Returning to the notion of tribes being united by Islam, it must be noted that the Hashemites were not born and raised in what is now Jordan. Rather, they hail "from another genealogy and another region. They came from the Hijaz [now Saudi Arabia]. They have a history of their own; they have ancestors and origins of their own" (ibid.). In other words, in a culture that is wary of external actors, the Hashemites were originally outsiders. However, their religious lineage and a controlled, centralized narrative allowed the Hashemites to be accepted "as a breed of 'super shaykhs' who have the power to impose their own history on others" (ibid.).

The "dynastic nationalism of the Jordanian state" means Hashemite control of "an immemorial past" that serves as the narrative of the present (ibid., p. 354). For this reason, government portrayals of Jordan's history make "not a single reference to any of the nation's tribes" (ibid., p. 353). Ultimately, the rise of the Hashemites in Jordan is the official tale of the perennial kingdom and "the history [...] students [should] know about and admire" (ibid.).

The narrative of Hashemite unity was tested after the 1967 War with Israel and Jordan's subsequent loss of the West Bank (Culcasi, 2016, p. 9). From 1948 to 1967, Jordan had already absorbed almost 800,000 Palestinian refugees, including displaced persons and West Bank settlers (ibid.). With Israel annexing the West Bank from Hussein's kingdom in 1967, a further 140,000 Palestinian refugees were now absorbed into a truncated Jordan that until 1988 preached the motto "Jordan is Palestine and Palestine is Jordan". By this period, it was estimated that as "a result of both granting citizenship and natural demographic growth, [...] more than 50% of Jordan's total population was of Palestinian origins" (ibid.). The growth of a Palestinian populous had ominous implications for Jordan's nationalism.

Losing the West Bank seriously dented King Hussein's Religious Legitimacy. With Hashemite custody of Mecca now taken by the Kingdom of Saudi Arabia, Jordan's monarchs had at least enjoyed custodianship of Jerusalem's holy sites (Said, 2018). The most significant of these Jerusalem sites was Al Aqsa Mosque, which held strong connections to the Prophet Muhammad, and where a young Prince Hussein witnessed the assassination of his grandfather, Emir Abdullah I in 1951 (AFP, 2014). With the 1967 annexation of the West Bank, the Hashemite family lost the prestigious title of Custodianship over Holy Sites in Jerusalem. For this reason, the 1967 loss of the West Bank is commonly referred to in Jordan as *al-Nakba* or The Disaster of 1967 (Stead, 2018).

At the same time, although most Palestinians were granted Jordanian citizenship, they were not treated as well as their East Bank counterparts. The original Jordanian tribes of the East Bank were part of a generous social contract that saw them enjoy socio-economic benefits in exchange for supporting the Crown (Alshboul & Oudat, p. 66). Palestinians, however, were viewed as external refugees and with suspicion. Indeed, local literature written by Bedouin authors symbolized East/West Bank tensions by portraying a "Bedouin patriotism" that emphasized "a privileged form of national identity which only Jordanians of tribal descent can claim" (Shryock, 1995, p. 325). Such patriotism excluded Palestinian-Jordanians and popularly "echoed long-standing concerns that the growing Palestinian population would weaken the position of East Jordanians who saw themselves as the original inhabitants of Jordan" (Culcasi, p. 9).

The darkest stain of Hashemite rule and Jordanian nationalism is inevitably linked to the East Bank-West Bank relationship. Under King Hussein and especially after 1967, there was a national dialogue of internal division. Despite sharing the same passport, East and West Bankers co-resided "as two different nationalities within the Jordanian state and social structure, the question of national allegiance lying at the heart of [being Jordanian]" (Gallets, 2015, p. 117). The refugee flood of 1967 brought not only innocent refugees but hardened militant groups loyal to the Palestinian Liberation Organization (PLO) (ibid.). Jordan's adjacent position to Israel and increasingly numerous Palestinian intake encouraged militias to see Jordan as a launching base for future attacks against Israel (ibid., p. 118).

Influential groups loyal to the PLO and operating under the umbrella branch Palestinian Resistance Movements (PRM) infiltrated conspicuous refugee camps. Much as Egypt's Muslim Brotherhood or *Ikhwan* had gained popularity through providing welfare services (Nagarajan, 2013, p. 33), the PRM militias offered welfare and education to camp inhabitants. The *Ikhwan* expected votes in return for such socio-economic services (al-Awadi, 2005, p. 67). For PRMs, camps gladly accommodated their offices, training facilities and recruitment centers. King Hussein tacitly referred to a Natural Hashemite Kingdom of Jordan and Palestine, implying eventual West Bank unity and Palestinian return (Culcasi, p. 13). In the meantime, PRMs "in the Wahadat and Husseini refugee camps" were growing in strength and support until they became popularly known as independent republics. With their own "mini-state" structures and increasing clashes between their militias and the military, it was clear that Hashemite control was weak in the camps that now stood as combative headquarters of popular resistance movements (Gallets, 2015, p. 118).

A civil war was simmering. By 1970, PRMs were operating with brazen disregard for Jordanian law, engaged in open militant activity and a "constant cycle of making agreements with the government before breaking them shortly afterwards" (ibid., p. 120). Reflecting two years later on what was to become the conflict of Black September, King Hussein was frank in his assessment. "Right to the very last possible second, we tried to prevent the clash from occurring. But Jordan had unfortunately turned into the battlefield of [...] different ideologies. [...] [T]hen came a time when I nearly lost control" (Thames TV, 1972). That loss of control rang out with the sudden attempt on Hussein's life.

On September 1, 1970, the prevalent Popular Front for the Liberation of Palestine (PFLP) attempted to assassinate Hussein (Gallets, 2015, p. 118). In a 1972 interview, King Hussein described his brush with death in vivid detail. "[T]here was a military-police check-post. We found that one side of the road was closed. And the other side was blocked by an Army lorry. No one inside. We stopped [...] and at that precise moment, heavy machine gunfire opened [upon] us. [...] I was stunned for a little while and angered. And then I realized what had happened, so I jumped out of the vehicle and rolled into a ditch and we fired back" (Thames TV, 1972).

The King claimed in the same interview that he has never feared death (ibid.). Nevertheless, the attempt on his life and the hijacking and detonation of three planes two weeks later hardened his stance to the Palestinian militias. The Jordanian Armed Forces responded to the buildup of militia operations "by shelling the Wahadat and Husseini refugee camps, which housed the PRM headquarters and was their primary bastion of support" (Gallets, 2015, p. 118). By the end of fighting on September 27, 1970, Palestinian deaths totaled around 3,400 (ibid.). By the summer of 1971, Jordan had taken a page from the PDM book and ignored an agreement to allow Palestinian militias to remain in Jordan. All Palestinian Resistance Movements had been expelled by 18 July (ibid.). In addition to cracking down hard on such militants, Hussein's government would shift its policy from accommodating West Bankers to purging them from the political sphere (ibid.).

A month after the events of Black September, Hashemite loyalist Wasfi al-Tal was appointed for his third term as Jordan's Prime Minister (ibid., p. 118). While previous governments had distinguished between Palestinian refugees and residents versus the need to expel militants, al-Tal's administration considered the entire Palestinian populous as potentially problematic. al-Tal effectively oversaw the "Jordanization" of Hashemite bureaucracy and the start of political segregation inside the kingdom. Within the state structure, al-Tal's policy directed the dismissal of Palestinians from government posts, including health, education and tourism appointments. Jordanians loyal to the Crown replaced them. The Armed Forces and *mukhabarat* or intelligence services were subjected to the same purge (ibid., p. 119). Further, civil society was reined in under al-Tal's purview. All NGOs under Palestinian leadership were co-opted by the state and scrutinized, while Palestinian-run or pro-Palestinian papers were shut down. In an effort to present this reshuffle as a positive affirmation of Jordanian nationalism, two Jordanian papers were established under government supervision (ibid.).

King Hussein also encouraged the partnership of Palestinian and Jordanian activists under the Jordanian National Union in an attempt to ease further tensions after the clashes of Black September. While not an enduring structure, the Union seemed to succeed in preventing escalated hostility between West and East Bank communities (ibid., p. 120).

The purging of the *mukhabarat* was especially pertinent to the long-term political landscape of the Hashemite Kingdom. While Egypt's Hosni Mubarak relied on military might, Hashemite rule in Jordan loosely paralleled security developments in Ben Ali's Tunisia. Ben Ali's Constitutional Democratic Rally party and marginalized police forces had engineered coup rumors under the so-called Barrakat Essahel Affair (Grewal, 2016, p. 4). However, King Hussein's early years saw the very real fomentation of dissent within the ranks. Stoked by Gamal Abdel Nasser's Arab nationalism and the perceived dependence of Jordan on Britain, leading military figures had conspired to overthrow the Hashemite dynasty in the spring of 1957 (Cavendish, 2007). The early intervention of loyal officers allowed King Hussein to detain coup leader, General Ali Abu Nowar, and tour the main military base in Zarqa, eleven miles from Amman. There, "he was mobbed by excited supporters, hugged and embraced" (ibid.).

This event not only deepened the importance of tribalism to regime security but also paved the way for the rise of Jordan's secret police (ibid.). The *mukhabarat* became a pervasive shadow of state surveillance, mirroring their status in Ben Ali's Tunisia (Sadiki, 2002b, "The Search for Citizenship", p. 506). The purge of Palestinians from the *mukhabarat* was all the more significant when considering the tools of control assigned to the secret police. In time, the *mukhabarat* would have the means to arbitrarily detain any Jordanian for vague offenses and strip them of their passport (*The Economist*, 2003). Further, no Jordanian citizen could pursue employment or higher education without a reference of good character from the state's secret police—a document that can be withdrawn for any supposed offense (ibid.). In addition, it is interesting that the *mukhabarat* offers scholarships to the most active informants, allowing officers to penetrate, inter alia, the education sector, a sphere dominated by Palestinian bureaucrats before Black September (ibid.).

In the final decade of Hussein's rule, the *mukhabarat* stood as one buttress out of several in Hashemite security. These "power partners" included business elites that, mirroring Mubarak's management style, were co-opted over time. By 1989, the ruling class was composed of:

- The monarchy and its regime elite.
- The military and *mukhabarat*.
- Business elites and East Bank tribal leaders (Robinson, p. 387).

Although coexisting with the Armed Forces and tribal and commercial circles, the *mukhabarat* continues to exercise both surveillance and political control over the public sphere. As business elites are co-opted, so too are political candidates vetted by the *mukhabarat* during elections to ensure that, no matter the choice of the people, no victory can threaten loyalty to the Crown or create a parliament unwilling to comply with monarchical will (Human Rights Watch/Middle East, 1997, p. 21; Robinson, p. 406).

Although elections may be manipulated, the existence of parties has traditionally allowed groups like the Muslim Brotherhood to enjoy open engagement with the public sphere rather than furtive operations as in Egypt before Mubarak (al-Awadi, p. 73). The Muslim Brotherhood was not only legalized by King Abdullah I but enjoyed exclusive status as "the only tolerated public political grouping in Jordan for decades" (Robinson, 1998, p. 401). Under King Hussein's rule, cooption of the Muslim Brotherhood became a tool to counter the rising fervor of Nasser's anti-monarchical Arab nationalism. This tactic was, of course, in contrast to the banning or marginalization of the Muslim Brotherhood by three of Egypt's presidents (ibid.). However, what Egypt's pharaohs and Hashemite monarchs had in common was leveraging the Muslim Brotherhood to contain radical fundamentalists. This latter element was all the more important in Jordan. Many Muslim Brotherhood members hailed from "well-established political families" and would therefore oppose rather than joining revolutionary or anti-monarchical cells (ibid.).

Despite the utility of the Brotherhood, the state has been wary of including them in any democratization process. The fear behind this policy is twofold. First, by using the *Ikhwan* to sideline more radical parties, the regime had inadvertently created a situation in which the Muslim Brotherhood would be the most organized political opposition to regime policies. This opposition became quite real from the late eighties to the mid-nineties. By that time, the Muslim Brotherhood's exclusive social contract with the regime (i.e., fending off radical political groups in exchange for open political engagement) made them "the only significant power in Jordan that [could] strongly oppose the two most significant policies driving the [Crown's] democratization campaign: the IMF-mandated austerity measures [...] and the normalization of relations with Israel" (ibid., pp. 401–402).

Second and especially after the Peace Treaty with Israel, there was the deep fear shared by regime supporters and democratic parliamentarians that a majority of the Brotherhood in parliament would threaten further liberalization. As one parliamentary official put it: "[We] fear democracy may be a vehicle only, for one group to reach the number-one status; one group which sees all truth in one book. Then there will be room for no other book, no other view. If that happens, where will I be? It will be time for people like me to go, [...] but one cannot say this here. One would be accused as a *kafir* [non-believer] or as so many Salman Rushdies. It could be the democratic path to authoritarianism" (Ryan & Schwedler, 2004, p. 142).

This fear of the Brotherhood's Islamic Action Front (IAF) party using democracy to subvert liberalization and/or Hashemite plans encouraged their marginalization. The manipulation of tribal lines during elections was complemented by regime loyalists forming coalitions in parliament to dilute involvement of elected Islamists. Such measures also included using regime loyalists to block Muslim Brotherhood appointments and to minimize their involvement in cabinet activities and deals (Robinson, p. 392).

Overall, it cannot be denied that elections in Jordan have served as a form of window-dressing, as with Ben Ali's Tunisia (Driesbach & Joyce, 2014) and Mubarak's Egypt (Nagarajan, pp. 30–31). Jordan's political liberalization program began at a time when the kingdom was attempting to gain access to IMF credit (Robinson, p. 140). Further, it appeared that the liberalization process was initiated as a form of "defensive democratization" for the regime. In other words, democratic transition has not been a bottom-up process but a regime-controlled response to socio-economic pressures. Returning to the ruling bargain, the Hashemite elite gain support from key circles in exchange for socio-economic benefits (not political openness). Hence, Jordan's liberalization program was a response to a fiscal crisis that affected the Crown's ability to maintain the rentier cash flow required for their ruling bargain (Robinson, p. 389). As with Egypt, financing for patronage networks and basic subsidies was drawn externally and when such aid from proximate Gulf States declined in 1990, the resultant financial gap provoked a severe economic downturn (ibid., pp. 389–391). It was this downturn that encouraged a liberalization program amid royal pleas to access IMF loans (ibid.). IMF demands for austerity measures meant the regime would need to partially withdraw subsidies, "thereby indirectly attacking key bases of its support" (ibid., p. 391).

Rather than meeting IMF criteria solely through the withdrawal of elite gift-giving, the Hashemite Crown also imposed taxation upon the masses. This shift in the social contract (i.e., taking rather than providing financial benefits) meant that by "relying more on its citizenry than on external rents for its government revenues, [the monarchy] was simultaneously compelled to incorporate a greater public voice in decision-making" (ibid.).

In reality of course, the monarchy and its pillars of power were very aware that the deeper the liberalization and democratization process, the greater the risk to the existing ruling structure (ibid., p. 390). As explained by Glenn E. Robinson, this balancing act set against financial frugality presented a socio-political challenge. "Societal depolitization is a hallmark of rentier states. Conversely, if a rentier state is compelled by budgetary realities to permanently extract greater resources from its own society (i.e., through taxation), then demands for greater inclusion and substantive political restructuring would be difficult to resist" (ibid.).

Returning to the main pillars of regime security, the austerity measures of IMF loan requirements actually gave the regime a chance at further cooption. Wasfi al-Tal's earlier purge of the public sector inadvertently had the long-term effect of driving West Bankers into the business elite of the private sector. Knowing that subsidy cutbacks would provoke East Bank resentment that could be directed toward Palestinian businesses, the Crown easily co-opted dominant business elites in exchange for protection from possible "East bank retaliation" as East Bankers suffered from IMF austerity measures while West Bankers "benefited the most from IMF structural adjustment in Jordan" (ibid.). Hence, cooption allowed regime control of the business elite, ensuring they would "champion economic, but not political, liberalization" (ibid.).

In addition to regime cooperation with West Bankers of the business elite, election results were often countered if not in the regime's favor. On top of manipulating tribalism to ensure votes were often cast along clan rather than ideological lines, the monarchy also installed strong regime loyalists as parliament speakers and in some cases also appointed retired *mukhabarat* leaders as prime ministers. This two-tier reaction emphasized control over what should ideally be a pliant parliament (ibid., p. 392). Furthermore, the involvement of *mukhabarat* figures as early as the first democratic elections of 1989 foreshadowed the increasing role of the *mukhabarat* and its infiltration of the liberalization program. Knowing the dangers of democratization and balancing mass approval with retained privileges, the regime used the *mukhabarat* for a policy of contained liberalization. One former PM argued it was for containment that "[n]othing, nothing is decided on any topic without the *mukhabarat*. No policy, political or otherwise, is uninfluenced by them" (Ryan & Schwedler, 2004, p. 143).

While the attacks of 9/11 gave Mubarak and Ben Ali a chance to exploit the War on Terror against domestic enemies (Sadiki, 2002a, "Democracy by Non-democratic Means", p. 75; Thaler, 2004, p. 98), this did not appear to be the case in Jordan. Across the Jordan River, while some Palestinian militants expressed satisfaction with injury done to the imperialist Americans, the majority of Palestinians saw 9/11 as a hijacking of both Islam and related Arab causes for unjustifiable murder of innocent civilians (Thaler, p. 117). At the same time, 9/11 happened amid an atmosphere in Jordan of multiple election postponements that lasted from November 2001 until June 2003 "in the aftermath of the 2003 Iraq war and in the context of attempts to revive the Israeli-Palestinian peace process" (Ryan, 2004, p. 47). In addition, the 1994 Peace Treaty with Israel had, among other things, encouraged further control or even reversal of freedoms linked to the liberalization process. For the *mukhabarat* especially, "the events of September 11 did not so much change the course of domestic politics in Jordan as accelerate them by providing a Washington-friendly justification for increased political repression" (ibid.).

Islamists in Jordan did not seem to find any advantages or major policy shifts to be undertaken in the aftermath of 9/11. However, the Arab Spring presented an interesting example of cooperation between Jordan's Islamic Action Front and the Muslim Brotherhood in Cairo. According to King Abdullah II, Mubarak's overthrow strongly influenced Brotherhood instructions from Cairo for the IAF to boycott Jordan's January 2011 elections. "I think they thought the revolution was going to happen in Jordan, and they didn't need to be part of the national [dialogue]", explained the King. "They thought they'd won. They had decided that they'd won" (Goldberg).

Between September 11, 2001 and Jordan's brush with the Arab Spring in 2011, the most pressing challenge was the 2003 U.S. invasion of Iraq.

The impending invasion placed deep pressure on the kingdom's economic ties with Iraq's Saddam Hussein. Not only was Iraq Jordan's sole source of hydrocarbons, the Hashemites also enjoyed the "lucrative nature of the specific Jordanian-Iraqi oil deal", which effectively meant that "half of [Iraq's supply to Jordan] was provided for free while the other half was provided at severely reduced prices (usually half price)" (Ryan, p. 46). Nonetheless, the combination of 9/11 and the U.S. stance on Iraq provided Jordan with an opportunity to leverage their indirect support for U. S. policy in exchange for aid. Returning to the monarchy's tactic of patronage distribution, key external donors included not only proximate Gulf States but also Western supporters, especially the United States (ibid., p. 45). Hence, the kingdom played a delicate balancing act between the anti-U.S. stance of its Arab brethren and providing minimal logistical support for the invasion (Greenwood, 2003, p. 106).

The starting date of U.S. operations in Iraq was March 2003. By May of that year, Jordan was rewarded with the U.S. "release of $700 million in emergency aid to compensate [...] for the negative economic impact of the war in Iraq", bringing total U.S. aid to Jordan to "the highest level of economic aid ever given to Jordan by the United States" (ibid., p. 107). Further, a new investment agreement was signed between the Hashemite Kingdom and the United States Republic that would increase American investment in Jordan, while U.S. allies in the Gulf were to provide Jordan with oil "free of charge until July 2003" (ibid., p. 107).

Aid has always been linked to patronage, and the 2003 U.S. package was no exception to the ruling bargain. A Hashemite Fund for Jordanian Development was established in June 2003. With a combination of the aid package and "$4.2 million of [the King's] own personal funds", the purpose of such Hashemite generosity was to increase job creation and patronage to key tribal leaders. The result of increased economic pledges and security was "high levels of voter turnout among the regime's rural Transjordanian supporters in the upcoming elections", with "candidates emphasizing 'services' over ideology" securing votes. In the process, it did not hurt the regime to know that the Islamic Action Front received diluted votes that ultimately marginalized their presence in parliament (ibid.).

Within the context of the Iraq War and maintaining nationalism in the face of East/West Bank division, King Abdullah II launched the Jordan First campaign. Jordan First was announced as early as 2002. While officially "shifting national discourse [...] to actively unite Palestinian-Jordanians and East Jordanians living to the east of the Jordan River

(Culcasi, p. 7)", it is no coincidence that the government-led movement was launched at a time when "Abdullah [was] working for a diplomatic solution to the critical situation in the region of the US-Iraq conflict" (Alshboul & Oudat, p. 84). Furthermore, Jordan First gave King Abdullah II a new platform for foreign policy with regard to the U.S. invasion of Iraq. Under the patriotic slant of Jordan First, Abdullah was able to publicly attack opposition parties with regional political ties (including to Saddam Hussein's Ba'ath party). As argued in his own words: "[the] programs, objectives, membership and financing of every party operating in Jordanian territory ought to be purely Jordanian...In recent decades, Jordan has given priority to Arab interests and not to its national interests...We have a right to be concerned first for our own people, as every country in the world does, which is where our "Jordan first" slogan comes from" (Ryan, p. 55).

In other words, any political opposition with loose ties to external parties can be branded as unpatriotic. Indeed, in 2002, the logic of patriotism encouraged arrests of journalists, scholars, activists and the shutting down of media stations critical of the regime and its support for U. S. policies (ibid., p. 56).

Jordan First ultimately emphasized regime security under the guise of national unity. The narrative of national cohesion triumphing over regional troubles allowed the regime a veneer of legitimacy in altering laws for the 2003 elections. Subsequently, in addition to jettisoning ideology in favor of increased welfare, many elected candidates "emphasized local and national issues over regional ones" (Greenwood, 2003, p. 107) in the aftermath of "increasing [...] military deployments in civilian areas" to pre-empt public discontent regarding U.S. involvement in Iraq and other regional crises (Ryan, p. 51).

As the self-immolation of Bouazizi spread across the region, Jordan found itself under pressure once more. By February of 2011, street protests had spread across the capital, with marches in late February attracting up to 6,000 participants (and 3,000 police officers for deterrence) on Amman's so-called day of anger (Gavlak, 2011). Demands that year included a reduction of Abdullah's powers but also employment and price restrictions on basic goods (ibid.). The socio-economic aspect of protests was further emphasized in the autumn of 2012. Amid Hashemite efforts to secure a $2 billion credit line from the IMF, necessary cuts to fuel subsidies provoked price rises and popular resentment (al-Khalidi, 2012). By 2014, Jordan's proximity to warring Syria had flooded the Hashemite state with over

600,000 refugees. In a kingdom of 6.3 million, Syrians comprised 10% of the population that year, worsening competition for already scarce access to public services, including schools and health care. The pressure of refugee absorption and willingness of Syrians to work for less in semi-skilled labor provoked sporadic protests in the summer of 2014 (Hartlaub, 2014).

Scattered protests have continued into 2017 amid further austerity measures (Williams, 2017). Nonetheless, it would appear that the monarchy has been stirred but not shaken. Why? The answer to this question is a multilayered strategy of Hashemite survival that draws on financial aid from external parties while also exploiting ostensible weaknesses, namely Jordan's geostrategic position amid revolutions, instability and the refugee crisis. As one Jordanian journalist put it, Jordan has escaped the Arab Spring by taking advantage of "the chaos in the region to guarantee the perpetuation of the status quo" (Murad, 2014).

From a regional perspective, both King Hussein and the current King Abdullah II have relied heavily on external aid to continue the ruling bargain for patronage networks. Indeed, within six months of his father's passing, the young monarch "visited the leaders of [...] the Group of Seven (G-7) states – the world's seven most industrialized and most wealthy countries" that, in turn, have strong links to global money lenders such as the IMF (Ryan, p. 45, 44). In addition, Abdullah also visited proximate oil states, including Libya and naturally the Gulf States that buttressed Hussein's patronage network until the Gulf War in the 1990s (ibid., p. 45).

Both Gulf Wars in Iraq brought streams of refugees into the Hashemite Kingdom. By 2007, UNHCR figures placed them at 500,000 or almost 10% of Jordan's population (UNHCR, 2007, p. 198). After the outbreak of Syria's civil war, refugees fleeing Assad's violence also sought shelter in Jordan. By 2016, the Hashemite Kingdom was hosting up to 1.2 million Syrian nationals (Ghazal, 2016). In time, the intake of refugees would become a tactic to ward off serious discontent during the Arab Spring. However, in the years between 9/11 and the Arab Spring, the monarchy has ruled through temporary laws and partially-managed protest movements via a licensing regime. This system officially tolerated protests if written permission had been obtained from the government three days in advance. In practice, however, few such permits were granted (Ryan & Schwedler, pp. 144–145).

Amid socio-political demands from 2011 to 2012, the King has complemented a partial reversal of liberalization with a pattern of dismissing prime ministers and cabinet members, placing blame for nepotism, corruption and socio-economic malaise upon their shoulders (Tobin, 2012). Indeed, this tactic seems to have been somewhat successful, as certain protests in 2012 concentrated anger against then Prime Ministers Samir Rifai and later Marouf Bakhit, calling for their successive resignations in a climate of "rising food and fuel prices, inflation and unemployment" (ibid.). In addition, the government has not underestimated the symbolism behind public spaces where protests have occurred. As Jillian Schwedler explains, there is a political science behind not only regime security but popular discontent. "Protestors want to operate in places that will make the most impact. A heavily populated [...] neighborhood [...] becomes a [prominent] space to disrupt" (Schwedler, 2012).

The importance of symbolism and popular public spaces was attacked early on during Jordan's containment of the Arab Spring. As witnessed by a university student, authorities responded quickly to protests held in *Dakhlia* Square in the populous Jebel Hussein area. "[It happened in] 2011, right when the [A]rab [S]pring began. The night after those protests were shut down [in Jebel Hussein] the government immediately rebuilt the [*Dakhlia* Square] making it not fit for crowd gatherings. The next morning the plaza or the square that held people was turned into fountains and they planted trees and other plants and they made passages in between [...] fit for [only] 3 people walking side by side" (Facebook, 2017, *Personal Correspondence with Student from University of Jordan*).

In addition, new development projects like the shopping district of Abdali Boulevard (close to Jebel Hussein) are transforming large swathes of public space into "private commercial spaces, which can be policed and controlled more stringently, as citizens have no right to be there. If you are not buying a $4 coffee in an upscale café, you are not really welcome in that space. This elitism helps the government, because it keeps those who do not "belong" (those who might protest) out [of conspicuous public areas]" (Schwedler). It is perhaps a peculiar coincidence that the now-open Abdali Boulevard "stands near the site of the old *Mukhabarat* Building [...] [,] literally being built on the foundations of a security state" (ibid.). Abdali Boulevard stands as a new symbol of regime security meeting tourism and global investment. The glitter of high-price malls and luxury developments fosters a simulacrum of generic but safe materialism, in which "foreign investors can go to the sushi bars and beautiful hotels and get to their places of work" (ibid.).

Returning to the influx of refugees, their plight has added to the regime's resources for crowd control. At the start of protests in 2011, Iraqis who had fled Baghdad in 2003 warned of the consequences of overthrow in their homeland (Tobin). The fear of instability provoked by the presence of Gulf War victims was exacerbated by the Syrian civil war. Absorbing more Syrians than Iraqis by 2016, "Jordanians [became] fully aware that this is no time for their domestic concerns", with increasing refugees a constant reminder of what awaits should the status quo crumble. As one human rights activist explained, fear of instability means that Jordan's "ruler is best served by the status quo. The regime is comfortable today and is sitting on its podium surveying the scene. It doesn't need to make any serious effort to fix or improve [things] because the status quo is stable" (Murad).

Tracing Hashemite rule from Hussein to today's Abdullah II reveals a multilayered form of regime security that draws heavily on external aid. While it is true that the Hashemites may boast some Religious Legitimacy though lineage to the Prophet Muhammad, their ultimate survival comes from the trappings of a patronage network and the ruling bargain of a rentier state financed by proximate oil sheikhs and access to global aid bodies through powerful Western allies. This ruling bargain is heavily linked to tribal support, which in turn has influenced manipulation of elections and the infiltration of the pervasive *mukhabarat* to ensure any democratic opening does not threaten elite interests. At the same time, King Abdullah seems to express a desire for democratic openness and some regret for inheriting the electoral tactics of his father.

During 2013 election campaigns, Abdullah met with leaders of the National Current Party only to discover that "what the party stood for [...], beyond patronage and the status quo, was not entirely clear" (Goldberg). Emphasizing his disappointment in how such parties were approaching the democratic vote, Abdullah explained that he "read [their] economic and social manifesto, and it scared the crap out of me. [It made] no sense whatsoever. If [they're] going to reach out to the 70 percent of the population that is younger than me, [they've] got to work on this. [The party manifesto] [...] didn't have anything. It was slogans. There was no program. Nothing. [...] It's all about 'I'll vote for this guy because I'm in his tribe'" (ibid.).

Such sentiments and the public desire of Abdullah for "a Jordan where [the people] love the monarchy, just like [...] the outpouring toward Queen Elizabeth in England" may very well be genuine (ibid.). However, in a desert kingdom dependent on external aid and rentier agreements, it would seem that the Hashemite tribe continues to practice regime survival above all else, exploiting regional chaos rather than pushing sincere reform. Their goal: to stay afloat and keep the state under their name.

An overview of Jordan under the Hashemites explains further how Jordan as a monarchical case study is strongly tied to the assumption that monarchies draw on religion and traditionalism. Jordan's dependence on external aid highlights the nature of a limited socio-economic ruling bargain, with "defensive democratization" linked to Korany's discussion in Chapter 2 of how the ruling bargain is not static and can change or become politicized when material distribution is limited. In addition, Jordan's history under the Hashemites emphasizes Religious Legitimacy, which is strongly emphasized in Abdullah II's speech in response to the Arab Spring, as will be discussed in Chapter 4. The major themes of Religious Legitimacy and the ruling bargain are most apparent in Jordan as a case study and from Abdullah's speech, with Chapter 5's analysis of political factors from Jordan's Constitution further bolstering rule through traditionalism and religion.

3.3 The Kingdom of Bahrain

> Our dear people[,] […] [National Day] is in recognition of your outstanding performance and achievement […], producing common values of co-existence, tolerance and enlightenment. [We] should proudly recall memories of those who had set sails up and planted palm trees, and excavated for oil […] in order to implement prosperous life on each inch of […] Bahraini soil. Our appreciation goes as well to […] the Bahrain Defense Force (BDF) and other security bodies who safeguard gains, freedom […] and stability of the nation. […] The march of welfare, reform and modernization will never be halted. (Bahrain News Agency, 2004)

A celebration of monarchical rule, oil wealth, regime security and welfare benefits. Thus, was the 2004 National Day announced by King Hamad bin Issa al-Khalifa. It is the emphasis on oil wealth that will be examined as a major theme in Chapter 4's main analysis. To reiterate, we assume that republics will emphasize the socio-economic ruling bargain as the main source of their non-democratic legitimacy in response to the Arab Spring, due to most republics being the result of coups rather than established familial rule. Consequently, many republican rulers have weaker ties to traditional (religious) institutes and popular support and rely on a ruling bargain to maintain legitimacy. Monarchs, on the other hand, will draw on Religious Legitimacy more than the ruling bargain due to their longevity and ties to traditional institutions and accepted socio-cultural norms. However, Bahrain's oil wealth and monarchical system present a partial reversal of this hypothesis. As will be expanded upon in Chapter 5 and discussed in this chapter, Bahrain is a monarchy but one that draws on oil wealth to ensure consistent welfare provisions. Such a factor of Political Legitimacy provides a case study of monarchical rule that emphasizes a socio-economic ruling bargain. Yet, as with its Jordanian counterpart, Bahrain is also a case study that draws on religion, albeit via the divisive lens of sectarianism. It is this mix or themes of traditionalism and oil wealth that places Bahrain after Jordan when addressing the hypothesis and answering the questions: What are the factors Arab leaders use in discourse justifying their rule within the context of the Arab Spring? To what extent does this discourse support a (socio-economic) ruling bargain and Religious Legitimacy?

In 2002, Bahrain's ruler had transformed the island state into a kingdom. A 2001 constitutional amendment had re-crowned the former emir as king by 2002, an ostensible move toward constitutional rather than absolute rule (Henderson, 2017, p. 2). This progressive image was in keeping with the nascent period of King Hamad. Ascending to the throne in 1999, the mature monarch was a rumored reformer (Diamond, 2013, p. 85). Deep rather than cosmetic reforms were offered as concessions by the new king, intended to mark a departure from a restrictive predecessor. Akin to the pragmatic Mubarak and soft-spoken Ben Ali, Hamad released up to 320 political prisoners and pardoned political dissidents (Wehrey, 2013, p. 118). Tight security laws were revoked. In addition, civil society was tentatively awakened under a new right to form political "associations" and the creation of a parliament with up to forty elected members (ibid., pp. 118–119).

The aforementioned changes seemed indeed to lead to a less absolute autocracy. In 2001, Hamad's National Action Charter formally called for Bahrain to progress into a constitutional monarchy. The same document also deepened citizen relations with the state and their political involvement through parliament. An elected lower house would complement an appointed upper house, kept in check by an independent judiciary. As Ben Ali presented himself as an advocate for women (Hawkins, 2011, pp. 45–46), Hamad called on the engagement of Bahrain's females in the political sphere and gave men and women over twenty the right to vote (Wehrey, p. 119). The National Action Charter was overwhelmingly endorsed when put to vote in February 2001 (ibid.). Verily, the island nation "and particularly its large numbers of relatively impoverished [Shia'as], worked itself into a state of near-euphoria over these initiatives" (ibid.).

Such excitement was short-lived, however. By 2002, many of these initiatives had been reversed. Amid renewed press censorship, King Hamad also sought to severely reduce the legislative rights of the elected lower house (ibid.). Already in these early days of power, it was becoming clear that Bahrain's monarchy was not progressively constitutional but a firm family affair. While other Gulf States centralize rule around one head, Bahrain's House of Khalifa is distinguished by a triumvirate. This ruling arrangement sees King Hamad as the premier decision-maker, seconded by his elder uncle as Prime Minister (Henderson, p. 2). This partnership is followed by Crown Prince Salman bin Hamad al-Khalifa as the third ruling member and a moderating presence against royal hardliners who "oppose any concession toward the country's [Shia'a majority]" (ibid.).

Reform reversal seemed to garner little international outcry. Indeed, years of human rights gaps and political regression did not seem to draw attention from the power corridors in London or Washington D.C. (Diamond, p. 85). As put by American geopolitical firm Stratfor, "Bahrain's importance to [the West] as a regional ally in the Middle East is inversely proportional to the kingdom's size" (Stratfor Enterprises, LLC, 2017). Bahrain's proximity to Iran provides the oil kingdom with a "geostrategic trump card" akin to Jordan's politically sensitive location in the Arab world (Diamond, 2013, p. 85). For the United States, access to the Persian Gulf, Arabian Sea and Indian Ocean has encouraged naval bases on Bahraini shores since 1947. By 1995, this presence had been expanded to include the U.S. Fifth Fleet and U.S. Naval Forces Central Command. With a population of almost 10,000 American military, DoD and civilian staff (including family members), the Fifth Fleet has been a U.S. entry point into MENA conflict participation since shortly after the reform regression of 2002. Hence, Bahrain became the "[primary] naval base for U.S. War in Afghanistan" and in 2003 complemented Jordan's logistics support geography by becoming the primary Gulf base for the 2003 invasion of Iraq (Stratfor, 2017).

In addition to strong U.S. ties, Bahrain and the Hashemite Kingdom of Jordan share British relations as another commonality. Rulers of both states received military training at the U.K.'s prestigious Sandhurst Royal Military Academy (BBC, 2014b, "Sandhurst Sheikhs"). Known as the Sandhurst Sheikhs, past graduates include Gulf and Levant monarchs. Both King Hussein and current King Abdullah II of Jordan attended the "grueling 44-week course testing the physical and intellectual skills of officer cadets and imbuing them with the values of the British Army" (BBC, 2014b, "Sandhurst Sheikhs"). Such values extend to an "Officer Commissioning Course [that] covers counter-insurgency techniques and ways to manage public disorder" (ibid.). The Sheikhs of Sandhurst are also ruling sheikhs in their home countries, with the majority of Sandhurst's royal graduates heads of GCC (Gulf Cooperation Council) states. In addition to training Jordan's Hashemite kings, Sandhurst also trained "King Hamad of Bahrain, Sheikh Tamim, Emir of Qatar, [late] Sultan Qaboos of Oman [and] [...] Sheikh Saad, [fourth] Emir of Kuwait [until 2006]" (ibid.).

Common factors between Jordan and Bahrain are contrasted by one resource taken in the Gulf for granted: oil. However, Bahrain's oil reserves remain modest compared to its GCC brethren. As of 2016, proven crude volume stood at 100 million barrels with a production capacity of 50,000 barrels per day (CIA World Factbook, 2017; U.S. Energy Information Administration, 2016a, *Bahrain*). Along with Oman, Bahrain is the only Gulf State that does not belong to OPEC and stands as the smallest oil producer in the GCC (U.S. Energy Information Administration, 2016a, 2016b). With a population of around 1.3 million, Bahrain's energy outlook is easily rivaled by its neighbors, Kuwait and Qatar (CIA World Factbook, 2017). As of 2016, Kuwait boasted 102 billion barrels of proven crude reserves and a population of just under 4 million (U.S. Energy Information Administration, 2016b, *Kuwait*; World Bank, 2015). Qatar, on the other hand, enjoys proven oil reserves of 25.7 billion barrels for a population of around 2.2 million (Oxford Business Group, 2017; World Bank, 2015). Naturalized citizens number a fraction of this total. While recent official estimates are lacking, a 2010 survey by the Qatar Statistics Authority placed the natural populous at around 240,000 (Winckler, 2015).

In addition to its one onshore field, Bahrain shares a second offshore field with Saudi Arabia. Known as the Abu Safah field, the partnership between the two kingdoms sees Bahrain refine and market half the field's output, while Saudi Arabia oversees all production. Profits are split evenly between the House of Saud and the House of Khalifa. Nevertheless, the dominance of Saudi production involvement symbolizes an asymmetric political relationship between both Gulf States. This unequal partnership would prove pivotal during Bahrain's Arab Spring (U.S. Energy Information Administration, 2016a, 2016b).

Since the 1970s, Bahrain has emphasized economic diversification, building up a regional base for industry, Islamic banking and global appeal as a foreign investment hub and global banking center in the Middle East (Hamdi & Sbia, 2013, p. 119). Nonetheless, oil profit remains the principle source of state income, accounting for up to 87.85% of revenues in 2011 (ibid.). In addition, the government appears to draw on oil wealth, however meager, to maintain a high level of expenditure. This expenditure includes development projects for long-term infrastructure and raising living standards, linked to welfare and Beneficial Consequences under the ruling bargain (ibid.). High expenditure on long-term goals draws heavily on hydrocarbon riches, making expenditure vulnerable to oil price fluctuations. At the same time, state commitment to long-term projects and spending almost prevents a reduction in expenditure if and when oil prices decrease (ibid.). This conundrum is framed within the context of the ruling bargain and Beneficial Consequences expected by GCC citizens, with governing tactics straddling "the need to build modern state institutions [with] the [government's] urge to retain control over the political and public sphere" (Sika, 2013, p. 7).

Government control through the ruling bargain, as in many Arab states, is primarily solidified through subsidies and welfare benefits. Subsidies often target daily consumer goods and other items that affect living costs and standards. Hence, the monarchy provides total or partial subsidies for:

- Commercial petrol.
- Basic foodstuffs, including fresh meat.
- All utilities.
- Prescription medicine.

In addition to the aforementioned subsidies, health care and education are provided to the populous free of charge and the state constantly intervenes in domestic markets to keep prices stable and sheltered from any economic shocks that can alter the cost of (imported) consumer goods (Epstein & Miller, 2015, p. 29). The importance of such constant Beneficial Consequences appears to supersede long-term infrastructure projects on, e.g., roads, bridges and even schools and hospitals. Indeed, it would seem that while the state attempts to shelter its citizens from economic shocks through price control, any spike in oil demand sees an across-the-board increase in grants, subsidies and wages as opposed to the bulk of increased profits being invested (Hamdi & Sbia, 2013, p. 123).

At the same time, Bahrain's leadership appears to understand the curse of finite resources. Four years before the Arab Spring, a royal decree established the Future Generations Reserve Fund (FGF). The Fund was ostensibly founded to strengthen long-term fiscal management and preserve what little remains of Bahrain's oil wealth. However, the Fund's coffers are lined by oil profits only when payment for hydrocarbon exports are higher than predicted. The fact that oil profits are consistently spent on subsidies while the Fund's growth assumes non-projected surplus implies that maintaining the ruling bargain and related benefits takes precedent (ibid.).

Oil wealth is not given to all, however. Just as the Hashemite Kingdom of Jordan is ruled by a minority and populated by a majority of Palestinian origin, so too does Bahrain suffer from its own sectarianism. The Sunni al-Khalifas are a minority elite ruling a population that is 70% Shia'a (Wehrey, p. 116). The fear of a Shia'a takeover buttresses Bahrain's relations with the rest of the Gulf, especially the Saudi Kingdom. As a Sunni government, Saudi Arabia contains its own Shia'a minority in the oil-rich eastern provinces (ibid., p. 124). Hence, Saudi Arabia fears not only its own minority but how political reform in Bahrain may empower local Shia'as to the extent that a challenge to Sunni rule is possible (Henderson, p. 4). Such a shift in Bahrain's political relations would in turn inspire Saudi Arabia's Shia'as to seek the same liberation from their Sunni masters (ibid.). It is for this reason that Saudi Arabia attempts to hold political sway in Bahrain. In addition to oil income, the al-Khalifas enjoy Saudi oil subsidies (ibid., p. 118). This economic penetration of Bahrain symbolizes deeper political involvement, under which Saudi Arabia acts as "the al-Khalifa family's chief economic and political patron" (ibid., p. 123).

It would seem that Saudi Arabia exercises its own ruling bargain over the al-Khalifas. In exchange for Saudi financial and political backing, the conservative Saudi Kingdom is granted dominant influence in Bahrain's parliamentary affairs. As with Mubarak, Saudi Arabia considers true liberalization dangerous but welcomes "*calibrated* political reform as a means to release pressure and marginalize more hard-line elements of [Shia'a] opposition" (ibid.). As such, Riyadh's strategy since 2006 has been to shape and limit the political path of Bahrain's parliament. Saudi Arabia funded the Sunni Islamist al-Asala group in 2006 while also welcoming the participation of moderate Shia'a groups in elections. At the same time, while such moderates may be manipulated to counter militant Shia'a groups in Bahrain, Riyadh has also sent Sunni voters with dual citizenship to cast votes in Bahrain, complementing al-Khalifa tactics of naturalizing foreign Sunnis for ballots during elections (ibid., pp. 120, 123–124). By the time of Bahrain's Arab Spring, naturalized Sunnis were referred to as "mercenaries" for being granted citizenship in order to augment Bahrain's Sunni population (al-Rawi, 2015, p. 35).

While Egypt and Jordan have seen the *majlis* become an arena of (Sunni) Islamist-government collaboration (al-Awadi, p. 63; Robinson, p. 401), Bahrain's own parliament augments such relations through the fragile lens of sectarianism. Returning to the 2002 reversal of reforms, a subsequent rise in public cynicism toward al-Khalifa rule punctuated a year of increasing restrictions. The weakening of parliament's elected lower house and subsequent strengthening of the royally-appointed upper council was presented as a necessary step for national stability. As explained by an upper house member, the parliamentary framework was revised "so it couldn't be hijacked by extremists. We don't want a forty-person elected house composed of religious clerics who will ban alcohol, forbid women from driving, take Bahrain backwards, and drive away the foreigners who enjoy our liberal society" (al-Rawi, p. 119).

However, when the weakening of the lower house was combined with fixed elections, it was increasingly obvious that more important than mitigating religious conservatives was the continuation of Sunni political dominance (ibid.). The subsequent boycott of 2002 elections by Shia'a groups strengthened the numbers of Sunni Muslim organizations in parliament, including Muslim Brotherhood affiliate al-Minbar and the Salafist al-Asala. The strengthening of ties between the regime and (Sunni) Islamists is in contrast to the persecution of the Muslim Brotherhood in the nascent years of the Egyptian Republic (Nagarajan, p. 33). However, it is also a collaboration tactic utilized by the Hashemite kings of Jordan, intended to strengthen not only cooperation between the regime and mainstream Islamists but also as a strategy to marginalize fundamentalists. In Bahrain, however, the same political stratagem illustrates the use of Religious Legitimacy through empowering the Sunni minority elite. A strong Sunni bloc in parliament and their rapport with Hamad would eventually weaken Shia'a involvement twofold.

First, such a Sunni partnership would ensure that Shia'a entrance into parliamentary elections in 2006 would face the de facto obstacle of fewer seats and hence diluted political clout. Second, such marginalization from 2002 to 2006 fragmented Shia'a opposition regarding involvement in elections. The moderate al-Wifaq group decided to participate in 2006 elections, while the militant al-Haq group refused. Compared to other Arab regimes, Bahrain's Sunni-Shia'a divide affects parliamentary partnerships between parties and the regime. Hence, al-Khalifa collaboration with parliament ensures the political dominance of Sunni moderates. At the same time, King Hamad allows Shia'a representation and political activity through al-Wifaq, the candidates of which are "backed by senior Shia'a clerics" (al-Rawi, p. 119). This Sunni-Shia'a relationship provides a veneer of religious tolerance in the political sphere while in reality fragmenting Shia'a political opposition. The split between moderate al-Wifaq participation and al-Haq refusal ensures that any elected Shia'a member is "still short of the majority needed to pass laws" (ibid., p. 120).

In addition to manipulating Shia'a numbers in parliament, the Shia'a majority face other forms of discrimination. Such marginalization can be divided into political and religious forms. Political discrimination includes underrepresentation not only during elections but in national surveys and district representation. This form of populous manipulation carries hidden discrimination for Shia'a communities. Underreported district numbers guarantee reduced aid and benefits, forcing Shia'a leaders to fill a services gap. While Egypt's Muslim Brotherhood had the luxury of plugging such a gap to gain popularity, Shia'a leaders find their political opportunities reduced as they "must sacrifice the basic work of governing in order to respond adequately to the citizens they represent" (ADHRB, 2015, p. 19).

Returning to the previous discussion of naturalized Sunnis, the regime complements this practice by denying citizenship to eligible (Shia'a) residents. At the same time, the monarchy has not hesitated to strip Shia'a activists and clerics, even youth, of their passports to further augment Sunni numbers (ibid., p. 20). Equally telling when it comes to distribution of power has been work discrimination, with Shia'as routinely barred from government positions, including police and military (Wehrey, p. 125). Much as Jordan's similar treatment of Palestinians was meant to ensure East Banker and royalist dominance in the public sector, Bahrain's own hiring practices are intended to preserve Sunni dominance and the elite status of the ruling minority (ibid.).

Older still and perhaps less covert is religious discrimination toward the Shia'a populous. It is ironic indeed that the ostensible equal rights of Hamad's National Action Charter encouraged many exiled Shia'a clerics to return (ADHRB, 2015, p. 23). The political openness of the Charter saw many such clerics band together to form the Shia'a al-Wifaq group that became Bahrain's largest political organization and Shia'a opposition. After 2002, openness became authoritarianism with reform reversal, and since 2011, religious discrimination of Shia'a leaders has worsened. After the start of February protests that year, the regime arrested and tortured prominent Shia'a clergymen before sentencing them to several years or life imprisonment. Their crimes were: insulting the ruling family and guilt by association (ibid.).

To complete retaliation against the Shia'a majority, government forces have also targeted landmarks and sites of cultural importance to Shia'a' Bahrainis. Throughout 2011, up to 38 Shia'a mosques were demolished across the country, some up to several hundred years old. The majority of such structures appear to have been crushed due to their public visibility and/or proximity to Shia'a neighborhoods (ibid., p. 24).

The bulldozing of Shia'a shrines and physical violence toward Shia'a clergy punctuated the regime's sectarian response to protests in 2011. However, these acts also symbolize Shia'a discrimination and the dangerous balancing act of sectarianism that was present years before such demonstrations. The strongest symbol and source of failure have been the parliament amid flirtations with reform that reverted to authoritarianism. Amid these reversals were the alteration of the 1973 Constitution and the legislative powers of the elected lower house. As discussed, this shift was intended to preserve power for the royally-appointed upper house but also deepened "a government strategy of using the legislature to incite sectarianism so that the monarchy could play the role of arbiter" (Wehrey, p. 125).

By 2006, the regime tactic of playing mediator was having harmful effects on Bahrain's political outlook. The partnership between the regime and Sunni Islamists provoked increasing sectarianism that, in turn, created a weakened parliament. Amid regional tensions that highlighted Sunni-Shia'a hostility, the sectarian squabbling in parliament and inability of al-Wifaq to push reforms was provoking growing frustration among Bahrain's younger Shia'a majority (ibid., p. 120). Regional tensions filtered into Bahrain's parliament to the point where legislation became highly politicized. As explained by GCC scholar Frederic Wehrey, "[in] the wake of the 2006 Lebanon War and Iraq's Sunni-Shia violence, Bahraini MPs adopted increasingly sectarian positions on the dramatic events unfolding around them. Instead of legislating reforms that might improve the lives of their constituents, deputies tried to pass parliamentary expressions of solidarity with the defenders of Fallujah, Najaf, or Beirut. During loud and heated debates, Sunni MPs [exchanged insults with] their Shia'a counterparts and were called al-Qaeda' in return" (ibid., p. 121).

Examples of sectarian impasse such as the aforementioned cases were used by the monarchy as proof that only the House of Khalifa could truly rule Bahrain and, as mediators of sectarianism, prevent the island nation from descending into the chaos of the next Iraq or Lebanon (ibid.). Yet, while claiming to be arbiters of sectarianism, the regime was also pushing al-Wifaq into a corner over a significant parliamentary issue that contributed to protest: corruption. Unfortunately for al-Wifaq, corruption was one of the few political issues it could fight as a way of promoting both itself and what should have been non-sectarian interests. However, as in Jordan's parliament, such a campaign threatened to interfere with royal socio-economics and provoked the monarchy into a caustic response. One year before Bahrain's Arab Spring, Shia'a activists found themselves at the mercy of mass arrests, loss of citizenship and jail terms. The most prominent victims of this campaign were Shia'a clerics and cabinet members. By portraying the accused as Iranian agents, the al-Khalifas once again framed political issues in deeply sectarian terms, while also issuing a warning to MPs: examining how the royal family uses public funds or lands was crossing a red line (ibid., p. 122).

This real threat against political investigations emphasizes al-Khalifa power in a parliament that is ultimately disempowered. Since the 1990s, Bahrain's political life has been subject to the same "reforms" as the parliaments of Ben Ali's Tunisia and Mubarak's Egypt. Cosmetic changes marked the 1990s, which saw the creation of the unelected *majlis* in 1993 (ibid., p. 118). The promise of true democratic progress was cut short with the 2002 reversal of reforms. This period of revived authoritarianism preceded the 2006 sectarian tensions in parliament amid Saudi influence and vote manipulation.

Sectarianism punctuated the al-Khalifa strategy of keeping parliament weak. It would also punctuate their successful attempts to quash revolution. On February 14, 2011, protestors inspired by the movements in Tunis and Cairo gathered to make their own demands known. Their requests included non-sectarian albeit generalized ideals such as freedom, democratic transition and equality, with Bahraini Sunnis (outside the royal circle) participating in demonstrations for such universal values (Diamond, 2013, p. 85). The regime's response would not only be brutal but utilize regional allies and media as the al-Khalifas hijacked Bahrain's protests to transform them into sectarian threats that emphasized internal differences over political unity.

Initial protests began to coalesce around February 14, 2011. On February 17, Bahrain security forces sent a brutal message. As Jordan's *Dakhlia* Square became a rallying point and symbol for unrest, so too did Bahrain's Pearl Roundabout in the capital, Al Manama become a symbol of resistance to authority (al-Rawi, p. 25; Wehrey, p. 122). And just as Jordan's monarchy was quick to deconstruct *Daklia* Square, the al-Khalifas responded in kind. A pre-dawn raid of the Roundabout saw the immediate deaths of four sleeping protestors amid a flurry of "rubber bullets, birdshot and tear gas" (ibid.). The act and subsequent arrests, killings and denial of medical care were justified by the state as a necessary response to sectarian threats (ibid.). One day after what became known as 'Bloody Thursday", government forces tore down the (in)famous pearl that had become the symbol of protest at the Pearl Roundabout (Bronner, 2011). Officials claimed the move was intended to ease traffic congestion in an often-crowded part of the capital. However, it is impossible to accept this explanation if analyzing the shifting meaning of symbolism.

The pearl sculpture was originally a defining landmark symbolizing GCC unity and Bahrain's relations with "the six gulf states whose economic life was based, before oil, on pearls" (ibid.). By 2011, however, the same symbol loomed over the tent-camp of popular protest movements "with free food and a carnival atmosphere modeled on Tahrir Square in Cairo" (ibid.). For demonstrators, the pearl monument had become a defining rallying point, changing the symbolism of the Pearl Roundabout from a government-controlled GCC narrative to one of popular resistance. Indeed, Bahrain's Foreign Minister at the time, Sheikh Khalid bin Ahmed al-Khalifa contradicted excuses of easing congestion. "We did it", he explained, "to remove a bad memory". Referring to the protests, Sheikh Khalifa went on, "[the] whole thing caused our society to be polarized. We don't want a monument to a bad memory" (ibid.).

In addition to expunging altered symbols of national unity, the regime also paid attention to how social media was presenting Bahrain's Arab Spring. Of note has been the use of popular video search engine YouTube, often used by Bahraini activists to spread their filmed activities (al-Rawi, p. 25). However, activists were not the only political actors to use social media to spin their own narrative. While protestors in Al Manama may have brought universal demands, underlying sectarianism turned Bahrain's troubles into a public opportunity for regional and domestic groups to frame the island nation's divide as a Sunni-Shia'a split for their own political motives. This opportunistic hijacking of the protest narrative would slowly aid the al-Khalifas in their own media campaign (ibid., p. 26).

The al-Khalifas were assisted in their campaign by fellow GCC allies, who framed the demonstrations as the work of Shia'a "traitors [who were] supporting an Iranian agenda" (ibid.). In addition, Qatar-owned Al Jazeera was accused of under-reporting protests and presenting a Sunni-biased slant of unfolding events. Four of Al Jazeera's employees ostensibly resigned over the lack of neutral reporting (ibid., p. 27). At the same time, Al Jazeera's biased coverage and the Sunni support of GCC partners were contrasted by the coverage of Shia'a satellite channels, including those of Iranian origin. This was especially true of the Iranian Al-Alam station, which devoted much time to coverage of "Shia'a protests" in Bahrain and Saudi Arabia. Al-Alam encouraged dissent against monarchy in both the al-Khalifa and Saudi kingdoms, an alarming fact considering that Al-Alam is watched by up to 90% of Bahrain's Shia'a populous (ibid., p. 27). Al-Alam's supposed voicing of Shia'a concerns at the expense of objectivity allowed the regime and its GCC allies to frame the protests as a sectarian threat and activists as Iranian agents. The fact that such Sunni accusations were linked to real broadcasters in Iran gave the government's sectarian campaign partial legitimacy (ibid.).

The government's campaign of sectarianism spread to social media to deepen the religious chasm so vital to the al-Khalifa narrative. In particular, regime operatives traced Bahraini users of Facebook and Twitter, constantly monitoring political expressions "using sophisticated and expensive equipment provided by Western companies" (ibid., p. 30). Traced activists faced jail terms or worse in state-run social media campaigns that were, in some cases, disturbingly overt. One Facebook page ostensibly linked to authorities encouraged visitors to reveal the name and workplace of Shia'a activists "and let the government take care of the rest" (Voice of America, 2011). Another page seemed designed to intimidate, boasting photos of individual demonstrators. Each photo would be checked off once the person in question was detained by authorities (ibid.).

The regime's manipulation and monitoring of social media was effective in sowing sectarian distrust online. Sunni and Shia'a users became suspicious of one another, ensuring that rather than national unity (against the regime), Facebook and Twitter became arenas for fueling sectarianism, creating "suspicion between people who work together or live together or are in the same society or club" (ibid.). The ease of monitoring Twitter and Facebook drove many activists toward posting their narratives on YouTube. As of 2015, no reported arrests had been linked to YouTube posts (al-Rawi, p. 31). However, this supposedly "safer" online platform was not immune to sectarian divide. Even on YouTube, activists appeared split into pro- or anti-Shia'a communities (ibid., p. 36). Indeed, YouTube activity saw Bahrain's protests take on a regional and even global slant that reflected al-Khalifa-Saudi relations and the interest of GCC states and the West.

In a 2015 analysis of YouTube videos posted by Bahraini activists, it was revealed that seven channels sharing just over 3,500 videos on protests had garnered over 12 million views and over 14,000 subscribers (ibid., p. 32). Further analysis of video comments exemplified regional and Western interest in Bahrain's woes. 41.4% of examined comments were from inside Bahrain. However, over 20% of video comments came from Saudi Arabian users and 4.1% from Kuwait (ibid.). Interestingly enough, only 0.2% of comments were from Iran, with U.K. comments providing 3.6% and comments from the United States just behind Saudi Arabia at 20.3% (ibid.).

Complementing regional involvement was the act of "flaming" or insulting another person based on, inter alia, religious and political affiliation. The act of "flaming" is often topic sensitive but also thrives on anonymity, which may encourage uninhibited online behavior (ibid.). The greater anonymity of YouTube users when compared to Facebook and Twitter may also have contributed to the hurling of insults across videos (ibid.). Returning to al-Khalifa accusations of Iranian interference, YouTube comments made on Bahrain's Shia'a populous appear linked to Iran, implying the supposed conspiracy and regime fear that Shia'a communities sought the overthrow of Sunni royalty under Iranian influence (ibid., p. 34).

On the other hand, comments also provided an interesting example of Religious Legitimacy. While the Hashemite monarchy of Jordan drew on lineage to the Prophet Muhammad, in Bahrain it appeared to be the protestors who saw themselves as blessed by their links to their faith. Comments are often laced with common religious phrases such as "Allah's blessing", "by Allah" and "my Allah" (ibid., p. 32). These religious supplications are linked to anti-government phrases such as "down with Hamad" and other slogans used by overwhelmingly Shia'a users and protestors (ibid., pp. 33–34). In other words, protestors see their cause as just under God, with some users going so far as issuing "Allah's curse" against King Hamad and also Saudi Arabia (ibid., p. 34). At the same time, the phrase "Allah's curse" is also directed by some users toward "Bahraini Shiites". Such comments seem provoked as a counter response to anti-Hamad comments and appear to stem from "hardline Sunnis" in Bahrain and Saudi Arabia (ibid., p. 35). Countering anti-Shia'a comments, some "flaming" took a politico-economic as well as religious slant through frequent use of the term "mercenaries". The word "mercenaries" was used to refer to naturalized Sunnis in Bahrain and the al-Khalifa strategy of providing foreigners with Bahraini citizenship to augment Sunni numbers, reflecting demands of Shia'a protestors to end said practice and revoke citizenship of such "mercenaries", who are also accused of being incorporated into Bahrain's security forces (ibid.).

In addition to violent crackdowns and manipulating sectarianism, it is possible to return to the ruling bargain to understand why Bahrain's Arab Spring never blossomed. The ruling bargain includes subsidies and free benefits (health care, education) that are associated with general living costs. It must be recalled that many movements under the Arab Spring were provoked not only by political suppression but by the desire for bread, which came before freedom, social justice and human dignity (Pin, p. 3). As mentioned earlier, Bahrain's government ensures fixed food prices and hence controls consumer expenses linked to living standards—for, as Bouazizi himself put it, citizens will not tolerate being unable to make a living. In the case of a Gulf ruling bargain, oil wealth may create expectations for a subsidized living, however (Epstein & Miller, p. 2, 8).

The subsidies and welfare benefits of Bahrain's ruling bargain represent a constant service that should be maintained by the state in exchange for political support or at least apoliticism. Clearly, Bahrain's unrest illustrated that for many, especially the marginalized Shia'a, this agreement was not enough. Indeed, Shia'a discontent is a reminder of their discrimination and receiving less of such benefits than their Sunni counterparts (ADHRB, 2015, p. 19). When oil benefits, albeit unevenly spread, did not prove enough, the state responded with the manipulation of sectarianism and the brutal crackdown that became known as "Bloody Thursday". However, such violence did not stem demonstrations. In less than a week, over 100, 000 Bahrainis or 15% of the population occupied the streets of Al Manama once more, in honor of the victims of "Bloody Thursday". King Hamad offered concessions in response that were "too modest, too late. [...]

Bahrain's aroused majority would settle for nothing less than a purely constitutional monarchy, and militants were calling for an end to the monarchy altogether" (Diamond, 2013, p. 86).

Bahrain is a tiny kingdom, but its neighbor is not. The media campaign of sectarianism pushed by Bahrain was not the only countermove supported by Saudi Arabia and the GCC. On the morning of March 17, the Pearl Roundabout was once again invaded by 5,000 soldiers, tanks and aerial assault vehicles. In a tragic twist of irony, this crackdown was also on a Thursday, deepening the violent memories of "Bloody Thursday" just a week before. Further, Bahraini troops were supported by soldiers of the United Arab Emirates and Saudi Arabia. Around 1500 GCC troops entered Bahraini soil, thus complementing the online sectarian warfare led by the al-Khalifas with military force. Saudi Arabia especially was eager to extinguish the fires of rebellion due to the event taking place next door to their own Shia'a populous (Mcevers, 2012).

The King Fahd Causeway connects both nations, symbolizing Saudi-Bahraini unity (perhaps under Saudi leadership) and is enjoyed regularly by Saudis seeking a Friday night in less uptight Bahrain, where they can "drink alcohol in bars and clubs" (Mabon, 2012). However, the Causeway also serves as a strong political symbol of Saudi concern regarding Iran and Bahrain's Shia'a majority. The Causeway's primary political purpose is therefore not to increase Saudi-Bahraini economic ties (or "tourist trips" to bars and clubs) but rather "to engender easier access [for Saudi Arabia] in case of trouble for the [al-Khalifas]" (ibid.). This political motive accelerated completion of the Causeway after the Islamic Revolution of 1979, reflecting "suspicion of Iranian interference [...] within Bahrain [...] and [suspicion of] Khomeini's desire to export the revolution". A worst-case scenario for the House of Saud is that Iranian interference and subsequent "increasing Shia power in Bahrain may lead to an empowered Shia community in [Saudi Arabia's] Eastern Province" (ibid.).

And so it was that on March 17, 2011, Saudi troops crossed the border with ease, with the King Fahd Causeway also welcoming "police and troops from the UAE and Qatar" (ibid.). Under a GCC-crackdown, resistance to al-Khalifa rule began to buckle. Completing the media war and militarized repression was socio-economic retribution (Diamond, p. 86). Just as Jordanian authorities have been willing to revoke citizenship of disloyal subjects, Bahraini activists suddenly found themselves stripped of their passports (Amnesty International, 2016). Worse still, some victims found that revocation of citizenship was only the first stage, followed by deportation. Expulsion appeared to be an increasingly favored method of silencing dissent by the spring of 2016 (ibid.).

Amid sectarian-framed crackdowns bolstered by GCC military might, King Hamad appeared to remember his initial image of reform. In the summer of 2011, a royal decree established the Bahrain Independent Commission of Inquiry (BICI). On the one hand, this act went deeper than the democratic window-dressing of Ben Ali and Mubarak. A report by BICI concluded that security forces during 2011 events were guilty of systemic abuse, torture and other forms of physical and psychological harm amid "a culture of impunity for the perpetrators" (Diamond, 2013, p. 88). Such outspokenness indeed makes the BICI appear independent. On the other hand, few of the reforms suggested by the BICI have been implemented (ibid.). Moreover, the BICI's suggestions seemed solely focused on government responses to protests. Its report lacked any mention of how to address structural issues of long-term governance, in particular the weak parliament that played a large part in provoking protests by shielding the al-Khalifas from public accountability (Wehrey, p. 117).

With GCC and Saudi support, it would appear that the al-Khalifas have countered the Arab Spring through a sectarian media campaign that framed state brutality as a necessary evil against Iranian and Shia'a threats. As the BICI report found Bahrain's security forces acting with impunity, so too has the al-Khalifa family been able to freely press sectarianism as a dividing tactic under the guidance of Saudi Arabia and the GCC's military arm, aptly named the Peninsula Shield Force (Obaid, 2014, p. 13). It would seem that sectarianism is taking on a new political tint in Bahrain. As of 2017, regime officials were pursuing previously permitted political organizations in the name of national security (Middle East Eye, 2017).

In 2016, al-Khalifa administrators took a hard line with Shia'a opposition groups, banning the al-Wifaq organization it had been willing to work with in parliament (ibid.). Later bans extended to secular opposition groups. In an official statement about the liquidation of the Waad group, formally the National Democratic Action Society, authorities claimed said group incited hatred against the state and against "factions of society" (ADHRB, 2017). Outside observers, however, argue that GCC might and Saudi military assistance has emboldened the al-Khalifa administration to engage in a "de facto ban on all opposition" (Middle East Eye, 2017).

An overview of Bahrain's history as an oil monarchy punctuates the importance of welfare and the manipulation of sectarianism. These themes partially contrast the assumption that monarchies will rely on traditionalism as opposed to a socio-economic ruling bargain. However, the overview of Bahrain's politics also emphasizes how the use of oil can be used to justify non-democratic legitimacy precisely through a socio-economic ruling bargain. This notion will be further explored in the main analysis of Chapter 4.

3.4 Mubarak's Egypt

> I swear by Almighty God to sincerely safeguard the republican system, respect the Constitution and law, fully look after the people's interests and safeguard the independence of the fatherland and the integrity of its territory (Farrell, 15 October, 1981). The time for work has come [.] [...] Egypt is for all – it is not a community of the privileged few who would monopolize influence and impose a guardianship on the people. [...] Every national of this country should know that the home front is quite safe, and the institutions of this country are quite on the alert and dedicated to protect this country (Farrell, 9 November, 1981). [...] We shall build and not destroy, we shall protect and not threaten, we shall safeguard and not dissipate. Guide me, God Almighty, and may God guide you all. (Farrell, 15 October 1981)

Mubarak's succession to Egypt's presidency was provoked by the violent consequences of a militant plot. A week before Mubarak's ascendance, President Sadat was gunned down by fundamentalists posing as officers during a military parade. Seated next to Sadat at the time, Vice President Mubarak escaped unharmed (BBC, 2017). The attempt was brief, successful and plunged the parade into chaos. As one eyewitness reported, "[within] seconds of the attack, the [Armed Forces] review stand was awash in blood. [...] Screams and panic followed as guests tried to flee, tipping over chairs. Some were crushed underfoot. Others, shocked and stunned, stood riveted" (Farrell, 7 October 1981).

The element of threat was quickly seized upon by the uncharismatic Mubarak. An emergency law was imposed that was to last until the end of his regime, allowing his government to target any potential rivals for the sake of security (Shehata, 2011, p. 28). At the same time, Mubarak needed to create a name for himself and mark the new presidential era as his own. As with Ben Ali, Mubarak hence started his term by creating the image of a more contemporary and liberal leader than his predecessors. Mubarak wanted to be his own president and not in the shadow of Egypt's first republican head, Nasser or the balding Sadat. "I am neither Gamal Abdel Nasser nor Anwar el Sadat", he insisted shortly after inauguration. "My name is Hosni Mubarak" (Nagarajan, p. 28). Political prisoners were released in the thousands and the press enjoyed fewer restrictions. Even civil society appeared to be welcomed, with NGOs flourishing (ibid., p. 29).

But the reality of ruling Egypt was a far cry from Mubarak's self-image and pragmatic optimism. For Mubarak could not escape that he was third in a line of modern pharaohs, and as such, he inherited Egypt's growing socio-economic burdens that originated in the curse of Nasserism (Shehata, p. 27). The Arab Republic of Egypt was not built on political liberalism but on a skewed ruling bargain by the military elite. Nasser's popularity after overthrowing the monarchy was not due solely to charisma but his apolitical "ruling bargain with labor and the middle class. All political parties were banned and all civil-society organizations [...] came under the direct control of the regime. In return, the state provided social and welfare services in the form of government employment; subsidies for food, energy, housing, and transportation; and free education and health care" (ibid.).

This generous social contract in one of the Arab world's most populous and poorer states could not last without pushing governments deeper into debt and structural difficulties. Indeed, economist K.V. Nagarajan points out that "[the] system ran into difficulties within a few years. [Under Nasser], [while] consumption continued to rise, domestic savings and investment failed to materialize, leading to a huge fiscal gap. To cover the gap, the state had to resort to massive external borrowing. On top of that, [...] a severe balance of payments crisis also developed" (Nagarajan, p. 24). Under Sadat, debt continued to rise while economic progress stalled. Sadat's liberalization initiatives to spur private sector activity had little effect and a desperate Sadat turned to the 1973 war with Israel as a socio-political distraction that could restore government support. While successful in provoking national pride, military operations also increased Armed Forces expenditure at the expense of an already exhausted civilian economy (ibid., p. 26). Hence, while Mubarak would try to step out of the shadows of his predecessors, he would ultimately fail to do so. Mubarak would inherit Egypt's growing debt and an unsustainable ruling bargain that could not bridge the wealth gap or address the eventual concerns of domestic and external forces. How Mubarak would attempt to address such concerns and his inability to escape the legacies of Nasser and Sadat would in turn define his relationship with Islamism, Egypt's powerful Armed Forces and ultimately the nation itself (ibid., p. 29).

The history of Egypt's socio-economic ruling bargain connects with the major recurring theme of material Beneficial Consequences as a key aspect of the ruling bargain, as examined through the assumption that republicans will emphasize a socio-economic ruling bargain as a key source of non-democratic Political Legitimacy. At the same time, Chapter 4's analysis reveals limited religious references in Mubarak's final address. The context of a republican partially drawing on religion challenges the assumption that only monarchs will draw on traditionalism. This context and Egypt's history of a material ruling bargain as a republican state provide a case that emphasizes the socio-economic themes of a ruling bargain while also providing a minor example of Religious Legitimacy. It is for this reason that Egypt is presented as the first republican case study, ahead of Ben Ali's Tunisia.

Muhammad Hosni Sayyid Mubarak had much in common with his predecessors. Like them, he was a military man, and it was thanks to Sadat that he made the transition from military to statecraft (Al Jazeera, 2011, *Profile: Hosni Mubarak*; BBC, 2017). In 1972, Sadat appointed Mubarak as Air Force commander. By 1975, Mubarak found himself in the post of Vice President and also a senior head of the National Democratic Party (Al Jazeera, 2011, *Profile: Hosni Mubarak*). Just as Ben Ali had been PM before gaining national leadership (Grewal, p. 2), so too Mubarak found himself in a position of high governance before tasting real power (ibid.). However, while Ben Ali was to turn his back on the military and craft a police state, Mubarak heralded from a military elite that could not be marginalized (ibid., p. 4). After all, Egypt's 1952 Revolution and republican birth was a product of the Armed Forces. Nasser's ideological mission and socialist policies placed military officers in the ranks of government (Nassif, 2013, p. 511). Sadat used the military as a tool to ensconce himself and isolate political competitors (ibid., p. 513). Mubarak's leadership, on the other hand, lacked ideological vision and his new post was devoid of entrenched political rivalry. A depoliticized military meant little competition in a simplified system of apolitical officers, but the Armed Forces still expected reward (ibid., p. 513).

Lengthening a page from Nasser's book, Mubarak wedded military and government through "the *carrots* of material largesse, rather than the *sticks* of permanent purges and reshuffles" (ibid., p. 515). In other words,

Mubarak would not focus on Nasser's ideational link with the army or Sadat's arbitrary redistribution of disloyal competitors. He would instead focus on how his predecessors used financial reward to intertwine the Armed Forces to the personage of the president. In particular, Mubarak deepened "the promotion of the military elite's private interests" under a "system of control [that] was built on a promise of the accumulation of pecuniary rewards and a postretirement career for officers who had remained reliable throughout their tenure" (ibid., p. 516) (Table 3.1).

Within a year of Mubarak's tenure, military spending rose exponentially and accounted for 26% of GDP. New and junior officers began their careers enjoying free health care and housing arrangements reserved exclusively for the Armed Forces. As they climbed the ranks, they knew that loyalty to Mubarak would mean profitable appointments that allowed unchecked opportunities for wealth building and even direct cash payments (Nassif, 2013, p. 516). Under such a system, officers knew "their turn could come if they complied with the system" (ibid.). Hence, Mubarak created a separate social contract between ruler and military, outside of the general arrangement between the ruler and the ruled. The fact that such a contract rewarded personal loyalty and represented the private interests of the Armed Forces illustrates how necessary military might was to political power. Abandoning Nasserism and other ideology was fine by the military elite, but no president of Egypt's Republic could remain pharaoh without offering economic privileges to the top brass (ibid., p. 509).

Table 3.1 Mechanisms of controlling the Egyptian Armed Forces, by President

Era	*Promoting the material interests of senior officers*	*Ideational links*	*Frequent purges in the officer corps*	*Frequent reshuffles of armed forces commanders*
Nasser (1952–1970)	Yes	Yes	Yes	No
Sadat (1970–1981)	Yes	Yes	No	Yes
Mubarak (1981–2011)	Yes	No	No	No

Source Nassif (2013)

The parallel social contracts of subsidies for the masses and wealth for the Armed Forces were a drain on public expenditure (Nagarajan, p. 22). As Ben Ali created a democratic image of Tunisia, so too did Mubarak manipulate the existence of NGOs for the same purpose: access to external aid. Under Mubarak, the NGO sector was actually expanded. From 1993 to 2011, NGOs in Egypt grew from 14,000 to over 30,000. This growth model was akin to Ben Ali's controlled liberalization or a form of governance termed as a "liberalized autocracy" (Herrold, 2016, p. 192). In other words, the expansion of NGOs was supervised by Mubarak as a form of civil society cooption, which itself was part of a scheme of (skewed) economic restructuring (ibid., p. 195). As charities, NGOs were expected to provide bread and related foodstuffs to the poor, lowering state expenditure on basic subsidies and providing the required image of democratic progress. This cooption tactic allowed Mubarak access to the World Bank and other external lenders for much-needed credit (ibid.).

At the same time, cooption was as much political as financial. Restrictive laws minimized NGOs to social welfare work, ensuring apolitical activity (that still required government approval and supervision). NGOs with a desire to promote human rights were not officially recognized, required to register as civil companies or law firms and often harassed to ensure their marginalization (ibid., pp. 196–197). As civil bodies often become the locus for political opposition, limited and fragmented dissidence was tolerated to the extent that any such NGOs "[served] as the release valve of society, providing 'opposition groups a way to blow off steam [...without] undermining the regime's ultimate control'" (ibid., p. 192). Mubarak thus controlled civil society, ensuring NGOs existed as part of his window-dressing campaign for external aid but also allowing the state to keep an eye on the masses and any collective action that could be perceived as a challenge to the regime (ibid.).

While Ben Ali's Tunisia saw the state control NGOs to minimize Islamist involvement in welfare projects (Sadiki, "Democracy by Non-democratic Means", p. 59), the reverse was initially true in Mubarak's Egypt. Under Nasser, the Muslim Brotherhood had been persecuted, and following Sadat's assassination, countless members were arrested for suspected involvement (Nagarajan, p. 33).

However, Mubarak's need to begin a stable rule turned state scorn into cooperation. As part of his "liberal" policy to release political prisoners, the Muslim Brotherhood found their members free and their group recognized in the political and civic arena (al-Awadi, p. 63). As a socio-political group, the Muslim Brotherhood were known for their welfare activities and extended network across Egypt's vulnerable social classes. Hence, during Mubarak's nascent period of political diversity, Mubarak was happy to use the Muslim Brotherhood both as a shield against more radical Islamist groups and as a socio-economic "partner" that could ease state weaning of subsidies through their own welfare program, including "schools, health clinics and financial aid" (Nagarajan, p. 33).

This tactic of transferring welfare responsibility to the Muslim Brotherhood was a socio-political balancing act, allowing the Muslim Brotherhood to flirt with Political Legitimacy. After all, as Islamists the Muslim Brotherhood were not apolitical. On the one hand, the Brotherhood or *Ikhwan* had to be regarded by the masses as politicized to a moderate degree in order for Mubarak to utilize their moderation against more extreme Islamists (al-Awadi, p. 62). On the other hand, the *Ikhwan* had their own (religious) views on what it meant to be a good Egyptian. For the Muslim Brotherhood, nationalism held two elements. As with Nasser and successive Arab nationalists, the Brotherhood regarded "nationalism [as] a response to Western imperialism and the rule of European colonists", allowing Brotherhood and government to agree on an Egypt First policy and the belief that Western interference had to end (Liu, 2008, p. 71). However, since its inception, the *Ikhwan* had been a political body rooted in fundamentalism. Hassan al-Banna, founder of the Brotherhood, declared that Islam was the "all-embracing system which regulates all aspects of human life. [...] [It] is religion and state; and Q'uran and sword" (Ansari, 1961, p. 7).

Indeed, while Mubarak used the Brotherhood for welfare, the Brotherhood used the state for indirect legitimacy. The Muslim Brotherhood had historically been acutely aware of the socio-economic needs of the masses. This awareness was, ironically, a partial result of their suppression by the state. Unable to gain votes in the political sphere, they resorted to charity and welfare activities to gain loyalty from the poor and underprivileged, a majority of Egypt's classes (al-Awadi, p. 63). Hence, when Mubarak offered an open-door policy toward the *Ikhwan*, it allowed them to make already active services more conspicuous and better organized. Rather than mobilizing their network to provide furtive charity in hidden city quarters, the Brotherhood enjoyed "the opening up of social, political, and economic spaces and opportunities, which [they] at once began to utilize" (ibid.).

By penetrating the major spheres of society, the Brotherhood began to engage with the masses and adjust their image accordingly. Gone were the traditional Islamic body robes and beards, replaced with the Western suits and jeans modern Egyptians seemed to favor. Obvious talk of religion and political aims was suppressed in order to focus on their ability to service the needs of major social groups from all backgrounds (ibid., pp. 63–64). The *Ikhwan* may not have been welcome in parliament, but by addressing student and teacher needs, they began to proliferate in student and teacher unions across Egypt, in some cases securing majority seats at Cairo University and other major institutes (ibid., p. 64). The Brotherhood organized student-run healthcare schemes and even pushed for affordable housing for teaching staff (ibid., p. 65).

Internally, the *Ikhwan* restructured their organization, decentralizing management so as to better spread themselves across Egypt's major cities and provinces. By allowing regional branches to make decisions rather than taking orders at the top, coordination of services improved, and the Brotherhood was able to informally partner with local unions, social clubs and civic organizers without drawing state alarm (ibid., pp. 67–68). As they built up social endorsement, the Brotherhood maintained a professional, not political veil. "In the initial years of our presence […]", confirmed one member, "we did nothing but services, services, services. We did not speak politics, because we realized that if we did so from the outset, people would not listen. We needed to provide services first. As a result, people began to gather round us. It was only then that we could talk to them about our political views. We would expect them to support us, since by then they knew us better" (ibid., p. 67).

Indeed, just as Mubarak had an exclusive social contract between himself and the Armed Forces, so too did the Muslim Brotherhood develop their own tacit contract between themselves and the beneficiaries of their generosity. Hence, "students who benefitted from the Brothers' services on university campuses were expected to vote for them in student union elections, and also, if [possible in the future] vote for them in parliamentary elections" (ibid., pp. 69–70). With their own understanding of nationalism and the ability to build up informal or social legitimacy, it started to become clear to the state that cooption of the Brotherhood through open tolerance was a tight balancing act. Mubarak was aware of the risk that the Brotherhood could gain more popularity than the state. While tolerating Muslim Brotherhood involvement in social spaces, student unions and civic organizations, Mubarak ensured that all such bodies were ultimately governed through the state's own control mechanisms, thus allowing the use of the Muslim Brotherhood for welfare dispersion (and alleviation of state spending) while monitoring their interaction in social and political spaces (ibid., p. 70).

By 1992, it became clear to the state that the Brotherhood was growing, in terms of both popularity and politicization. The early nineties saw both American involvement in the Gulf War and an Islamist victory in Algeria's elections (that was to prompt civil conflict) (ibid., p. 71). Having built support across several socio-political arenas, the Brotherhood now made their political views public. Their influence ensured multi-party boycotts of Egypt's 1990 elections, "an approach that particularly angered Mubarak" (ibid.). The Brotherhood also publicized their opposition to U.S. involvement in the Gulf War, a position that was popular among the masses, allowing the *Ikhwan* to use "student unions, university teachers' clubs, syndicates, and [their] organized network to mobilize their constituencies against the [pro-Western] policies of Mubarak" (ibid., p. 72).

The final straw for Mubarak came during the 1992 Earthquake Disaster that wreaked havoc across Cairo. The greatest disaster for the Mubarak regime was not the human casualties but rather how the event became "an interesting example of how the *Ikhwan* merged services with political propaganda" (ibid., p. 73). The vast social network of the Muslim Brotherhood allowed for a rapid response in victim rescue that was "notably superior to and surpassed that of the state", a fact addressed by domestic press and "the Western media, whose coverage highlighted the growing impact of the Muslim Brothers in Egypt, in contrast with the receding role of the state" (ibid.). The Brotherhood used such publicity to present their political core. All relief offices, tents and related buildings controlled by the Brotherhood proudly displayed their slogan "Islam is the Solution" (ibid.).

It was the combination of politicized welfare and statements challenging regime policies that condemned the Muslim Brotherhood to Mubarak's wrath. The state had allowed the *Ikhwan* to operate openly under the assumption that Brotherhood activities would be apolitical and charitable. In other words, there was (from the government's perspective) a tacit social contract between the state and the *Ikhwan*. The Brotherhood could plug the state's "welfare gap" with their social services, in exchange for tolerance in various socio-political spheres. By not only politicizing its welfare services but also organizing political committees to publicly condemn Mubarak's policies, the Brotherhood broke this contract, using its social legitimacy to directly challenge the political standing of the state and "undermine the legitimacy of Mubarak's leadership" (ibid., p. 72). Retrospectively, Brotherhood members themselves agreed that their increasingly provocative stance against state policies incited repercussions. One member recalls: "I consider the second statement that condemned the Egyptian involvement in the [Gulf War] to have been the straw that broke the camel's back. I remember that [...] we wrote it in a provocative manner. I think that after we issued the statement, the regime said to itself: 'That is enough. The [Muslim Brotherhood has] crossed the red line'" (ibid.).

The result of the Muslim Brotherhood's provocation was that its rhetoric on the Gulf War was used against its members. Mubarak labeled the *Ikhwan* as disloyal, funded by Iraqi dictator Saddam Hussein and thence proceeded to end his honeymoon with the Brotherhood through mass arrests (ibid., p. 73). Egypt's nationalism was not for the Brotherhood to decide. Nationalism was not mosque and country, as al-Banni declared. Rather, nationalism was the state. It was the military and its might that "courageously took part in war and peace" (Menshawy, 2017, p. 120). In time, as Brotherhood influence was forcibly reduced, nationalism would also be a return to subsidization, launched under Nasser's modern republic. "[Egypt must] abandon any talk of abolishing subsidies", Mubarak declared long after the *Ikhwan* were crushed. "Subsidization will remain an established right for Egyptians. We will never abolish subsidies or reduce them" (Nafaa, 2010).

Under Mubarak's emergency law, systemic attempts were made to abolish the Brotherhood. Prior to September 11, Mubarak attempted to control the Muslim Brotherhood as part of his "symbiotic relationship with the opposition mainstream Islamist movements" (Thaler, p. 98). Such control was not solely via cooption but also "legal manipulation and internment of the movement's leaders" (ibid.). As Ben Ali used 9/11 and the War on Terror to pursue his political opponents, so too did Mubarak exploit said events and "the imminent war on Iraq to stifle dissent by arresting opposition figures" (ibid.). Such actions were often pre-emptive, intended to target potential protestors that voiced opposition to regime policies. In addition, countless Brotherhood supporters were detained right before 2002 legislative elections on charges of "rioting, illegal gathering, and attempting to hinder public balloting, among other things" (ibid.).

At the same time, 9/11 appeared to have a conspicuous effect on Islamist groups themselves. Previously militant organizations like

Al-Jama'a al-Islamiyya publicly denounced the use of violence and even *takfir*, "the act of accusing the government of apostasy" (ibid., p. 99). This decision to renounce both terror tactics and government clashes "was [ostensibly] based on a careful, exhaustive review of Islamic law and [appeared] to be an authentic revision of [the group's] ideology" (ibid.). However, Mubarak's initial openness with other Islamic groups and willingness to accommodate their apolitical existence may have convinced *Al-Jama'a al-Islamiyya* that a social contract with the regime, however skewed, could mean that "operating within the existing institutional framework is a more effective way of achieving its long-term goals" (ibid.).

Mubarak's uncharismatic succession in a line of militant pharaohs saw him continue the core management techniques of his predecessors. The military elite had to be appeased, subsidies for the poor maintained the social contract between the ruler and the ruled, and apolitical accommodation of Islamist forces balanced both welfare needs and, at least in theory, Islamist aggression. Finally, the appearance of democratic willingness, as with Ben Ali, gave Egypt access to external aid to ensure economic growth. Mubarak's Egypt was hailed by external lenders, including the IMF for its implementation of economic structural adjustment programs in exchange for credit. "Egypt [...] is a remarkable success story. [...] Egypt's economy has come a long way since the 1980s. Growth is recovering and confidence is rising. Tough macroeconomic policies and deep structural reforms are doing the trick", insisted one IMF policymaker (Nagarajan, p. 30). Mubarak projected the image of a prosperous Egypt that, under his leadership, could balance differing interests and still carry the nation down a path of moderate prosperity. As with Ben Ali, however, Mubarak's days were numbered.

Ultimately, Mubarak could not serve as an effective political manager in two roles: President of Egypt and Senior Chairman of the National Democratic Party (NDP), Egypt's ruling political faction (Heiss, 2012, p. 156). As head of the NDP, Mubarak led a forum for Egypt's political elite. This forum allowed Mubarak to present Egypt with a face of political unity for his rule. In addition, the NDP served as a cooption model for the business elite. The National Democratic Party was "an exclusive political apparatus that [...] [became] the only vehicle for attaining financial, political or social success" (ibid., p. 157). Hence, the NDP ensured not only Islamists but rising business tycoons were co-opted. This arrangement allowed Mubarak to extend political control into influential economic and commerce spheres. All moguls and industrialists "were forced to comply with NDP desires and expectations to gain additional power" (ibid., p. 159).

The NDP also bolstered Mubarak's image of political strength by creating a portrait of a president supported by a cohesive and powerful political elite (ibid., p. 165). In reality, of course, the NDP was not always unified by Mubarak but instead split into one or more factions, often the old guard of politicians that had been active since Nasser and the new guard of foreign-educated and business savvy young bloods. As Mubarak attempted to leverage the Muslim Brotherhood against other political groups to dampen Islamist threats, the same fragmentation tactic was applied to party politics. Hence, he sided with "the old guard (his peers and long-time allies) and the centrists (his son, Gamal and his supporters)" in order to "secure his legacy as president by installing his son as president after his death" (ibid.).

The NDP not only represented a shell for Mubarak's political authority among the elite. It also served as the "talent pool" from which all government administrators had been drawn since the 1950s. Hence, any appointments to the state bureaucracy often meant a revolving door of aged political elites that drew not on new talent but the same loyal members of the NDP. This endless cycle of antiquated appointments in a nation of growing youth would present a blow to Mubarak's political support base during the 2010 protests. Under intense pressure to prove he could oversee real change, a cornered Mubarak felt that only by disbanding the NDP could he calm popular aggression. However, his "last-ditch efforts to stay in power betrayed every principle and assumption of his managerial strategy" out of fear of what was to come: his overthrow. By disbanding the NDP, Mubarak partially realized his own downfall. Disbanding both government and party meant the end of "his key supporting institutions" (ibid., pp. 167–168).

The final blow of party disunity and collapse of political support came atop larger structural economic gaps that gradually pushed Egypt to breaking point and Mubarak off his throne. Indeed, the IMF's praise for Mubarak's performance could not have been more wrong, for Egypt's IMF-led Structural Adjustment Program (SAP) hid liabilities rather than assets to the regime. On paper, Egypt's fiscal performance was stabilizing throughout the nineties and beyond. Mubarak's macro-economic slant curbed inflation from 21% in the early nineties to 7% by 1996 (Nagarajan, p. 30). The introduction of sales tax in 1991 meant extra revenue that allowed Egypt to eliminate trade barriers and join the World Trade Organization (WTO). Finally, a state-supervised auction of cellular networks illustrated a willingness to privatize sluggish sectors and netted "$1 billion in revenues, $3 billion in foreign direct investment and [encouraged developments in] the latest technology". Ironically, the same technological progress "would play a major role in [coordinating protests and] bringing down the Mubarak regime in 2011" (ibid., p. 31).

Mubarak, as with Ben Ali, did not focus on long-term prosperity for the masses. Rather, eyeing access to IMF and other external loans meant a slanted focus on using macro-economic policies to satisfy the "short-term fiscal parameters" of external lenders (ibid.). In other words, Mubarak's ability to satisfy superficial economic criteria gave him financial credit but "did nothing to boost productivity of the economy and increase [resource] supply which is needed for long-term prosperity for Egypt" (ibid.). Worse still, the sole macro-economic focus of the SAP ignored the plight of ordinary Egyptians to the extent that poverty levels were rising. More alarming were World Bank reports that noted how rising food prices were barring many families from the "minimum cost diet", which by the early nineties had "increased by 216 percent in urban and 242 percent in rural areas" (ibid.). Despite the awareness of such social ills by external lenders, Mubarak seemed all too happy to oblige only the short-term targets of the SAP, while IMF evaluators themselves "rarely touched the [urgent] subjects of employment, unemployment and human development" (ibid., p. 32).

While the regime appeared to respond to World Bank concerns with a Social Fund for Development, such moves were not enough to undermine the entrenched corruption of domestic statecraft. The Social Fund itself was internationally financed yet vulnerable to political manipulation by public officials (ibid.). Furthermore, while the military elite drained the nation's resources through their own social contract with the state and the NDP acted as a gentlemen's club for quid pro quos rather than public service, the privatization of state assets was also to blame. Just as Ben Ali ensured his family and associates dominated the business economy (Driesbach & Joyce, 2014), so too did Mubarak permit "the emergence of family-owned huge conglomerates" that catered "to the rich elite who formed about 5 to 10 percent of the Egyptian population" (ibid.). While the masses existed in a "triangle of poverty", Mubarak allowed subsidized property deals and other auctions that created the illusion of stable financial growth through "a frenzy of speculation and quick profit schemes", each gamble being played in a financial sector that "was bailed out by the government to avert defaults and bankruptcies [of the elite]". In other words, "government intervention was shoring up the fortunes of the rich and the politically connected, [while] the rest of the population was facing withdrawal of government support and erosion in their standard of living. [...] The ranks of the poor were swelling" (ibid.).

The increasing wealth gap acted as a contrasting reminder of the basic social contract between state and subjects since Nasser. While the rich could get richer, it was expected that Mubarak at least continues the legacy of subsidies implemented by his predecessors. How ironic that such socialist generosity had been started by Nasser both for political support and "to raise the living standards of people in the lower rungs of the economic ladder" (Nagarajan, p. 24). By Mubarak's time, subsidies and military gift-giving had set Egypt on the road to an economic crisis, while Mubarak also faced the long-term prospect of being challenged by the Muslim Brotherhood. Though Mubarak used the *Ikhwan* to plug social services gaps, he was aware of their building support. When the Brotherhood began to raise a political voice against the regime, Mubarak felt forced to crack down on them, which also meant that the state could no longer rely on them to plug the gaps in welfare for the masses (al-Awadi, p. 75).

With rising poverty, entrenched corruption across all political spectrums and withdrawal of efficient and much-needed social services, the stage was set for the pharaoh to fall. As Tunisia's spark was provoked by state mistreatment, so too did Egypt see its own Spring blossom in a similar manner. In the summer heat of 2010, twenty-eight-year-old Khaled Said was targeted for his ostensible exposure of police corruption. In June, the baby-faced activist was "dragged out of an internet café and set upon by [officers] in the northern city of Alexandria" (BBC, 2014a, "Egypt Police Jailed over 2010 Death of Khaled Said"). As video footage of Bouazizi's self-immolation galvanized Tunisia, so too did the images of Said's body shock Egypt. At the hands of police, his close-cropped hair and oval face had been reduced to a battered corpse, open mouth revealing smashed teeth and scarred lips (Meky, 2014).

The leaked evidence of his broken body contrasted with the state's post-mortem investigation, which "concluded that he had died of suffocation after trying to swallow a packet of drugs he had been carrying" (BBC, 2014a, "Egypt Police Jailed over 2010 Death of Khaled Said"). The blatant implausibility of the regime's explanation for his death prompted the creation of a Facebook page, "We Are All Khaled Said".[1] The page was dedicated to Said's memory and campaigned against police corruption. Hundreds of thousands rallied to its cause and followed its message to "participate in the nationwide anti-government demonstrations on 25 January 2011", which would in time force Mubarak's resignation (BBC, 2014a, Egypt Police Jailed over 2010 Death of Khaled Said').

The regime's stubbornness and loss of elite support are key to understanding Mubarak's defeat. It is obvious that Mubarak's skewed economic policies and revolving door of aging NDP members for governance alienated youth and the poor (in other words the bulk of the population). However, there were several opportunities missed by Mubarak to minimize political damage and perhaps even salvage his position to retain power. First, while it is true that many attended protests at Tahrir Square, political opposition groups were not united in their political agendas (other than freedom from detainment, the emergency law and other basic factors). Indeed, some movements were even "divided over whether to participate in demonstrations" (Shehata, p. 30). Further, even when protests intensified, they were composed of large political groups with opposing agendas "that had previously competed with one another—Islamists and secularists, liberals and leftists" (ibid., pp. 30–31). It is thinkable that had Mubarak negotiated compromises with the largest of these groups instead of stubbornly refusing "to make any real concessions" while continuing violent crackdowns on gatherings, the movement against him would fragment and "the protests would begin to lose steam" (ibid.).

Second, Mubarak placed himself in a position of overdependence on his Armed Forces. While the military had backed Mubarak, they had also showed restraint against their fellow Egyptians. In other words, the Armed Forces had teetered between the ruler and the ruled for a reason shared by the protestors: neither the traditional elite nor the masses wanted a dynastical presidency through the succession of Mubarak's son, Gamal (Hiro, 2013). While Mubarak did remove Gamal from his influential position at the NDP, Mubarak did so by disbanding the party and government, leaving only the military as the last buttress of his rule. The removal of two-thirds of his supporting system left him in a very precarious

[1] As of April 2017, this page remains active on Facebook and holds just under 300,000 likes. Source: Facebook (2017) *We are all Khaled Said*. Available at: https://www.facebook.com/elshaheeed.co.uk?filter=3 (accessed 21 April 2017).

position. The third and fatal mistake Mubarak made also revolved around succession and was the tipping point that united protestors and the military against their "father". Rather than giving the nation time to absorb Gamal's removal and that of his cronies from key socio-economic positions, Mubarak waited less than twenty-four hours to declare that he himself would not step down until elections in September. Immediately after this announcement, "security forces and hired vigilantes violently cracked down on the protestors—11 were shot and killed in Tahrir Square alone" (ibid., p. 31). These orders of violence were hardly the actions of a ruler who intended to reverse ambitions of succession or listen to popular demands. With increasingly bitter protestors urging the military to side with the people, Mubarak's departure was imminent.

On February 10, 2011, Vice President Omar Suleiman spoke to Egypt's millions through a televised address projected in Tahrir Square:

"In the name of God, the merciful, the compassionate. [Citizens], during these very difficult circumstances Egypt is going through, President Hosni Mubarak has decided to step down from the office of the president of the republic and has charged the high council of the armed forces to administer the affairs of the country. May God help [us all]" (*New York Times*, 2011).

From a sixty-second speech, Tahrir Square and Egypt "prayed, wept and chanted [...] [in] a deafening roar" (McGreal & Shenker, 2011). The Armed Forces would go on to administer Egypt on and off until their 2013 coup against elected Islamist President Mohamed Morsi (Elmasry, 2015). This move acted as a reminder of Egypt's militant nationalism and the role of the powerful military elite in national governance. Further, the coup marked a transition in how the Armed Forces perceived this role. Under former General and now President Abdel-Fattah al-Sisi, the military has emerged "from behind the curtain of influence to openly [govern] Egypt" (Aziz, 2016).

An overview of Egypt under Mubarak reveals the importance of a socio-economic ruling bargain, especially through subsidies, which connects with the assumption that republicans will rely on a socio-economic ruling bargain. In addition, Chapter 4's analysis of Mubarak's speech will also examine his use of Religious Legitimacy.

3.5 Ben Ali's Tunisia

> In the name of God, the Clement, the Merciful. [...] The great sacrifices made by the Leader Habib Bourguiba, first President of the republic [...] for the liberation and development of Tunisia, are countless. [...] But the onset of his senility and the deterioration of [his] health [...] called us to carry out our national duty and declare him totally incapable of undertaking the tasks of President of the Republic. [...] We shall see that the law is correctly enforced in a way that will proscribe any kind of iniquity or injustice. [...] We shall give Islamic, Arab, African and Mediterranean solidarity its due importance. [...] Fellow citizens, [by] the Grace of God we are entering [...] a new era of efforts and determination. Love of our country and the call of duty requires this of us. Long live Tunisia! Long live the Republic! (Ben Ali, 1987)

The "self-inauguration" of President Zine al-Abidine Ben Ali in 1987 appeared to highlight social justice for all and Islamic unity. Yet, underneath Ben Ali's words lay a complex transition that was provoked by numerous socio-economic failings during President Habib Bourguiba's tenure and his inability to address them through his personal management style (Ware, 1988, p. 587).

Ironically, it was precisely these failings that gave Ben Ali his chance to become the new president, albeit with the consequence of also inheriting them. Bourguiba's original legitimacy and right to rule drew heavily on his leading role in Tunisia's anti-colonial movement. Upon liberation from France, Bourguiba relied on his political credentials to draft the independent state's constitution and assume its presidency (Hawkins, pp. 39–40).

Nonetheless, his past successes as an anti-colonialist were nullified by Bourguiba's refusal to accommodate Islam as a public platform and by his failure to ensure minimal economic growth. When it came to Islamist movements and their desire to be given a political voice, Bourguiba appeared to be quite the violent reactionist. While supportive of Tunisia's Islamic faith during French oppression, upon independence Bourguiba declared Islam the state religion yet also "spoke out against the fetters of traditional religion as retarding modernization" (ibid., p. 39). Bourguiba's hatred of politicized Islam crystallized the year of his overthrow. In response to a 1987 hotel bombing, Bourguiba arrested leading figures of Tunisia's Al-Nahda party (then known as the Islamic Tendency Movement or MTI). A show trial against the party's leader, Rashid Ghannouchi backfired when the defense convincingly portrayed the MTI as a moderate group and any extremist cells as being the result of Bourguiba's suppression of political Islam (Ware, p. 589).

Bourguiba's personal ruling style was a double-edged sword, for personal control also meant the masses were more likely to place responsibility for failure at his feet. Bourguiba's refusal to acknowledge his involvement in radicalizing fringe MTI members did much damage to his public image. Worse was yet to come, however, as his Tunisia continued to struggle with economic uncertainty. A young populace demanded work and higher wages at a time when European market crashes had drastically cut down tourist numbers to Tunisia and when steady but weak GDP growth did not raise living standards but ironically barred Tunisia from external aid earmarked for underdeveloped states (ibid.). In a further twist of irony, Bourguiba's expanded education programs developed unemployed youth with increasingly higher aspirations that could not be fulfilled (ibid.).

The pressures on Bourguiba would unite to give Ben Ali his path to power. Ben Ali was not a fervent nationalist and anti-colonialist. Rather, he was a quiet military man (ibid., p. 6). His career rise in such a capacity was aided by security incidents that provoked Bourguiba to expand Tunisia's Armed Forces. The post-independence coups across the MENA region had convinced Bourguiba to confine Tunisia's military might. The formation of the Tunisian Armed Forces (1956) was thus somewhat haphazard and with limited staff. A 1961 coup attempt entrenched Bourguiba's belief that the military should be apolitical and weak (Grewal, p. 2). However, poor economic performance and external threats soon changed his mind.

A nationwide worker's strike in 1978 was followed only two years later by a 1980 rebellion instigated by Libya's adjacent Muammar Gaddafi (Ware, p. 589). Both incidents were soon followed by widespread riots over price rises in basic foodstuffs. Taking note of how overwhelmed police had been in such instances, a panicky Bourguiba reversed his military stance. It was time to enlarge Tunisia's Armed Forces. By the mid-eighties, "[m]ilitary spending quadrupled and arms imports—especially from the United States—skyrocketed" (Grewal, p. 2).

The 1980s saw not only the rising significance of the military but the increasing influence and authority of Ben Ali. Already appointed to the Directorate of Military Security in 1964, Ben Ali became Director General of National Security in 1977 (ibid., p. 3). Relations between Ben Ali and Bourguiba were ambiguously distant. Ben Ali flirted with displeasure on two occasions, resulting in exile in 1977 and 1980. However, the 1984 bread riots saw Ben Ali hastily recalled from Poland amid Bourguiba's military expansion (Reich, 1990, p. 79). His appointment as Secretary of State that same year was soon followed by the post of Interior Minister in 1986 and finally Prime Minister in 1987 (Grewal, p. 2).

The peak of Ben Ali's authority under Bourguiba coincided with continued socio-economic unrest and Bourguiba's increasing impulsiveness that seemed to push the elderly statesman toward forging his personal legacy while ignoring mounting resentment (Ware, 1988, p. 590). In less than a year, Ben Ali deposed Bourguiba. Despite his military background, the move was regarded by some as "hardly [...] a "coup de force", or even a "coup de théâtre"" (Ware, p. 592). Rather, it was a soft coup justified by the existing constitution against a nationalist mentally unfit to lead (ibid., Grewal, 2016, p. 3). As explained by Ben Ali in a French interview one year later, "[on] the seventh of November [1987], [...] I had to re-establish law and order. I did what I had to do". For Ben Ali, his decision was less a military coup than a "medical coup". "[Bourguiba] was sick", Ben Ali insisted at the time. "His poor health prevented him from governing" (Press TV Doc, 2016).

Ben Ali carefully crafted the image of a liberal leader during the beginning of his rule, in contrast to his predecessor. This image included emphasizing both a break with Bourgubism through the formation of a new government and implying a temporary role as a "caretaker" president. The latter was hinted at by two elements. First, the Tunisian Constitution at the time held clauses that would ensure Ben Ali held "[...] legal power until 1991, when legislative elections [would] once again take place" (Ware, p. 592). Second, Ben Ali promised constitutional revisions that would expunge both lifetime presidency and "the automatic succession of the prime minister to the presidential post" (ibid.).

As for Islam's public role, Ben Ali had learned from the mistakes of his predecessor. While Bourguiba had emphasized secularism to the point of alienating Islamists, Ben Ali increased the presence of faith in politics and daily life. Such measures included increasing the legal protection of mosques and religious sites and implementing the broadcast of the *athan* or call to prayer on T.V. and radio (ibid., p. 599). In addition, Ben Ali adopted formal Islamic introductions in his speeches, a mark of religious respect that gave Islamists a reminder of his piety both as a fellow Tunisian and as head of state (ibid., p. 592). Further, Ben Ali borrowed from Bourguiba's anti-colonialism by switching from French to *Fusha* or Formal Arabic. This shift could be regarded as both anti-colonialist and nationalist but also implied stronger connections to Islam, as *Fusha* is the language of the Quran (Hawkins, p. 40).

Despite talk of pluralism and political inclusiveness, Ben Ali was still a military man, and in the early days of his rule, it clearly showed. Upon seizing power, Ben Ali ensured that the military gained more political influence. This transition was signaled not only by the promotion of fellow officers but by his creation of the military-led National Security Council, a forum that met weekly with the ambiguous aim of "safeguarding internal and external state security" (Grewal, p. 3). Under Ben Ali, the military had experienced a reversal from barracks to bureaucracy. Even traditionally civilian posts were filled by Ben Ali's comrades (ibid., pp. 3–4). However, such a shift would not last long. The rising influence of the Armed Forces would provoke rival institutes into engineering a conspiracy to transform Ben Ali's Tunisia into the police state it was to become until the Arab Spring.

A 1991 "discovery" by the Interior Ministry of a coup plot against Ben Ali was broadcast, using the coerced testimony of one Captain Ahmed Amara, who outlined the plot on live television (ibid., p. 4). Captain Amara confirmed that Ben Ali's beloved military was in cahoots with the Islamist Al-Nahda party, supposedly meeting to advance their goals at the coastal town of Barrakat Essahel. The Barrakat Essahel Affair was nothing more or less than a fabricated rumor instigated by sidelined police forces and Ben Ali's own Constitutional Democratic Rally party. Nonetheless, it resulted in the arrest of 244 officers, including senior soldiers connected to the Army Chief of Staff (ibid., p. 4). The scandal had its intended effect: Ben Ali's trust in his comrades was permanently shattered. The President responded by assuming personal command of the Armed Forces as its Chief of Staff and curtailing senior posts that would allow coordination between the army, navy and air force (ibid.).

Personal oversight of the military did not give the military a second chance. From 1991 until his overthrow, Ben Ali starved the Armed Forces of funds and armaments, retiring any remaining generals or colonels in senior political posts and appointing no further officers in positions of power. Instead, Ben Ali turned his trust to the police and Ministry of Interior, as both had planned. From 1992 until Tunisia's Arab Spring, the Interior Ministry was lavished with 165% of the defense budget, morphing Tunisia into the "modern" police state (ibid.; Sadiki, "The Search for Citizenship", p. 506). The resultant increase in police officers over military staff, in addition to budget cuts, would come to haunt Ben Ali in 2010. Popular resentment among the military was a key reason troops did not come to his aid during the uprising against him (Grewal, pp. 4–5).

In his first year, Ben Ali had hinted that democratic pluralism would become a greater reality. One year after the September 11 Attacks, the MENA region appeared to undergo a shift nudging autocracies toward keeping pluralist promises. Access to uncensored satellite television and other forms of global information were spreading at a time when Arab regimes appeared to concede to either the succession of younger leaders or structured parliamentary elections (Sadiki, "Democracy by Non-democratic Means", p. 57).

For Ben Ali's Tunisia, the trend of increasing parliamentary elections would be tailored rather than openly followed. Hence, the illusion of democracy was headed by Ben Ali under what Sadiki termed "tightly controlled liberalization" (ibid.). This form of pseudo-liberalization saw Ben Ali ensure political pluralism that was diluted and artificially birthed, preventing any opposition from altering his oversight of core state institutions (ibid.). This method of the regime permitting yet dominating the electoral process allowed Ben Ali to compose the façade of democratic choice while retaining all power. This carefully tailored balancing act was intended to ensure domestic, regional and international Political Legitimacy.

Monopolizing the electoral process and coopting potential rivals allowed Ben Ali to claim pluralism without fear of losing power to political competition. Rival candidates were often hand-picked by the regime and limited parliamentary seats for opposition party members ensured "the veneer of democracy without having to be democratic". Hence, Ben Ali controlled all major policies and political processes against a weakened opposition. No checks and balances or power sharing was necessary (ibid., p. 64). Further, Ben Ali's media mouthpiece *Le Renouveau* would reproduce quotes from Arab neighbors abroad favorable to the regime in order to demonstrate the regional legitimacy of Ben Ali's Tunisia. This tactic also allowed for regional legitimacy by comparison, as the regime often highlighted Tunisia's stability in contrast to the impulsive militancy of Gaddafi's Libya and the civil bloodshed of adjacent Algeria (ibid., p. 67). Finally, Ben Ali reversed the "aid contradiction" inherent under Bourguiba. While Bourguiba's tenure saw weak growth that barred the country from receiving external aid, Ben Ali's democratic façade was constructed to specifically meet International Monetary Fund (IMF) and World Bank criteria for aid à la Mubarak that no doubt lined his own coffers and maintained his inner circle (ibid., p. 64).

At the same time, Islamists would see a reversal in fortunes just before Ben Ali's downfall. While the new President appeared to embrace the public role of religion in his early years, post-9/11 this openness was no longer the case. The image of fundamentalism linked to Islamists gave Ben Ali the excuse required to increase already extensive policing and related activities (ibid., p. 68). By definition, such a strategy required the marginalization of Islamists, both politically and publicly. Indeed, Algeria's civil war allowed Ben Ali to publicly justify his attack on Islamists by arguing that "greater democracy does not lead to greater liberalism, because it leaves the way open to the rule of Islamic fundamentalism" (ibid.). The hostility toward Islamism also extended to the charity sector. Knowing full-well that Islamist parties such as the Muslim Brotherhood traditionally used charity to gain support from the masses, the regime took "no chances with welfarism" and thus monopolized charity events, suppressing the existence of any NGOs (ibid., p. 59). It appeared that Ben Ali was more than aware of the fact that non-state pluralism "in this domain opens up space for not only proactive Islamist-led grassroots social engineering, but also for all kinds of other non-State activism" that could threaten the regime's controlled pace of liberalization (ibid.). Complementing his aggressive turn on Islamists, Ben Ali also took advantage of the War on Terror by cooperating with French authorities to detain and extradite exiled opponents, often under false accusations of illegal activities (ibid., p. 75).

Yet, the role of men and women in Tunisia's Islam was not entirely sidelined but used by the regime for validation in contradictory ways. Ben Ali's donning of religious garb allowed him to argue that Islam still held sway in Tunisia and also allowed him to merge Religious Legitimacy with paternalism. In many portrayals of the faithful President, traditional attire is used to construct piety and generosity. Hence, "Ben Ali often appears as a paternal figure, receiving the thanks of aid recipients or sagely listening as they describe their lives and problems" (Hawkins, 2011, pp. 45–46). On the other hand, women are often constructed by the state as models of Tunisia's modern secularism. Hence, religious garb worn by elderly females is often accepted as a form of (religious) tradition, but younger women are expected to embrace clothing that is modest yet without obvious religious connotation (ibid., pp. 45–46). Under Ben Ali, the hijab was thus banned at public institutions and state images of female youth often rendered educated *hijabis* invisible (ibid., p. 46). As education is linked to secularism in the state's narrative, the very existence of pious but educated female youth "represents a challenge to the state's model of modernity" while also risking that the public visibility of Islam encourages its politicization (ibid., p. 46).

As with any dictatorship, Ben Ali's Tunisia had gaps in governance that went unsolved by democratic window-dressing and associated balancing acts. The most arresting of such gaps was how Ben Ali tailored economic growth laws to benefit himself and his circle at the expense of the masses. Such laws allowed Ben Ali's family to control up to 21% of private sector profits through 220 firms that provided 3% of economic output (Driesbach and Joyce). All competition was blocked, while business ownership regulation also allowed Ben Ali to ensure familial ownership of Tunisia's largest media outlets, guaranteeing political censorship of anything that cast doubt on the regime (ibid.). Any legal revisions during Ben Ali's tenure only served "the interests of his family and those close to him to the detriment of the rest of Tunisia" (ibid.). Ben Ali's corruption would eventually be reflected in his final speech. It is that speech's scant references to the socio-economic ruling bargain that places this case last as the weakest confirmation of the assumption that republicans will rely on a socio-economic ruling bargain for non-democratic legitimacy. This fact will be further analyzed in Chapter 4.

Adding insult to injury was the practice of regional favoritism, both politically and economically. While the tourist-friendly coastal regions (and the birthplace of Ben Ali and Bourguiba) enjoyed lavish development, the interior regions suffered from socio-economic neglect and unemployment (Arieff, 2011, p. 18; Grewal, p. 4). Further, until the Barrakat Essahel Affair, enlargement of the military drew upon officers from Ben Ali's Sahel region along the eastern coast. The towns of the region "mounted to just 24 percent of Tunisia's population yet claimed nearly 40 percent of the officers promoted [...] under Ben Ali" (Grewal, 2016, p. 4). The combination of socio-economic and political isolation no doubt fueled interior resentment that exploded in 2010 (ibid.).

When the Arab Spring sparked in the interior and spread to the capital Tunis, Ben Ali urged calm. "Citizens, citizens", he declared, "[t]hese incidents are the work of a small group of hostile elements who are offended by the success of Tunisia and who are filled with resentment and grievance, because of the progress and development achieved by the country" (Ben Ali, 2010). Ben Ali was right to recognize the dangers of resentment and grievance but unable to understand not only the extent of popular anger but how he had sowed the seeds of his own downfall. While widespread discontent and Bouazizi's self-immolation sparked the Arab Spring, it was resentment within the Armed Forces that dealt the final blow to his regime. Still remembering the injustice of the Barrakat Essahel scandal and the favoritism bestowed upon coastal officers, the majority of troops in Tunisia's Armed Forces felt no loyalty toward their President and no remorse upon his ouster (Grewal, p. 5).

As the origin point of the Arab Spring, Tunisia remains a litmus test for the transition out of dictatorship. In yet another reversal of fortunes considered "a healthy phenomenon for Tunisia's young democracy", the military received a state apology for the Barrakat Essahel Affair and has begun to play a more politicized role in governance (ibid., pp. 1, 11). This role has allowed experienced military officers to address security gaps, including terrorist threats and the dismantling of Ben Ali's *mukhabarat* (government spying) apparatus, bringing Tunisia out of its police state (ibid., p. 1). At the same time, Islamists were given a second chance in the public sphere, with their 2011 election under a tripartite government, in partnership with two secular parties (ibid., p. 6). Inclusion is indeed at the center of democratic belief. Nonetheless, as a state with a legacy of secular-religious tension and almost 30 years under dictatorship, both the involvement of Islamists and the Armed Forces will be carefully observed (ibid., p. 2).

3.6 Understanding MENA Monarchies

An overview of each case study should reveal how the monarchical nations of the Levant and the Gulf have survived the Arab Spring, with King Abdullah II of Jordan and King Hamad of Bahrain still perched on their thrones. It is therefore imperative to further explore the nature of monarchical systems in the Middle East. Are they truly different from their republican counterparts? Do they possess a gravitas or political leeway that presidents-for-life do not?

Of note across MENA monarchies have been greater promises of reform (economic or otherwise), especially in non-oil states such as Jordan (Tobin, 2012). These reforms include limited economic liberalization to increase working-class purchasing power while also allowing for controlled political speech. Yet this process is often accompanied by a revolving door of government officials that are hired and fired at Abdullah's behest to deflect blame during protests (ibid.). At the same time, such promises may or may not be met. Moreover, they may or may not cover comprehensive popular political desires, which can include the transition from absolute monarchy to constitutional monarchy (King, 2011, p. 4). The option of such a transition is a path unavailable to republics led by a single leader and remains an exclusive choice for monarchies (ibid.).

Critics like Linz et al. argue that such a transition can be measured and formalized. Taking the older European monarchies as a model, Linz et al. explain that such monarchies evolved over time from absolute ruling monarchies under which only the monarch "forms and terminates government" to constitutional monarchies under which the "formation and termination of government needs support of both the monarch and elected parliament" (Linz et al., 2014, p. 37). While monarchies are typically seen as falling into one of these two categories, Linz et al. further argue that European monarchs have transitioned to the third and final classification of democratic parliamentary monarchy, under which only "the freely elected parliament forms and terminates government" (ibid.). The European connection to understanding Arab monarchy is most pertinent, as many Arab states established monarchical constitutions upon independence that were based on European legal structures (Brown, 2001, p. 62).

Linz et al. argue that these transitions away from autocracy and toward constitutional and in time democratic parliamentary monarchy are encouraged or undermined by five key factors:

- Political pressure from the masses for a transition to constitutional monarchy or democratic parliamentary monarchy can increase the chances of such a transition taking place. However, the likelihood of transition is itself affected by the remaining criteria.
- Monarchical family: Differences between small ruling families and large dynastic families can affect how a monarch responds to political pressure for transition from subjects. Under small families, a single monarch often rules alone and can make the decision to accept a constitutional or democratic parliamentary system. However, in a large dynastic family as seen in the Gulf (and Bahrain), relatives often fill high-ranking and influential posts and if transition threatens their power, they will form internal coalitions to block the current ruler from yielding to popular political demands.
- Taxes or no taxes: The more taxes a monarchy needs, the more vulnerable their political position. This situation can be linked to

earlier discussions of Jordan's defensive democratization, in which the Hashemites responded to socio-economic pressures through a controlled, top-down liberalization process after imposing taxation. This shift in the social contract and "relying more on its citizenry than on external rents for its government revenues, [meant the monarchy] was simultaneously compelled to incorporate a greater public voice in decision-making" (Robinson, p. 391). By contrast, a Gulf oil sheikhdom can ignore and even retaliate against popular political demands through the carrot of well-funded welfare as part of the ruling bargain and the stick of well-equipped security services.

- Ethnic and religious division: As with differences between dynastic and single monarchies discussed above, the likelihood of a transition to constitutional or democratic parliamentary monarchy hinges on access to political power. If transition will quell sectarian/ethnic conflicts by increasing, e.g., political representation, it may be considered by the monarchy. However, if such a transition is considered by a minority elite as augmenting the political position of an ethnically or religiously marginalized majority, it will be resisted by said elite, as illustrated by Bahrain's sectarianism (Middle East Eye, 2017).
- International actors: A monarchy's link to international political actors can also influence transition. Global political allies hostile to transition will empower monarchies to resist popular political will, while influential global allies that value democracy may pressure monarchies into accepting transition (Linz et al., 2014, p. 39). The importance of international allies and their promotion of democracy is again illustrated by the Western response to the al-Khalifa crackdown on Bahrain's protests. As a geostrategic ally of Western powers hosting the U.S. Fifth Fleet, King Hamad received little pushback from the Whitehouse, with diplomatic officials more concerned with preserving good relations with both Bahrain and its patron Saudi Arabia (Birnbaum & Warrick, 2011; Linz et al., p. 38).

Linz's explanation and factors of monarchical transition also connect with Huntington's discussion of "the king's dilemma". In his 1968 book *Political Order and Changing Societies*, Huntington argues that traditional society undergoing modernization benefits from the leadership of a centralized monarchy (Lucas, 2011). Centralized administration can maximize progressive development, but modernization will also see the creation of groups that are not fully incorporated by traditional monarchy (ibid.). The king's dilemma is considered within the context of the Arab Spring by Lucas (2011), with youth as the product of modernization heretofore excluded from incorporation by traditional leaderships, a key factor of the Arab Spring (ibid.). As with Linz, Huntington considers how a monarch may respond to discontent due to the creation of new groups that are not incorporated by traditional institutes. These include:

- Abandoning absolutism for rule as a constitutional monarch.
- Reversing modernization and reasserting authoritarianism (as considered in Bahrain).
- Institutionalizing popular participation under a system of monarchical sovereignty (perhaps through parliamentary votes, as considered in Jordan) (ibid.).

This struggle between traditionalism and popular participation may also be linked to Weber's sources of legitimacy from Chapter 2. To reiterate, Weber's tradition draws legitimacy from acceptance of rule through established custom, while Weber's legality draws legitimacy from acceptance of a regime that rules through rationally created rules that establish said regime as "functionally competent" (Weber & Gerth, 2009, pp. 78–79). As considered by Huntington's king's dilemma, modernization may result in a tug of war between traditionalism and constitutionalism for monarchical rule, and it is possible that (monarchical) rulers are responding to the Arab Spring with a transition from Weber's tradition to legality as a manner of bolstering their non-democratic credentials (such as Religious Legitimacy) rather than abandoning absolutism altogether and fully embracing constitutionalism. Such a prospect will be further discussed in Chapter 5.

Returning to Linz's conditions of political transition, they can also be considered within the context of the ruling bargain. As has been previously addressed in Chapters 2 and 3, the ruling bargain varies from state to state. Nonetheless, it is intended to be apolitical in nature and can therefore be seen as a hindrance to any political transition toward constitutional monarchy or democratic parliamentary monarchy (Peter, 2016). This can certainly be true of Gulf States where oil wealth allows such a bargain to remain strong by providing the masses with Beneficial Consequences in the form of welfare and related socio-economic gifts, which can be augmented in response to potential unrest (Hertog, p. 401). Non-oil states like Jordan may be forced to engage in "defensive democratization"; however, such a move is still limited in its political liberalization and indeed intended to block full political transition, going hand-in-hand with a patronage network and ruling bargain supported by donor states (Robinson, pp. 389–391). The ability to maintain a ruling bargain is a strong incentive to preserve the status quo and hence resist political transition (Linz et al., p. 38).

In addition to the ruling bargain, it is appropriate to return to the role of Religious Legitimacy and how religion is drawn on to defer or neutralize serious constitutional transition. Both Jordan and the Kingdom of Morocco are non-oil monarchies. They can hence both be described as "lynchpin" kingdoms that attract much-needed external aid to maintain a less-than-lavish rentier model of "modest amounts of public spending and subsidies" (Bank et al., 2014, p. 165). Indeed, Jordan and Morocco may also share models of regime legitimation. These monarchies survive through a combination of "military and financial support by external actors combined with religious-traditional legitimacy claims" (ibid., p. 167). At the same time, symbols of Religious Legitimacy are often centralized around a single ruler in non-oil states rather than their family (as in the Gulf), making manipulation of traditional religious symbolism far more successful as a leadership ploy (Brumberg, p. 10).

Further, it would appear King Abdullah II of Jordan was influenced by his Moroccan counterpart in his response to the Arab Spring. When protests broke out in Morocco in March 2011, King Mohammed VI announced constitutional reforms (King, p. 4). While these reforms were considered substantial, they also augmented his Religious Legitimacy by reasserting "his supreme position as 'Commander of the Faithful'" and his leadership authority to "keep Islam as the basis of national identity" (Brumberg, p. 10). Within months, King Abdullah II announced his own constitutional amendments under a commission appointed by himself (Bank et al., pp. 170–171). In addition, a later address by Abdullah in October 2012 during further protest highlighted the King's "honour of being a descendant of our forefather Prophet Muhammad" (Abdullah II, October 2012). Just as Morocco's Mohammed VI assented to (controlled) constitutional reforms while reasserting his Religious Legitimacy, Abdullah II of Jordan used unrest as an opportunity to balance constitutional reform with a reminder of his religious credentials (ibid.).

Returning to Linz et al.'s discussions of factors for transition, it is worth mentioning that while the fourth factor of ethnic and religious divisions can influence or deter transition, unlike sectarian Bahrain, Morocco and Jordan enjoy a united Sunni populace, making assertions of religious authority more effective, as the ruler and the ruled are of the same Muslim branch (Brumberg, p. 10).

Understanding Arab monarchies through the lens of political transition does illustrate potential differences between kings and their republican counterparts. Monarchs, as hereditary rulers, can gracefully yield to the pressure for transition to constitutional or democratic parliamentary monarchy. The trade-off for such a long-term survival option is a reduction of royal power, be it personalized (Morocco and Jordan) or familial (the Gulf) "while maintaining considerable prestige, popularity and relevance" (King, p. 4). Nonetheless, it would appear that most if not all monarchs across the Arab world have rejected this option. For the Gulf States, oil wealth has allowed the continuation of a carrot-and-stick method or the ruling bargain, with little incentive to embrace transition. This seems especially true of dynastic or familial monarchies, under which many family members occupy influential political posts, preventing the monarch from considering transition at the expense of relatives who compose the political elite. On the other hand, even non-oil monarchies are not incapable of prioritizing a ruling bargain mixed more heavily with the use of Religious Legitimacy. Morocco's Mohammad VI acceded to popular demands for constitutional reform but also used the opportunity to augment his Religious Legitimacy, specifically his religious title as Commander of the Faithful. Jordan's Abdullah II runs a modest ruling bargain funded by external donors, including fellow Gulf monarchs. At the same time, Abdullah appears to have followed a similar pattern to his Moroccan cousin by introducing constitutional reforms through a panel under his own control. As with Morocco's Muhammad VI, these reforms were put in a (belated) context of Religious Legitimacyreligion and Abdullah's public reminder of his lineage to the Prophet Muhammad. In Bahrain, however, the tactic of drawing on religion has been fragmented by sectarianism, which gives King Hamad a different form of religious manipulation that, along with Saudi support, bolstered heavy repression.

3.6.1 Bahrain's Sectarianism and Jordan's Tribalism

As kingdoms, Jordan and Bahrain provide interesting parallels regarding how authoritarian rule may practice the inclusion of some groups and the inclusion of others, whether through the Sunni/Shia'a divide (Bahrain) or East Bank/West Bank discrimination (Jordan). The practice of such political segregation has been questioned within the context of the Arab Spring, with authors like Valbjørn exploring whether the Arab Spring has encouraged a deeper manipulation of sectarianism and ethnic differences as a regime response (p. 127).

To reiterate, Jordan's populous consists of original Jordanian tribes of East Bank origin who have enjoyed socio-economic privileges in exchange for loyalty to the throne (Alshboul & Oudat, p. 66). From 1948 onward, Jordan absorbed Palestinians of West Bank origin (Culcasi, 2016, p. 9). The growth of Jordan's Palestinian populous was mirrored by concerns over their potential political clout as their numbers increased within the Hashemite Kingdom and encouraged citizenship without the same privileges as their East Bank counterparts (ibid.). Such discrimination hardened during Amman's brush with the Arab Spring. While recognizing popular unrest as being led by East Bankers, some movements were attacked by the regime "[…] as being led by disloyal Palestinians and Islamists who wanted to overthrow the Hashemite monarchy in favour of Palestinian Islamist rule" (Valbjørn, p. 142). In Bahrain, the Sunni minority elite have historically blocked Shia'a numbers in parliament and reduced public services in Shia'a areas (ADHRB, 2015, p. 19). During the Arab Spring, the al-Khalifas fueled sectarian fears to successfully sow mutual distrust between Sunni and Shia'a neighbors, friends and colleagues (Voice of America, 2011).

The social phenomenon of political inclusion and exclusion can be addressed by Ibn Khaldun's *ʿasabiyya* (clannishness). *ʿAsabiyya* can be considered an element of Ibn Khaldun's framework for political relations, bolstered by religion and political institutions (Ra'ees, 2004, p. 159). According to Ibn Kaldun, religion is the highest good and when combined with *ʿasabiyya* encourages political and institutional transformations and state foundation, with the dominant force vacillating between religion and *ʿasabiyya* (ibid., p. 167). However, *ʿasabiyya* encompasses different types. These types can include natural *ʿasabiyya* encouraging strong bonds among family and tribe but also rational *ʿasabiyya* or social bonds among the ruling elite, who are meant to prioritize a common good but also the interests of the ruler (ibid., pp. 171–172). This latter aspect can connect with the monarchies of Jordan and Bahrain, including through a combination of rational *ʿasabiyya* and religion. If rational *ʿasabiyya* creates a bond among only the ruling elite, then there must be exclusion of those who are not of the ruling class (ibid., p. 172). Such exclusion can link to Bahrain's religious discrimination and Jordan's ethnic discrimination, respectively. In

Manama, a ruling Sunni elite practice inclusion/exclusion along religious lines with Shia'a discriminated against and decried as Iranian agents during the Arab Spring (Wehrey, p. 122). In Amman, a monarch with lineage to the Prophet Muhammad maintains a ruling bargain with East Bank Jordanians while also coopting Palestinian business elites during times of reduced aid and hence patronage cuts for the tribal elite (Robinson, p. 391). Jordan's model of rational *'asabiyya* is arresting as the fluctuation of the ruling bargain can mean that the ethnicity of the ruling elite can expand and contract according to cash flow (ibid.). However, the scape-goating of Palestinian protestors during the Arab Spring is a reminder that under rational *'asabiyya* the core of the ruling elite is monarchy and East Bankers (Valbjørn, p. 127). Ongoing Shia'a discrimination in Bahrain and ethnic discrimination in Jordan may reveal that the Arab Spring is strengthening such *'asabiyya* or clannishness as another form of regime security, with religion and ethnicity manipulated for regime survival.

3.7 Conclusion

A detailed overview of the four case studies for this project provides an understanding of how Political Legitimacy has been traditionally crafted in North Africa, the Levant and the Gulf. Republics and monarchies have drawn on democratic window-dressing and controlled parliaments to ensure the flow of aid into their coffers and the protection of their needed elite. In addition, both forms of government have manipulated religion and the image of piety to varying degrees. For Ben Ali's Tunisia, this included images of a pious but modern president, augmenting a state narrative of Islam being second to an educated youth that should regard Islamic garb as traditional rather than progressive. In the Levant, the Hashemites have enjoyed the stronger Religious Legitimacy of lineage to the Prophet Muhammad and also the related guardianship of holy sites in Jerusalem. In a twist of faith, however, Bahrain's al-Khalifas have seen the Shia'a masses draw on their own Religious Legitimacy, with many protestors decreeing their actions blessed by Allah.

Despite sharing strategies of manipulating religion and parliaments, the survival of family rule has been mixed across the Arab world. The old republics in Tunisia and Egypt have crumbled, ending the era of Mubarak and Ben Ali. At the same time, the nascent republics being birthed in

Tunisia and Egypt are seeing the military take center stage. For Tunisia, such a shift in a previously marginalized Armed Forces may actually help shape a stable democracy, as experienced officers address security gaps and help deconstruct Ben Ali's feared *mukhabarat*. In Egypt, however, the emergence of military rule has not expunged the suppression under Mubarak but rather enlarged it under President Abdel-Fattah al-Sisi, who now leads Egypt's Armed Forces as the new pharaoh of the land.

Republics may rise and fall, yet it seems that monarchies remain. The Hashemite Kingdom of Jordan is the last bastion of the Levant less for its religious lineage than for its ability to maintain the status quo through manipulation of tribal lines, regional fears and even the Arab Spring itself. Although King Abdullah II may want to transition the state toward a constitutional monarchy, it is clear from his public confessions that even he cannot alter the forces of the old elite, powerful tribes and his own *mukhbarat*. Further, he is limited in his reforms by the simple need for Hashemite survival, under which external aid and rentier bargains ultimately serve regime security. In the Gulf, the al-Khalifa monarchy of Bahrain appears to have also extinguished their own Arab Spring. Rather than exploiting regional threats, King Hamad has called on regional allies in the form of Saudi Arabia and GCC partners. A hard crackdown in the island state amid a smear campaign intended to deepen sectarianism appears to have been successful in sowing mutual distrust between Sunni and Shia'a. Just as Ben Ali and Mubarak engaged in democratic window-dressing, the establishment of the BICI did little to change the ruling tactics of the Sunni minority. Protected from accountability by parliament and the Peninsula Shield Force, the recent liquidation of political groups by an empowered monarchy illustrates a kingdom where survival of family rule continues in a regional atmosphere of impunity.

This chapter provides a detailed chronology of non-democratic political power as an established framework (albeit under the partial guise of democracy and/or civil society across all case studies) and how this framework was challenged by the Arab Spring. Such a detailed overview serves as an expedient analysis of the major political factors that are to be analyzed in Chapter 4, in which we explore how Arab leaders defended non-democratic legitimacy in public discourse in response to the Arab Spring.

References

Primary Data

Ben Ali, Z. (1987). *Speech to the Tunisian parliament by Zine el Abidine Ben Ali on 7 November 1987 After President Bourguiba Was Declared Unfit to Govern.* Available at: http://al-bab.com/documents-section/tunisia-overthrow-bourguiba (accessed 30 January 2022).

Ben Ali, Z. (2010). *Tunisia: Speech by President Ben Ali.* Available at: http://al-bab.com/documents-section/tunisia-speech-president-ben-ali-0 (accessed 4 April 2017).

British Broadcasting Corporation. (2011). *Egypt Unrest: Full Text of Hosni Mubarak's Speech.* Available at: http://www.bbc.co.uk/news/world-middle-east-12427091 (accessed 12 October 2021).

Facebook. (2017). *Personal Correspondence with Student from University of Jordan* (on file with author).

New York Times. (2011, February 11). Text of Omar Suleiman's Address. Available at: http://www.nytimes.com/2011/02/12/world/middleeast/12-suleiman-speech-text.html (accessed 21 January 2022).

Secondary Data

Academic Reports/Papers

ADHRB. (2015). *Apart in Their Own Land: Government Discrimination against Shia in Bahrain* (Vol. I).

al-Awadi, H. (2005). Mubarak and the Islamists: Why Did the "Honeymoon" End? *Middle East Journal, 59*(1), 62–80.

al-Rawi, A. K. (2015). Sectarianism and the Arab Spring: Framing the Popular Protests in Bahrain. *Global Media and Communication, II*(I), 25–42.

Alshboul, A., & Oudat, M. A. (2010). "Jordan First": Tribalism, Nationalism and Legitimacy of Power in Jordan. *Intellectual Discourse, 18*(1), 65–96.

Ansari, Z. I. (1961). Contemporary Islam and Nationalism: A Case Study of Egypt. *Die Welt Das Islams, 7*(4), 3–38.

Bank, A., Richter, T., & Sunik, A. (2014). Durable yet Different: Monarchies in the Arab Spring. *Journal of Arabian Studies, 4*(2), 163–179.

Culcasi, K. (2016). Warm Nationalism: Mapping and Imagining the Jordanian Nation. *Political Geography, 54*, 7–20.

Diamond, L. (2013). What Ever Happened to Bahrain? *Hoover Digest, 2*, 84–89.

Epstein, S., & Miller, M. S. (2015). Money, Inflation and the Arab Spring in Bahrain. *European Research Studies, 18*(1), 25–42.

Gallets, B. (2015). Black September and Identity Construction in Jordan. *Journal of Georgetown University-Qatar Middle Eastern Studies Student Association, 12*, 116–124.

Greenwood, S. (2003). Jordan, The Al-Aqsa Intifada and America's "War on Terror." *Middle East Policy, X*(3), 90–111.

Hamdi, H., & Sbia, R. (2013). Dynamic Relationships Between Oil Revenues, Government Spending and Economic Growth in an Oil-Dependent Economy. *Economic Modelling, 35*, 118–125.

Hawkins, S. (2011). Who Wears *Hijab* with the President: Constructing a Modern Islam in Tunisia. *Journal of Religion in Africa, 41*, 35–58.

Heiss, A. (2012). The Failed Management of a Dying Regime: Hosni Mubarak, Egypt's National Democratic Party, and the January 25 Revolution. *Journal of Third World Studies, XXIX*(1), 155–171.

Herrold, C. E. (2016). NGO Policy in Pre- and Post-Mubarak Egypt: Effects on NGOs' Roles in Democracy Promotion. *Nonprofit Policy Forum, 7*(2), 189–212.

King, S. J. (2011). *The Constitutional Monarchy Option in Morocco and Bahrain* (Policy Brief, 33).

Linz, J. J., Minoves, J. F., & Stepan, A. (2014). Democratic Parliamentary Monarchies. *Journal of Democracy, 25*(2), 35–52.

Liu, Z. (2008). The Relations Between Nationalism and Islam in the Middle East. *Journal of Middle Eastern and Islamic Studies, 2*(1), 69–78.

Lucas, R. E. (2011). Is the King's Dilemma Only for Presidents? Available at: https://carnegieendowment.org/sada/43333 (accessed 24 January 2022).

Nagarajan, K. V. (2013). Egypt's Political Economy and the Downfall of the Mubarak Regime. *International Journal of Humanities and Social Science, 3* (10), 22–39.

Nassif, H. B. (2013). Wedded to Mubarak: The Second Careers and Financial Rewards of Egypt's Military Elite, 1981–2011. *Middle East Journal, 67*(4), 509–530.

Obaid, N. (2014). *A Saudi Arabian Defense Doctrine: Mapping the Extended Force Structure the Kingdom needs to lead the Arab World, Stabilize the Region, and Meet its Global Responsibilities*. Cambridge, Massachusetts: Belfer Centre for Science and International Affairs. Available at: http://www.belfercenter.org/sites/default/files/legacy/files/Saudi%20Strategic%20Doctrine%20-%20web.pdf (accessed 8 June 2017).

Peter, F. (2016). *Political Legitimacy*. Available at: http://plato.stanford.edu/entries/legitimacy/ (accessed 18 January 2022).

Ra'ees, W. (2004). *Asabiyyah*, Religion and Regime Types: Re-reading Ibn Khaldun. *Intellectual Discourse, 12*(2), 159–180.

Robinson, G. E. (1998). Defensive Democratization in Jordan. *International Journal of Middle East Studies, 30*(3), 387–410.

Ryan, C. R. (2004). "Jordan First": Jordan's Inter-Arab Relations and Foreign Policy Under King Abdullah II. *Arab Studies Quarterly, 26*(3), 43–62.

Ryan, C. R., & Schwedler, J. (2004). Return to Democratization or New Hybrid Regime?: The 2003 Elections in Jordan. *Middle East Policy, 11*(2), 138–151.

Sadiki, L. (2002a). Bin Ali's Tunisia: Democracy by Non-democratic Means. *British Journal of Middle East Studies, 29*(1), 57–78.

Sadiki, L. (2002b). The Search for Citizenship in Bin Ali's Tunisia: Democracy Versus Unity. *Political Studies, 50*, 497–513.

Schwedler, J. (2012). *The Politics of Protest in Jordan*. Available at: https://www.files.ethz.ch/isn/170149/1701.201203.schwedler.politicsprotestjordan.pdf (accessed 11 January 2022).

Shehata, D. (2011). The Fall of the Pharoah: How Hosni Mubarak's Reign Came to an End. *Foreign Affairs, 90*(3), 26–32.

Shryock, A. J. (1995). Popular Genealogical Nationalism: History Writing and Identity Among the Balqa Tribes of Jordan. *Comparative Studies in Society and History, 37*(2), 325–357.

Sika, N. (2013). The Arab State and Social Contestation. In *The Evolving Ruling Bargain in the Middle East: Summary Report* (pp. 6–7). Georgetown University Center for International and Regional Studies.

Tobin, S. A. (2012). 'Jordan's Arab Spring: The Middle Class and Anti-Revolution. *Middle East Policy, 19*(1), 96–109.

Valbjørn, M. (2019). What's so Sectarian About Sectarian Politics? Identity Politics and Authoritarianism in a New Middle East. *Studies in Ethnicity and Nationalism, 19*(1), 127–149.

Ware, L. B. (1988). Ben Ali's Constitutional Coup in Tunisia. *Middle East Journal, 42*(4), 587–601.

Weber, M., & Gerth, H. H. (Eds.). (2009). *From Max Weber: Essays in Sociology*. Routledge Classics in Sociology. Routledge.

Wehrey, F. (2013). Bahrain's Decade of Discontent. *Journal of Democracy, 24*(3), 116–126.

Winckler, O. (2015). How Many Qataris Nationals Are There? *The Middle East Quarterly, 22*(2). Available at: http://www.meforum.org/5081/how-many-qataris (accessed 2 June 2017).

Media Reports

al-Khalidi, S. (2012, November). *Protests Erupt in Jordan After Fuel Prices Rise*. Available at: https://uk.reuters.com/article/uk-jordan-protests-idUKBRE8AD00F20121114 (accessed 10 January 2022).

ADHRB. (2017). *Bahrain Dissolves Wa'ad, Last Major Opposition Society*. Available at: https://www.adhrb.org/2017/05/bahrain-dissolves-last-major-opposition-society/ (accessed 04 January 2022).

AFP. (2014). *Fearing Backlash, Jordan Asserts Al-Aqsa Custodianship*. Available at: https://www.dailymail.co.uk/wires/afp/article-2836430/Fearing-backlash-Jordan-asserts-Al-Aqsa-custodianship.html (accessed 08 January 2022).

Al Jazeera. (2011). *Profile: Hosni Mubarak*. Available at: http://www.aljazeera.com/focus/2009/12/200912693048491779.html (accessed 18 January 2022).

Aziz, S. F. (2016, May 20). *Egypt's Unsustainable Military Regime*. Available at: https://www.alaraby.co.uk/english/Comment/2016/5/20/Egypts-unsustainable-military-regime (accessed 21 January 2022).

Bahrain News Agency. (2004, December). *King Hamad's Speech: National Day*. Available at: http://www.bna.bh/portal/en/news/380400 (accessed 29 May 2017, no longer online as of 21 January 2022).

BBC. (2014a, March 3). *Egypt Police Jailed over 2010 Death of Khaled Said*. Available at: http://www.bbc.co.uk/news/world-middle-east-26416964 (accessed 21 January 2022).

BBC. (2014b, August). *Sandhurst's Sheikhs: Why Do So Many Gulf Royals Receive Military Training in the UK?* Available at: http://www.bbc.co.uk/news/magazine-28896860 (accessed 2 January 2022).

BBC. (2017). *Profile: Hosni Mubarak*. Available at: http://www.bbc.co.uk/news/world-middle-east-12301713 (accessed 12 January 2022).

Birnbaum, M., & Warrick, J. (2011). *As Bahrain Stifles Protest Movement, U.S.* Muted Objection Draws Criticism. Available at: https://www.washingtonpost.com/world/as-bahrain-stifles-protest-movement-uss-muted-objections-draw-criticism/2011/04/14/AFziTofD_story.html?utm_term=.6f058ff44a70 (accessed 23 January 2022).

Bronner, E. (2011, March). *Bahrain Tears Down Monument as Protestors Seethe*. Available at: http://www.nytimes.com/2011/03/19/world/middleeast/19bahrain.html (accessed 7 January 2022).

Cavendish, R. (2007). A Failed Coup in Jordan. *History Today, 57*(4). Available at: http://www.historytoday.com/richard-cavendish/failed-coup-jordan (accessed 08 January 2022).

Driesbach, T., & Joyce, R. (2014, March27). Revealing Tunisia's Corruption Under Ben Ali. *Al Jazeera*. Available at: http://www.aljazeera.com/indepth/features/2014/03/revealing-tunisia-corruption-under-ben-ali-201432785825560542.html (accessed 03 January 2022).

Elmasry, M. (2015, July 3). *Morsi Myths: Re-examining Justifications for Egypt's Coup*. Available at: http://www.middleeasteye.net/columns/myths-about-morsi-examining-justifications-egypt-s-2013-cou-1248467631 (accessed 21 January 2022).

Fahim, K. (2013). Loyalists to Dominate Jordan's New Parliament. Available at: https://www.nytimes.com/2013/01/25/world/middleeast/jordan-elections-favor-government-loyalists.html (accessed 04 January 2022).

Farrell, W. (1981, October 15). *Mubarak, in Tears at Swearing In, Tells Egyptians, "This Is My Fate".* Available at: http://www.nytimes.com/1981/10/15/world/mubarak-in-tears-at-swearing-in-tells-egyptians-this-is-my-fate.html (accessed 12 January 2022).

Farrell, W. (1981, November 9). *Mubarak Pledges to Improve Living for All Egyptians.* Available at: http://www.nytimes.com/1981/11/09/world/mubarak-pledges-to-improve-living-for-all-egyptians.html (accessed 12 January 2022).

Farrell, W. (1981, October 7). *Sadat Assassinated at Army Parade as Men amid Ranks Fire into Stands; Vice President Affirms 'All Treaties'.* Available at: https://www.nytimes.com/1981/10/07/world/sadat-assassinated-army-parade-men-amid-ranks-fire-into-stands-vice-president-041355.html (accessed 09 September 2022).

Gavlak, D. (2011, February). *Middle East Protests: Jordan Sees Biggest Reform Rally.* Available at: http://www.bbc.co.uk/news/world-middle-east-12582869 (accessed 10 January 2022).

Ghazal, M. (2016, January) *Population Stands at Around 9.5 Million, Including 2.9 Million Guests.* Available at: http://www.jordantimes.com/news/local/population-stands-around-95-million-including-29-million-guests (accessed 11 January 2022).

Goldberg, J. (2013, April). *The Modern King in the Arab Spring.* Available at: https://www.theatlantic.com/magazine/archive/2013/04/monarch-in-the-middle/309270/ (accessed 24 January 2022).

Hartlaub, H. (2014, February). *The Dying Tide of Protests in Jordan.* Available at: http://muftah.org/dying-tide-of-protests-in-jordan/#.WRMmHdLyuM8 (accessed 10 January 2022).

Hiro, D. (2013, August 23). *Analysis: What Do Egypt's Generals Want?* Available at: http://america.aljazeera.com/articles/2013/8/23/what-do-egypt-s-generalswant.html (accessed 21 January 2022).

McEvers, K. (2012, January). *Bahrain: The Revolution That Wasn't.* Available at: http://www.npr.org/2012/01/05/144637499/bahrain-the-revolution-that-wasnt (accessed 8 January 2022).

Meky, S. (2014, January 25). *Remembering Khaled Saeed, Whose Death Sparked Egypt's Revolution.* Available at: http://english.alarabiya.net/en/perspective/features/2014/01/25/Khaled-Saeed-Egypt-s-Jan-25-icon-remembered-unlike-before.html (accessed 21 January 2022).

McGreal, C., & Shenker, J. (2011). *Hosni Mubarak Resigns—And Egypt Celebrates a New Dawn.* Available at: https://www.theguardian.com/world/2011/feb/11/hosni-mubarak-resigns-egypt-cairo (accessed 04 January 2022).

Middle East Eye. (2017, May). *Bahrain Heading for 'Total Suppression' with Secular Group Ban*. Available at: http://www.middleeasteye.net/news/secular-bahrain-opposition-group-says-it-has-been-dissolved-566223564 (accessed 8 January 2022).

Miller, E. (2013, March 19). *King Abdullah Chides Atlantic Interviewer*. Available at: http://www.timesofisrael.com/king-abdullah-chides-atlantic-interviewer/ (accessed 05 January 2022).

Murad, N. (2014, February). *Here Is How Jordan Escaped the Arab Spring*. Available at: https://www.aljazeera.com/opinions/2014/2/9/here-is-how-jordan-escaped-the-arab-spring (accessed 10 January 2022).

Nafaa, H. (2010, May 10). *An Alternative Mubarak May Day Speech*. Available at: http://www.egyptindependent.com/opinion/alternative-mubarak-may-day-speech (accessed 19 January 2022).

Press TV Doc. (2016). *Ben Ali: The Black Books* [film]. Available at: https://www.youtube.com/watch?v=xG50BvGQX9g (last accessed 30 January 2022).

Royal Hashemite Court. (2001a). *The Great Arab Revolt*. Available at: http://www.kinghussein.gov.jo/his_arabrevolt.html (accessed 05 January 2022).

Royal Hashemite Court. (2001b). *The Making of Transjordan*. Available at: http://www.kinghussein.gov.jo/his_transjordan.html (accessed 05 January 2022).

Said, W. M. (2018). *Jordan's Role Over Holy Sites in East Jerusalem Legal and Sovereignty Related*. Available at: http://www.jordantimes.com/opinion/walid-m-sadi/jordans-role-over-holy-sites-east-jerusalem-legal%C2%A0and-sovereignty-related (accessed 08 January 2022).

Stead, R. (2018). *Jordan Has a Duty to Defend Jerusalem and Al-Aqsa*. Available at: https://www.middleeastmonitor.com/20180714-jordan-has-a-duty-to-defend-jerusalem-and-al-aqsa/ (accessed 08 January 2022).

Thames TV. (1972). *King Hussein of Jordan—Interview* [film]. Available at: https://www.youtube.com/watch?v=rCYJchah3kY (accessed 08 January 2022).

The Economist. (2003, April). Jordan's Secret Police: Behave, or Else. Available at: http://www.economist.com/node/1682805 (accessed 08 January 2022).

The Economist. (2016). The Arab Revolt. Available at: https://www.economist.com/the-economist-explains/2016/06/03/the-arab-revolt (accessed 08 January 2022).

Voice of America. (2011, August). *Facebook Becomes Divisive in Bahrain*. Available at: https://www.voanews.com/a/facebook-becomes-divisive-in-bahrain-127958073/143943.html (accessed 7 January 2022).

Williams, S. E. (2017, February). *Jordan Austerity: Despite Rising Prices and Anger, Protests Limited*. Available at: http://www.middleeasteye.net/news/jordan-austerity-rally-amman-1693526432 (accessed 10 January 2022).

Printed/Online Books

Brown, N. J. (2001). *Constitutions in a Nonconstitutional World: Arab Basic Laws and the Prospects for Accountable Government*. SUNY Series in Middle Eastern Studies. State University of New York Press.

Menshawy, M. (2017). *State, Memory, and Egypt's Victory in the 1973 War: Ruling by Discourse*. Palgrave Macmillan.

Reich, B. (1990). *Political Leaders of the Contemporary Middle East and North Africa: A Biographical Dictionary*. Greenwood Press Inc.

International Organization Reports

Amnesty International. (2016, March). *Bahrain: Alarming Spike in Expulsion of Citizens Arbitrarily Stripped of Their Nationality*. Available at: https://www.amnesty.org/en/latest/news/2016/03/bahrain-alarming-spike-in-expulsion-of-citizens-arbitrarily-stripped-of-their-nationality/ (accessed 8 January 2022).

Arieff, A. (2011). *Political Transition in Tunisia*. Congressional Research Service.

CIA World Factbook. (2017). *Middle East: Bahrain*. Available at: https://www.cia.gov/library/publications/resources/the-world-factbook/geos/print_ba.html (accessed 2 January 2022).

Grewal, S. (2016). *A Quiet Revolution: The Military After Ben Ali*. Carnegie Middle East Center.

Henderson, S. (2017). *Beyond Islamists and Autocrats: Bahrain's Stalled Reforms and the Future U.S. Role*. Available at: https://www.washingtoninstitute.org/policy-analysis/bahrains-stalled-reforms-and-future-us-role (accessed 1 January 2022).

Human Rights Watch/Middle East. (1997). *Jordan: Clamping Down on Critics-Human Rights Violations in Advance of the Parliamentary Elections*. Available at: https://www.hrw.org/reports/1997/jordan/JORDAN97.pdf (accessed 08 January 2022).

Mabon, S. (2012). *The Battle for Bahrain: Iranian-Saudi Rivalry*. Available at: http://www.mepc.org/battle-bahrain-iranian-saudi-rivalry (accessed 8 January 2022).

Oxford Business Group. (2017). *Qatar Remains a Leading Player in Oil and Gas*. Available at: https://www.oxfordbusinessgroup.com/overview/market-share-matters-despite-global-price-volatility-country-remains-leading-player-oil-and-gas (accessed 2 January 2022).

Stratfor, LLC. (2017). *Bahrain's Importance to the United States*. Available at: https://www.stratfor.com/image/bahrains-importance-united-states (accessed 2 June 2017, offline as of 20 January 2022).

Thaler, D. (2004). The Middle East: The Cradle of the Muslim World. In *The Muslim World After 9/11* (pp. 69–144). RAND Corporation.

UNHCR. (2007). *Iraqis in Jordan: Their Number and Characteristics*. Available at: https://www.unhcr.org/455443a80.pdf (accessed 11 January 2022).

U.S. Energy Information Administration. (2016a). *Bahrain*. Available at: https://www.eia.gov/beta/international/country.cfm?iso=BHR (accessed 2 January 2022).

U.S. Energy Information Administration. (2016b). *Kuwait*. Available at: https://www.eia.gov/beta/international/country.cfm?iso=KWT (accessed 2 January 2022).

World Bank. (2015). *Population, Total*. Available at: http://data.worldbank.org/indicator/SP.POP.TOTL?locations=KW-BH-QA (accessed 2 January 2022).

Social Media

Facebook. (2017). *We Are All Khaled Said*. Available at: https://www.facebook.com/elshaheeed.co.uk?filter=3 (accessed 08 April 2022).

CHAPTER 4

The Speeches Defending Dictatorship During the Arab Spring

4.1 Introduction

As explained earlier, this book uses Searle's Speech Acts to examine cases relevant to the Arab Spring and to address the following questions: What are the factors Arab leaders use in discourse justifying their rule within the context of the Arab Spring? To what extent does this discourse support a (socio-economic) ruling bargain and Religious Legitimacy? As the Arab Spring can be regarded as a socio-economic movement or series of movements provoked by, inter alia, poverty and corruption (as discussed in Chapter 3), understanding how Arab leaders addressed the ruling bargain in their political discourses amid widespread discontent will allow examination of the assumption that republics will emphasize the socio-economic ruling bargain as the main source of their non-democratic legitimacy in response to the Arab Spring, due to most republics being the result of coups rather than established familial rule. Consequently, many republican rulers have weaker ties to traditional (religious) institutes and popular support and rely on a ruling bargain to maintain legitimacy. Monarchs, on the other hand, will draw on Religious Legitimacy more than the ruling bargain due to their longevity and ties to traditional institutions and accepted socio-cultural norms.

To complement the analysis of speeches and discourses, the present work also focuses on the constitutions from each case study in relation to the speeches. This investigation in Chapter 5 will ascertain what political processes of legitimacy are formally accepted, to what extent these

N. Due-Gundersen, *Non-Democratic Legitimacy During the Arab Spring*,
https://doi.org/10.1007/978-3-031-11882-1_4

processes are democratic or non-democratic forms of legitimacy (or processes of Religious Legitimacy) and whether these written processes are referred to in the speeches given by Arab leaders justifying their rule in response to the Arab Spring.

To reiterate, these constitutions include:

- Constitution of the Hashemite Kingdom of Jordan
- Constitution of the Kingdom of Bahrain
- Constitution of the Arab Republic of Egypt
- Constitution of the Republic of Tunisia

4.2 Speeches of Legitimacy During the Arab Spring

4.2.1 The Hashemite Kingdom of Jordan's Abdullah II

> In the name of God, the Most Merciful, the Compassionate. My brothers and sisters, I would like to welcome you all to your home, the home of all Jordanians. I wanted to meet with you today for a sincere talk at this particular stage in our beloved country's history, in order to highlight our reform roadmap. (Abdullah II, October 2012)

A discourse analysis of Jordan's Abdullah II reveals greater use of Religious Legitimacy than that of ousted republicans, while still highlighting the ruling bargain and socio-economic aspects of said bargain. At the same time, there is a turn toward political elements that appear to acknowledge that the non-democratic ruling bargain was limited since before the Arab Spring.

Abdullah II's speech opens with a Quranic phrase, "[…] [in] the name of God, the Merciful, the Compassionate" (ibid.). The use of a phrase familiar to all Muslims is arresting and can be linked back to Searle's mention of any speech act requiring mutual rules" (Searle, 1965, p. 3). The notion of mutual rules conveyed by Abdullah II as speaker can be compared and contrasted with the similar attempts of President Ben Ali in his address. For Ben Ali, the mutual rule between speaker and listeners is "[…] the language of Tunisians" (Ben Ali, 2011). For Jordan's King Abdullah II, however, the mutual rules are ones of religion. Here, Abdullah's opening passage indicates that he as a monarchical ruler may turn to religion more so than his republican counterparts (Abdullah II, October 2012).

Hence, religion can be regarded as the first preparatory condition and is followed by an interesting juxtaposition against Mubarak's paternalism. For the Egyptian President, his final address was "[...] a father's dialogue with his sons and daughters" (British Broadcasting Corporation, 2011). For Abdullah II, citizens of Jordan are not his sons and daughters but "[...] my brothers and sisters" who he invites not for "[...] a father's dialogue with his sons and daughters" as Mubarak does but for a "[...] sincere talk at this particular stage in our beloved country's history, in order to highlight our reform roadmap" (Abdullah II, October 2012). This "reform roadmap" refers to political reform programs that were launched "[...] a year and a half ago [...] [for] the home of all Jordanians" (ibid.). Such a preparatory condition is arresting.

Abdullah opens his address by (re)iterating political promises. As discussed in Chapter 3, the workings of the ruling bargain in Jordan have not always been apolitical. Reliant on regional and other external aid, Jordan has seen fluctuations in cashflow affect the non-democratic relations between monarchy and masses. The requirement of the Hashemites to maintain their patronage network by imposing taxation has meant that the maxim *no taxation, no representation* has been reversed at times, with the socio-economic shift in the social contract prompting citizens to demand a political voice (Robinson, 1998, p. 391). Abdullah II's reference to ongoing political reform can be understood as a reflection of this reality, allowing the preparatory conditions of Religious Legitimacy and democratic reform to act as a balance that is unseen in republican speakers: Abdullah II is not drawing purely on non-democratic factors and seems to understand the fact that the ruling bargain can change, as Jordan's history has revealed (ibid.).

At the same time, the fact that such promises are "[...] for all Jordanians" allows them to be restrictive within the context of Jordan's history. Again, as examined in Chapter 3, Jordan's geostrategic location has not only attracted fluctuating donations from Western powers but often leaves the Hashemite Kingdom "[...] between Iraq and a hard place", as described by the King himself when interviewed before the Arab Spring erupted (Lower, 2013). Jordan has endured waves of refugees since 1948, beginning with Palestinians after the creation of Israel and during the 1967 skirmish between Jordan's King Hussein and Israeli forces, which cost Hussein the East Bank and Jerusalem (including the loss of Muslim holy landmarks). Both Gulf Wars brought further refugees from Iraq and current events in Syria have augmented Jordan's refugee population to the point of sporadic unrest, as Jordanians began to fear for their socio-economic prospects. Within the context of continuing refugee flow, Abdullah's preparatory conditions of political promises for "[…] the home of all Jordanians" may act as a reminder that the ruling bargain's political elements prioritize Jordanians loyal to monarchy and of East Bank origin, while those of Palestinian and other origins may enjoy limited privileges or even be excluded from the ruling bargain, even if they have attained Jordanian citizenship (Culcasi, 2016, p. 9).

As Abdullah continues to make political promises, he does so while addressing citizens as equal "[…] brothers and sisters" who have "[…] focused on enhancing citizens' rights to participate effectively in the decisions that impact them and their future, and I am committed to guaranteeing this right for all" (Abdullah II, October 2012). Note the description in this passage of "[…] citizen's rights", again implying that democratic or political factors of the ruling bargain are not for all but only for those in Jordan who enjoy citizenship. At the same time, Abdullah draws attention to the enhancing of rights for citizens, implying that there is democratic Political Legitimacy in his rule and that the ruling bargain must acknowledge the political participation of citizens.

Abdullah also appears to engage, like Mubarak, in Democratic Approval through talk of constitutional reform and constitutional laws (British Broadcasting Corporation, 2011). Although political reforms include constitutional changes to "[…] make the people a true partner in the political process", King Abdullah II reminds Jordanians that he is the head of a "[…] constitutional monarchical system" and that hence his legitimacy is buttressed by "[…] our constitutional process" and that his very regime exists "[…] under the umbrella of the Constitution" (Abdullah II, 2012). Returning to discussions of Peter's Democratic Approval in Chapter 2, it is possible to consider the use of democratic proceduralism to formally validate a regime and its political decisions. Common institutions representing such Democratic Approval include the *majlis* or parliament, often used by Middle East monarchies. Abdullah emphasizes the role of parliament in his constitutional system, describing elections for parliament as representing "[…] the will of the people" and that reforms will be overseen "[…] under the dome of Parliament" (ibid.). This latter quote is arresting, as it merges Democratic Approval with Religious Legitimacy. The image of the parliament being under a dome will, for many Jordanians, evoke their faith and associations with the mosque. This image of Abdullah's parliamentary system being "holy" is augmented by the fact that domes are a central element of all mosques and related holy sites in Islam, symbolizing access to Heaven (Grupico, 2011).

Religious imagery associated with parliamentary procedure is significant in the context of Abdullah's speech. For Abdullah's preparatory conditions regarding political reform and Religious Legitimacy link directly with the essential condition issued to Jordanians: Abdullah does not desperately call for a halt to protests. Rather, he urges patience so that reforms already underway are "[...] allowed enough time for justice to take its course". More important than patience is his instruction that if citizens "[...] want to change Jordan for the better, [...] that chance is through the upcoming elections, and there is a way [for democratic involvement] and that way is through the next Parliament" (Abdullah II, October 2012). When compared to the speeches of his republican counterparts, Abdullah's essential condition can be considered more strongly tied to Jordan's ruling bargain: with a history of fluctuating aid, there is a formal recognition that Jordanians expect to be a part of the political decision-making process if (non-democratic) socio-economic benefits are reduced or unavailable. It would appear that Abdullah tacitly acknowledges this political aspect of the social contract, as his discussion of political reform is followed by a detailed account of Jordan's (recent) economic troubles. Indeed, in one passage Abdullah highlights that subsidies remain in place "[...] for some basic commodities" while contrasting this commonality across most ruling bargains with Jordan's "[...] increase in deficit and public debt", brought on, in part, by regional turmoil, including the end of subsidized oil agreements with Iraq and costly "[...] disruptions in the supply of Egyptian gas [to Jordan]". The effects of regional shifts have meant that regional aid "[...] barely covered the additional deficit" (ibid.).

With an admission of Jordan's financial difficulties, Abdullah seems to invite Jordanians to have a political voice in decision-making, thereby returning to Chapter 3's discussions on how the Hashemites have encountered political expectations from citizens when unable to deliver Beneficial Consequences of a socio-economic nature. However, this image of a more democratic social contract must be balanced with Jordan's tribal and political history. As discussed in Chapter 3, election results have often favored tribalism, royalists and leading *mukhabarat* figures due to electoral manipulation and gerrymandering. Considering Jordan's political profile and Abdullah's speech returns discussion somewhat to Korany's framework of the three Ms discussed in Chapter 2: the Military, the Mosque and the Masses (2014, p. 256). In Abdullah's case, perhaps the three Ms are the

Mukhabarat, the Mosque and the Masses, as Jordan's Hashemites have augmented the role of the security services more than the military when it comes to politics, while Abdullah draws on religious imagery and "[…] the honour of being a descendant of our forefather Prophet Mohammad" to represent his strong Religious Legitimacy to the masses (Abdullah II, October 2012).

Nevertheless, Abdullah seems to use Democratic Approval to remain aloof from socio-economic and political pressures. Returning to talk of political reform and elections, Abdullah outlines key "[…] policies and additional reforms" that an elected government should address. These include:

- Tackling poverty and unemployment
- Managing Jordan's debt and budget deficit
- Ensuring that the taxation system is adequately reformed
- Developing a more comprehensive voting system (linked to Abdullah's invitation for Jordanians to participate in the political process)
- Ensuring an improvement of public services, including health, transport and education (ibid.)

A detailed list of reform goals that connect with Jordan's socio-economic challenges and fluctuating ruling bargain differs markedly from the speeches of Ben Ali and Mubarak, as both offered last-minute reforms that involved vague political freedoms (of the press or the internet) and ambiguous promises for transitions of power. Nonetheless, Abdullah does not take responsibility for said reforms. As King, he is committed to the "[…] constitutional process" but political reforms themselves are left to the political parties that are campaigning for election (ibid.). In other words, Abdullah uses Democratic Approval to stay aloof from political demands, pushing such responsibility onto the next elected government while he himself will oversee the formalities of "[…] our constitutional process" and "respect the opinion of the majority" vis-à-vis whichever party is elected to government (ibid.). Such aloofness allows Abdullah's essential conditions to be understood in a new light. When Abdullah implores Jordanians to be patient with the parliamentary system and allow "[…] enough time for justice to take its course", his aloofness implies that even he as ruler must show patience alongside his Jordanian "[…] brothers and sisters" (ibid.). Again, this image can be linked to the notion of equality between ruler and citizens rather than paternalism. However, as discussed in Chapter 3, Abdullah's pushing reform and related demands onto successive governments must also be acknowledged as a common tactic used by the Hashemites to deflect popular discontent unto a revolving door of prime ministers (Milton-Edwards, 2017). Hence, Abdullah's use of Democratic Approval must be understood in such a context; legitimacy through proceduralism, as discussed by Peter, while also being used as a strategy to deflect blame.

Further, it is interesting to examine how Abdullah II acknowledges protests. Ben Ali describes demonstrations as "[...] protests against social conditions" (Ben Ali, 2011), while Mubarak did not even use the word "protest" but preferred to address Tahrir Square's demonstrations as "[...] the new Egyptian generation calling for a change to the better" that he, as father, could be proud of (British Broadcasting Corporation, 2011). Neither president appears aware of demonstrations calling for their overthrow. Contra to the republicans downplaying unrest, Jordan's Abdullah II acknowledges demonstrations and speaks "[...] frankly today about some slogans raised by a limited number of protestors—'overthrow the regime'" (Abdullah II, October 2012). In this passage, Abdullah takes the opportunity to draw on Religious Legitimacy in order to differentiate between positive opposition and negative opposition. Positive opposition plays "[...] a legitimate and needed role" by conforming with Abdullah's essential condition: showing patience and participating in the electoral process. Negative opposition, however, can be linked to specific Islamic concepts of disobedience that Abdullah draws on as a descendant of the Prophet Muhammad. Such opposition, Abdullah insists, does not "[...] serve the reform path, nor the country's future" and are "[...] attempts to incite chaos and *fitna* (sedition)" (ibid.).

The religious concept of *fitna* links back to Chapter 2 on how Muslim rule evolved through a social contract that included religious protection. Muslim jurists have discussed the notion that rebellion against a pious leader is forbidden, as such rebellion can threaten the community of believers. To engage in such specific rebellion is hence a sin in Islam known as *fitna* explored in Chapter 2 and by the idea of Political Quietism or fatalism explained by Brown (2000, p. 67).

Muslims must accept non-democratic rulers as long as they protect the Muslim faith and related territories or *Dar al-Islam*. At the same time, such reliance on Religious Legitimacy can be merged with Jordan's geopolitical situation. As discussed in Chapter 3, Jordan's location next door to unstable Iraq, conservative Saudi Arabia and warring Syria has meant that the fear of Jordan's collapse has provided the monarchy with the ability to exploit the status quo. Hence, the mention of *fitna* conjures not only religious connotations of protecting Islam through obedience to a pious ruler but also indirectly serves as a reminder of the chaos Jordan is surrounded by, especially as the Hashemite Kingdom continues to absorb increasing refugees from its neighbors.

Focusing further on Religious Legitimacy, Abdullah II has invoked Islamic sayings ("In the name of God, the Most Merciful, the Compassionate") and his lineage to the Prophet. The latter echoes Bulliet's discussions in Chapter 2 on Muslim leaders invoking Islamic titles and privileges, in this case the honor and subsequent (religious) authority of descending from the messenger of Islam (pp. 1, 12). In addition, the religious associations of *fitna* and Muslim territory connect with Bulliet's discussion of pious rulers maintaining territory that allows Muslims free practice of their faith (ibid.; Ayoob, 2004, p. 9). Finally, it is worth mentioning that, unlike Ben Ali and Mubarak, Abdullah II makes references to the Quran. Such references include deftly weaving Quranic verses and related religious concepts with non-democratic factors such as security and familial rule. Especially, Abdullah refers to the "[...] many martyrs" his family has sacrificed for Jordan's stability, while implying that he is ruler not out of choice but out of a sense of duty and the (divine) legitimacy of the Hashemite legacy (ibid.).

Moreover, before discussing acceptable and non-acceptable roles of the opposition, Abdullah paraphrases a Quranic quote, arguing that the Hashemites "[...] have to be objective and uphold the truth when we interpret things, and be honest in our words" (ibid.). This statement can be linked to Muslim critics of the Quran, who argue that honesty and truthfulness are natural and therefore exulted virtues (in the Quran). Hence, by linking his evaluation of the opposition to the Quran, Abdullah's message is that he is pious and therefore honest, while those who wish to overthrow him are, in contrast to his piety and honesty, guilty of *fitna* (Shahrur, 2009, p. 46).

Returning to Abdullah's promises and essential condition, reforms are discussed in his address as already underway, and Abdullah argues that those "[...] who want additional reforms" can gain them by again meeting his essential condition: participating in the voting process. It must be noted that although some critics consider Jordan to be ultimately stable due to the concern of outside powers over its geostrategic location, public reaction to Abdullah's instructions were mixed (Hawthorne, 2016). The month after King Abdullah addressed the nation, protestors clashed with police over the lifting of fuel subsidies (Luck & Warrick, 2012). This event came atop relatively peaceful and sporadic unrest but emphasized that widespread discontent was as much about socio-economics as it was about any desire by Jordanians for political involvement (ibid.). At the same time, the promised parliamentary elections went ahead in early 2013. Voter turnout was higher than expected. At 56.5%, the 2013 election turnout enjoyed greater popularity than the 2010 election, which had boasted only 52% (Greenfield, 2013). The 2013 turnout can be partially regarded as revealing that the Hashemites, after making political promises, continued to enjoy some approval that linked back to the ongoing reform process and hence maintained Political Legitimacy that merged non-democratic elements such as Religious Legitimacy and Democratic Approval with more democratic elements such as a parliamentary system.

Nonetheless, observers of the 2013 election concluded that voter turnout had less to do with democratic and political reforms and more to do with "[…] tribal loyalty and fears about regional instability" (ibid.). The latter element again augments previous comments that the Hashemite monarchy is exploiting regional chaos to maintain the status quo in Jordan and hence selling security as a further non-democratic factor that bolsters their legitimacy.

Abdullah II's address contrasts the speeches of republican counterparts in North Africa. As a monarch with direct lineage to the Prophet Muhammad, King Abdullah II draws much more on Religious Legitimacy than republican rulers. Further, his address provides preparatory conditions and essential conditions that are more strongly correlated and appear to take a long-term view. While Presidents Ben Ali and Mubarak make last-minute political promises and claim to offer moderate socio-economic incentives, they do so only with the aim of stopping unrest (Ben Ali, 2011; British Broadcasting Corporation, 2011). Abdullah, on the other hand, claims that political reforms are already underway and hence his promises and preparatory conditions reiterate an ongoing process, which can be linked to Peter's Democratic Approval. These promises are linked to Abdullah's essential condition or instruction: that Jordanians vote and participate in the political process rather than simply cease protesting. Moreover, the latter aspect differs markedly from Mubarak's use of Democratic Approval that is linked to constitutional amendments rather than an invitation for Egyptians to participate in political decision-making (ibid.). Further, Abdullah does not draw heavily on paternalism as Mubarak does, yet the Jordanian monarch merges the image of being equal to his "Jordanian brothers and sisters" with reminders of rule through tradition, describing how the Hashemite monarchy has provided stability long enough to offer "many martyrs", a reminder of the length of his family's rule that also uses religious language (Abdullah II, October 2012).

Analysis of Abdullah's speech reveals an address that shows a monarch drawing more heavily on Religious Legitimacy and tradition than the ruling bargain when compared to his republican counterparts. However, it must be noted that Abdullah's address devotes considerable time to explaining Jordan's fiscal problems and growing debt, thus acknowledging the socio-economic aspects of the ruling bargain and the expectation that a weaker socio-economic benefit structure should mean greater political participation for citizens through the voting and reform process, as discussed earlier in Chapter 3 by Robinson (1998, p. 389). At the same time, promises of political reform and citizen participation must be balanced against a voter turnout that some argue was encouraged by the same old tribal politics and the fear of instability rather than genuine democratic openings. From such a perspective, Jordan's King Abdullah II draws more greatly from non-democratic aspects, with heavy emphasis on Religious Legitimacy and Democratic Approval and the Beneficial Consequence of security amid a ruling bargain that relies on fluctuating external aid. Despite struggling socio-economics, an analysis of Abdullah's address appears to confirm the book's assumption: that monarchs draw more heavily on Religious Legitimacy than their republican counterparts.

4.2.2 *The Kingdom of Bahrain's Hamad Bin Isa Al-Khalifa*

> [The Bahrain Independent Commission of Inquiry] report deals with controversial matters of importance. You have sought to establish the true facts of a period of painful unrest which has affected all of us. You have understood the unprecedented challenges faced by our authorities as they confronted relentless provocation, from hostile sources both inside and outside the country. (Bahrain Independent Commission of Inquiry, 2011)

King Hamad's address contrasts that of his fellow Jordanian monarch by containing few religious references (Abdullah II, October 2012). Furthermore, Hamad's speech seems to address several diverse listeners rather than be only for domestic consumption (ibid.). Hamad's preparatory conditions are based on the findings of the Bahrain Independent Commission of Inquiry, a panel funded by the Bahraini government and headed by an Egyptian-American international law expert (BBC, 2011, "Bahrain Independent Commission of Inquiry excerpts"). Hence, much of Hamad's monologue forms a lengthy preparatory condition that encompasses ongoing promises of political reform and also further efforts toward ensuring security, a Beneficial Consequence (Bahrain Independent Commission of Inquiry, 2011). The fact that the address is based on conclusions from an independent investigation into Bahrain's unrest is a contrast to Ben Ali's address.

Ben Ali promises an independent investigation into Tunisia's upheaval and the corruption of nameless officials (Ben Ali, 2011). However, Bahrain's Hamad has already launched an independent investigation and is building promises of political and security reform upon this independent report. Such reform can also be regarded as a form of Democratic Approval, akin to Mubarak's address in which Mubarak promises constitutional amendments after reviewing a report in response to Egyptian unrest (British Broadcasting Corporation, 2011). Like Abdullah of Jordan, Hamad argues that political reforms are already ongoing and that even "[…] before receiving [the Inquiry's] Report, we have introduced proposals to amend our laws to give greater protection to the valuable right of free speech; and to expand the definition of 'torture' to ensure that all forms of ill treatment are sanctioned by our criminal laws" (Bahrain Independent Commission of Inquiry, 2011). Claiming to reform existing laws before being prompted (as Abdullah also insists in his address) augments the use of Democratic Approval. However, Hamad's speech draws the most on the Beneficial Consequence of security as a strong preparatory condition (ibid.).

Peter's Beneficial Consequences are purely utilitarian and can therefore consider factors such as security for citizens, even at the expense of liberties (Peter, 2016). What is interesting about Peter's view on Beneficial Consequences is that liberty can be all the more restricted if the stability the state provides in exchange not only protects its citizens but possibly extends to larger collectives outside the state's own borders (ibid.). This notion of "regional security" can be linked back to Hamad's address.

Hamad uses promises of security as a consistent preparatory condition. Of note is the fact that Hamad does not begin references to security with a focus on Bahrainis but rather the entire Gulf and the Gulf Cooperation

Council (GCC), of which Bahrain is a member. Regional security is placed within the context of an external threat, in this case Iran. Hamad admits to the Bahrain Commission of Inquiry that "[…] the Government of Bahrain was not in a position to provide evidence of links between Iran and specific events in our country this year" (Bahrain Independent Commission of Inquiry, 2011). However, in the same paragraph Hamad argues that Iran's propaganda and its influence on Bahrain's protests is "[…] an objective fact to be observed by all who have eyes and ears and can comprehend Arabic", implying that accusations against Iran are intended for a local and regional audience (ibid.). According to Hamad, Iran's influence and subsequent Bahraini unrest "[…] not only directly challenges the stability and sovereignty of our country, but also poses a threat to the security and stability of the GCC countries" (ibid.). In other words, if Bahrain is under threat, so too is the entire Gulf region (ibid.).

Hamad also takes this opportunity to address Bahrainis under the preparatory condition of security. He admits that security violations took place and assures citizens that "[…] we do not want, ever again, to discover that any of our law enforcement personnel have mistreated anyone" and that "[…] we are determined, God willing, to ensure that the painful events our beloved nation has just experienced are not repeated", implying that there has been a violation of the social contract's Beneficial Consequence of security that will be rectified (ibid.). At the same time, Hamad insists that "[…] we cannot fail to extend our gratitude to our armed forces and law enforcement agencies who restored public order in the face of intimidation and violence" and ends his speech by asserting that the House of Khalifa is committed to "[…] ensuring the safety and security of our nation and its people" (ibid.).

Again, it is emphatically apparent that security is being sold by the al-Khalifa monarchy as their main Beneficial Consequence (ibid.). This brief passage intended for domestic consumption leads to Hamad's essential condition for Bahrainis: continue to accept the ruling bargain in exchange for apparent security reforms but also "[…] a range of [financial] remedies, including the newly established Victims Compensation Fund" (ibid.). This socio-economic sweetener differs markedly from the address given by Jordan's Abdullah. Abdullah lists Jordan's financial struggles, increasing debt and reminders of its need for regional and Western aid, hence promising political participation during a period of socio-economic strain for the Hashemite Kingdom. Hamad, on the other hand, rules a kingdom of oil, allowing for a compensatory attitude that emphasizes the socio-economic aspects of the ruling bargain, again linking to Peter's Beneficial Consequences. It would seem that Hamad's speech emphasizes security and (financial) welfare as the main pillars of Bahrain's ruling bargain (ibid.).

Yet, Hamad's dedication to discussing security within a domestic context is somewhat brief. In the same passage in which he thanks the armed forces, he devotes more time to thanking "[...] our GCC allies who participated in protecting key installations by deploying the Peninsula Shield Force" (ibid.). Again, Hamad's comments on security appear to be taking a regional context. Ironically, expressing gratitude to the Saudi-led Peninsula Shield Force can be read as a tacit admission that the al-Khalifa monarchy cannot provide security without outside assistance from Saudi Arabia (Obaid, 2014, p. 13). However, the risk of such an image may also be why Bahrain is blaming unrest on external forces like Iran, which is regarded by Saudi Arabia and the GCC as a long-term political competitor (ibid., p. 8). In other words, an external threat requires external support (ibid.).

The notion of Bahrain's regional cooperation for stability can be linked to Peter's Political Cosmopolitanism or the belief that there can be an international legitimacy that is state-based. States will cooperate in an international system that prioritizes the stability of sovereign states over the rights of citizens of individual states (Peter, 2016). Peter's Political Cosmopolitanism links back to Chapter 2's discussion of international legitimacy and Ahram and Lust's "The Decline and Fall of the Arab State". In it, the pair emphasize how sovereignty is an artificial construct that requires the legitimation of an international system (Ahram & Lust, 2016, p. 8). It is such international legitimacy that Hamad seems to prioritize in his address (Bahrain Independent Commission of Inquiry, 2011).

Complementing Hamad's comments on regional security are extensive passages discussing Bahrain's involvement with international organizations. As Bahrain suffers from the influence of "[...] hostile forces both inside and outside the country" Hamad is able to use security as a connecting point to Bahrain's involvement with the international community (ibid.). Hamad compares the Bahrain Independent Commission of Inquiry to the European Court of Human Rights and its powers to "[...] frequently sanction European States for violations of human rights" (ibid.). Through the report issued by the Bahrain Independent Commission of Inquiry, Hamad draws attention to his preparatory condition and promise to the international community: that Hamad will "[...] reform our laws so that they are consistent with international standards to which Bahrain is committed by treaties" (ibid.). Hamad builds further on this promise with preparatory conditions that emphasize Bahrain's place in the international community. Hamad reminds listeners that Bahrain "[…] has taken the initiative to contribute to collective international action by providing facilities for multilateral organisations" and has received "[…] Mr. Ban Ki-Moon, Secretary-General of the United Nations" (ibid.). During said trip, Hamad reminds global listeners that "[…] we dedicated a significant plot of land in our capital Manama to serve the community of the United Nations; it now houses a regional office of the UN Development Programme" (ibid.). Hamad builds on Bahrain's relationship with the United Nations to imply that Bahrain enjoys international legitimacy through recognition from the United Nations and to introduce an essential condition to an international audience: that Bahrain "[…] would welcome other UN agencies" and hence Hamad invites the United Nations to deepen their already established relationship with the al-Khalifa family (ibid.).

The invitation to extend UN presence in Bahrain again links back to Peter's Political Cosmopolitanism by illustrating that the al-Khalifa regime is recognized by an international body (Peter, 2016). However, it also serves as a preparatory condition for a larger essential condition proposed by Hamad to the international community. Hamad proposes that Bahrain lead "[…] the creation of an Arab Court of Human Rights to take its proper place on the international stage" (ibid.). In this passage, Hamad merges the wish to deepen regional legitimacy with international legitimacy, desiring that Bahrain lead a regional court that will have international recognition. Returning to Peter's Political Cosmopolitanism, Hamad's approach illustrates an emphasis on state sovereignty within an international system. More important than domestic recognition of his regime is the fact that all states exist under a system of mutual recognition and from such recognition derive their legitimacy on the world stage (Peter, 2016). This consideration is augmented by the fact that Bahrain enjoys strong relations with Western states and United Nations members, including Britain and the United States, hosting the US Navy's Fifth Fleet in the Gulf since 1995 (BBC, 2018, *Bahrain country profile*); Saab, 2018).

An overview of Hamad's address reveals a speech that draws little on religion. This may hardly be surprising when taking into account Bahrain's sectarian nature and the fact that the ruling Sunni minority govern a Shia'a majority (ibid.). Rather, Hamad emphasizes security as a Beneficial Consequence of his rule and promises to address violations with appropriate (security) reforms. Further, the socio-economic nature of the ruling bargain is more apparent in this oil monarchy than in the Hashemite Kingdom of Jordan. The fact that Bahrain established a Victims Compensation Fund for Bahrainis augments the socio-economic rather than political reaction to unrest: the al-Khalifas are keen to enforce the ruling bargain and with oil wealth can afford to.

Hamad's instruction that Bahrainis accept compensation appears to have been partially successful. With his address given in late 2011, there seemed to be few major protest movements for the rest of the year (BBC, 2018, *Bahrain country profile*). Anti-government protests did occur in the spring of 2012; however, unrest was often sporadic and outside of the capital, Manama. Such demonstrations often blossomed in villages and were contained by security forces before they could spread (Mcevers). Nonetheless, 2012 and 2013 saw spikes in demonstrations (ibid.). It is worth noting that within the context of Hamad's November 2011 speech and Bahrain's relative stability before renewed protest in 2012, Hamad's emphasis on the Victims Compensation Fund does not automatically explain decreased unrest. Hamad's gratefulness in his speech to the Peninsula Shield Force is a reminder that protestors were not simply bought off but also confronted by a Saudi-led intervention that was the largest regional military deployment for the GCC (Wahba, 2017). The intervention of a regional force would explain Hamad's emphasis on regional legitimacy during his speech (ibid.).

Such a context of external intervention illustrates that Hamad's legitimacy for a domestic audience is drawn primarily from the socio-economic ruling bargain and welfare (or in this case compensation) as a Beneficial Consequence. Indeed, it is worth mentioning that the structure of the Victims Compensation Fund seeks to reinforce a non-political social contract that emphasizes socio-economic benefits. The Victims Compensation Fund was complemented by a two-year economic program that would pay out over one billion USD in wage increases for government employees (Reuters, 2011). In addition to the Victims Compensation Fund, a further fund was created in 2012 to compensate all victims of unrest, including expats (Trade Arabia, 2012). It is with this fund that the emphasis on legitimacy through the ruling bargain is augmented, as applicants of the fund must agree to drop any court cases against the Bahraini government to receive compensation (ibid.).

The fact that victims seem to have accepted buyouts under such circumstances illustrates that Hamad and the al-Khalifas have been able to maintain a non-democratic ruling bargain through material benefits (Kingdom of Bahrain, 2012). In addition to emphasizing the socio-economic ruling bargain, the creation of such funds also links back to Political Cosmopolitanism and international legitimacy. This is apparent from the fact that the compensation funds and related payouts were created upon the recommendation of the Bahrain Independent Commission of Inquiry and in accordance with UN principles on redress for human rights violations (ibid.). Once again, there is an emphasis on Hamad's appeal to the international community (ibid.).

Returning to Political Cosmopolitanism and international legitimacy, it would seem that Hamad's frequent references to international organizations and UN approval of Bahrain had the intended effect. Hamad's proposal that his nation lead the establishment of an Arab Court of Human Rights was met with approval by the Arab League, which selected Bahrain itself as the headquarters of such a court (Dickinson, 2013). Further, more recent events in 2018 saw Bahrain elected to the UN Human Rights Council (Arab News, 2018). As of writing, this election has proved an interesting turn of events. For Hamad sought regional and international legitimacy, what Peter would call Political Cosmopolitanism. While there have been no further concrete steps toward Bahrain hosting an Arab Court of Human Rights, it would appear that Hamad gained the international legitimacy his address seemed to emphasize (ibid.).

Finally, Bahrain's accusations of Iranian interference in Hamad's speech should be addressed. In his speech, Hamad emphasizes Bahrain's international status and links to regional security, especially the Saudi-led Peninsula Shield Force. Such a preparatory condition merges Political Cosmopolitanism with his accusations of Iranian interference. The Shia'a Iran is regarded by most Gulf monarchies as a threat to their Sunni rule. However, Bahrain's majority Shia'a population and Sunni minority rulers provides a far more sensitive context (BBC, 2011). While Hamad does not draw on Religious Legitimacy, a further difference between Jordan and Bahrain is sectarianism in the Gulf kingdom. Rather than relying on religious credentials as Abdullah II does, Hamad plays on sectarian fears by accusing the Shia'a Iran of influencing unrest, even though this goes against the findings of the Bahrain Independent Commission of Inquiry (Bahrain Independent Commission of Inquiry, 2011). Sectarian fears linked to Iran's interference are framed as a threat not only to Bahrain but "[…] the security and stability of the GCC countries", again invoking the fear of a Shia'a dominance across the Gulf that is felt by Bahrain's fellow monarchies (ibid.). Stoking such fears allows Hamad to reach out to fellow kings for military assistance through the Peninsula Shield Force but also serves as a warning to Iran that ties to Hamad's essential condition for the Islamic Republic: that Iran "[…] abandon [its] policy of enmity and discord […] inciting our population to engage in acts of violence, sabotage, and insurrection" (ibid.).

The actual involvement of Iran during 2011 protests has not been verified. However, Iran shares a history of tension with its Sunni counterparts, and it is this tension and the fears of a Shia'a spread into Bahrain that Hamad's address manipulates (Mabon, 2012). From this perspective, Hamad's essential condition for Iran can be regarded as a moot point. More important than whether or not Iran complies with Hamad's essential condition (or whether they did indeed influence unrest) is Hamad's use of Iran and the fear of sectarianism as another preparatory condition for a regional audience. Though not explicitly mentioned in the speech, Hamad's preparatory conditions that describe Iran as a threat and the importance of "[…] our GCC allies who participated in protecting key installations by deploying the Peninsula Shield Force" build up to an unspoken essential condition: that the GCC must buttress Bahrain's ruling family (Bahrain Independent Commission of Inquiry, 2011). The fact that the Saudi-led intervention occurred before Hamad's November address illustrates that sectarian fears in the region are real for the Sunni monarchies (Butler, 2011).

Hamad's address draws on the socio-economics of the ruling bargain to placate domestic audiences with some success, as the Victims Compensation Fund and related programs show. Security is also presented as a Beneficial Consequence, yet the fear of insecurity is used to reach a wider audience. More attention is given to regional and international listeners. Unlike republicans or Jordan's King Abdullah, there is little emphasis on Democratic Approval through extensive reforms or political changes (British Broadcasting Corporation, 2011). Hamad draws far more heavily on regional and international legitimacy, linked to Peter's Political Cosmopolitanism. Sectarianism is linked to security fears to secure regional support, which Bahrain appears to enjoy even as of 2018 with a 10 billion USD cash injection from Saudi Arabia, the UAE and Kuwait (Gambrell, 2018). Moreover, Hamad's emphasis on UN involvement in his country and Bahrain's links to the international community in general during his address appear to have also been successful, with Bahrain elected to the Human Rights Council in 2018. Such international legitimacy comes despite Amnesty International accusations of torture, arbitrary detention and the stripping of citizenship as common practices against Bahraini activists (Amnesty International, 2020).

Analysis of Bahrain's Hamad and his speech in response to unrest goes somewhat against the assumption that monarchs will rely on traditional values and religion above the socio-economic ruling bargain. Hamad draws on sectarianism rather than Religious Legitimacy to emphasize security as a Beneficial Consequence, while also linking security to a regional context. This context is augmented by his appeal to the international community and references to hosting the UN, which links back to Peter's Political Cosmopolitanism or a form of international legitimacy. Further, the establishment of more than one compensation fund that demands legal charges be dropped by applicants in exchange for a payout reinforces the socio-economic ruling bargain even more, illustrating how type of rule, be it monarchical or republican, may not be as important as oil wealth.

4.2.3 Egypt's President Mubarak

> I am addressing the youth of Egypt today in Tahrir Square and across the country. I am addressing you all from the heart, a father's dialogue with his sons and daughters. (British Broadcasting Corporation, 2011)

When compared to Ben Ali's final address, Egypt's Mubarak also uses religion sparsely (ibid.). However, there are greater factors of non-democratic legitimacy drawn on than in the speech by his Tunisian counterpart (ibid.). Returning to Searle's preparatory conditions and mutual rules, Ben Ali addressed his citizens "[…] in the language of Tunisians" (Ben Ali, 2011), reflecting Searle's belief that mutual rules govern clear communication and should ensure that the listener can thus provide transparent preparatory conditions that should maximize comprehension of essential conditions/instructions, with such instructions then being obeyed (Searle, 1965, p. 15). Rather than speaking to his youth in "the language of Egyptians", Mubarak frames the address as "[…] a father's dialogue with his sons and daughters" (British Broadcasting Corporation, 2011). The fact that Mubarak turns to paternalism rather than mutual (linguistic) rules is arresting. Mubarak frames his address through a non-democratic factor, paternalism. As discussed in Chapters 2 and 3, paternalism can be regarded as a non-democratic aspect of political rule common in the Arab world. Mubarak's invocation of paternalism thus sets the stage for his monologue on unrest to defend non-democratic legitimacy rather than offer desperate political reforms (that entail a change to the ruling bargain) à la Ben Ali (Ben Ali, 2011).

Mubarak acknowledges unrest and demands for reform early in his speech. However, such acknowledgment is mitigated by Mubarak's fatherly attitude toward such demands. "I am proud of you", he insists, "[my children] calling for a change to the better, dreaming and making the future" (ibid.). Paternalism marks the early passages of his speech and also serves to foreshadow how Mubarak downplays the political and democratic nature of popular demands (ibid.). While an acknowledgment of protests may serve as a preparatory condition and reference point, paternalism acts as a manner for Mubarak to attempt to portray demands as apolitical in nature (ibid.).

Contrary to Ben Ali's address, Mubarak's monologue appears less pleading in tone, as it does not begin with promises of political reform (Ben Ali, 2011). For his preparatory conditions, Mubarak asserts paternalism before making promises that reflect another non-democratic trait: security as a form of Peter's Beneficial Consequences. "I will hold those who persecuted our youth accountable with the maximum deterrent sentences", he insists, implying that as the head of state he will ensure that those who threaten citizen security will be punished (ibid.). Again, this promise is presented as paternalistic, Mubarak explaining that, as father of the nation, he mourns the victims of unrest as much as "[…] the families of those innocent [children]" and that is why he must punish those who harm them (ibid.).

Mubarak's paternalism seems to overshadow his comments that "[…] [protest] demands are just and legitimate demands" (ibid.), with promises of punishing those who breach security and the "promise" that protests are being acknowledged as legitimate acting as preparatory conditions for the essential conditions: Mubarak wants Egyptians to accept that "[…] mistakes can be made in any political system" and subsequently stop protesting and "[…] return the Egyptian street to its normal everyday life" (ibid.). Mubarak's instructions mirror those of Ben Ali's: stop protesting (Ben Ali, 2011). However, Mubarak's preparatory conditions and attempts to defend non-democratic legitimacy are more complex than those of his Tunisian counterpart. Mubarak repeatedly points to the need for security from (external) threats and his military accomplishments in defending Egypt's "[…] soil and sovereignty" from "[…] foreign pressure" (ibid.).

Further, Mubarak alludes to the religious notion of *Dar al-Islam* or defending Muslim territory, as discussed in Chapter 2. Mubarak emphasizes his "[…] lifetime defending [Egypt's] soil and sovereignty" while reminding his audience that his sacrifices have defended an Egypt that boasts "[…] the unity and cohesion […] of Muslims and Christians" (ibid.). This reference to Religious Legitimacy expands on Bulliet's discussions that an Islamic ruler must protect Muslim territory and the practice of Islamic laws and customs by reminding listeners that interfaith coexistence is a Muslim requisite for any pious ruler, as Christians are considered protected religious equals according to the Quran (Vajda, 2012).

Greater than Mubarak's turn to religion or security as a Beneficial Consequence is his discussion of constitutional amendments, which can be linked to Peter's Democratic Approval (Peter, 2016). Indeed, an entire section of Mubarak's speech is dedicated to constitutional reforms (British Broadcasting Corporation, 2011). This section of Mubarak's address sees the aging President engage in Democratic Approval as a form of non-democratic legitimacy. This strategic discourse allows him to both validate his non-democratic rule according to Peter and push blame for mismanagement upon Egypt's constitution (ibid.). It is important to note that although constitutional amendments have been discussed by a panel of independent "[…] experts in constitutional law and judges", it is ultimately Mubarak himself who will approve any and all constitutional amendments (ibid.). This aspect of the address highlights Mubarak's continuing leadership that is reliant on non-democratic legitimacy and circular via Democratic Approval (Peter, 2016). Mubarak justifies his leadership through security, religion (albeit minimal) and uses Democratic Approval as a form of non-democratic legitimacy, with constitutional amendments led by himself providing democratic proceduralism (and supposedly correcting "[…] mistakes […] made in [constitutional aspects] of [Egypt's] political system") that justifies his continued rule (ibid.).

Mubarak's reliance on Democratic Approval and promises of security contrast with Ben Ali's desperate offers of political reform. However, Mubarak appears to have a moment of clarity in his address and the brief cognizance to recognize the political nature of unrest. In a short passage, he promises his "[…] brother citizens" that he "[…] will not run for president in the next elections" (ibid.). It is interesting to note that in this (political) promise, Mubarak changes his tone of paternalism to one of equality. Suddenly, the Egyptian people are not his children but "[…] brother citizens", implying an equal relationship (ibid.).

An overview of Mubarak's speech reveals a greater reliance on non-democratic elements than Ben Ali's address. These include promises to punish perpetrators of violence and reminders of sacrifices Mubarak ostensibly made to ensure Egypt's security from external threats. The punishment of violent criminals is especially arresting, as it highlights the promise to restore security, a Beneficial Consequence of non-democratic rule. Religious Legitimacy is briefly alluded to, another (minor) difference from Mubarak's Tunisian counterpart (Ben Ali, 2011). Further, Mubarak engages extensively in Democratic Approval. The essential conditions of Mubarak's and Ben Ali's addresses are the same: they want protests to stop. However, their respective preparatory conditions differ. While Ben Ali hastily makes promises for political reform (indirectly implying that the ruling bargain has failed due to economic mismanagement) (Ben Ali, 2011), Mubarak emphasizes security and democratic proceduralism far more markedly.

Returning to Peter in Chapter 2, such proceduralism encompasses bureaucracy and related processes linked to the formalizing of democratic politics but can be de-facto non-democratic (Liden, 2014, pp. 52–53). In focusing on security and democratic proceduralism, Mubarak failed to address the political and socio-economic sources of popular unrest. Returning to Chapter 3, it must be recalled that Egyptians had become increasingly reliant on subsidies while struggling with widening wealth-poverty gaps. This fact is arresting, as Mubarak himself had insisted earlier in his career that subsidies were an established right that could never be abolished. He understood the socio-economic aspect of the ruling bargain when competing with the Muslim Brotherhood for political influence. Yet, in his final address there is no reference to be found to subsidies or the lowering of basic food prices. Ben Ali himself had ensured at least one reference to the lowering of food prices (Ben Ali, 2011), a reminder that the early rallying cry of the 2011 revolution was "Bread, Freedom, Social Justice, and Human Dignity" (Pin, 2016, p. 3).

A further point of discussion is the differences in attitude toward paternalism between Ben Ali and Mubarak. As discussed in Chapter 3, Ben Ali did play with the image of a paternal leader. However, equally significant were his efforts to construct modern feminism as secular, permitting elderly women to wear traditional garb while female youth were expected to project an image that expunged faith from the notion of being educated and progressive (Hawkins, 2011, pp. 45–46). Hence, any emphasis on paternalistic discourse would clash with Ben Ali's constant depiction of "modern feminism", which he emphasized more than paternalistic leadership (ibid.). It is likely for this reason that Ben Ali did not draw on paternalism during his final address (Ben Ali, 2011). Mubarak, however, engages heavily in paternalism as a form of non-democratic legitimacy in his final address.

This emphasis can be linked to the historical role of the state in Egypt and what Ashraf El-Sherif terms "authoritarian guardianship". The state centralized political administration of a society regarded as underdeveloped, with a populous that could not form politically aware and assertive individuals (El-Sherif, 2014, p. 6). Under such an ideal, the relationship between citizens and government was destined to be skewed. The military administrated all politics and regarded themselves as "[…] the guardians of the people", encouraging a paternalistic ruling style that disregarded individual rights and saw citizens as "[…] objects of state public policies" (ibid.). With Mubarak a military man who inherited such a skewed governance system, his tone of paternalism in his final address is hardly surprising.

Nonetheless, continuing a tradition of paternalism was a fatal mistake. Mubarak underestimated the political nature of the protests and the urgency of demands that he resign. He insisted that the "[…] current moment is not to do with myself, it is not to do with Hosni Mubarak" and had hence limited political promises regarding his transition out of power (British Broadcasting Corporation, 2011). Perhaps it was for this reason that his promises were disbelieved. Mubarak presented non-democratic credentials, including stability, Democratic Approval and to an extent Religious Legitimacy, with socio-economic Beneficial Consequences undiscussed and a timeline for his transition out of power mentioned in passing. In exchange for these credentials and promises, Mubarak delivers his essential condition: the end of unrest. The fact that protests continued, forcing Mubarak to resign one day after his final speech illustrates that his promises and credentials were not regarded as sincere by the millions of Egyptians in Tahrir Square (Al Jazeera, 2011, "Timeline: Egypt's Revolution").

4.2.4 Tunisia's President Ben Ali

> People of Tunisia: I am speaking to you today, to everyone, both inside and outside Tunisia. I speak to you in the language of Tunisians. I am speaking to you now because the situation demands deep change. Yes, deep and comprehensive change. (Ben Ali, 2011)

Ben Ali's final address contains scant references to religion. Only twice is religion mentioned, including as a way of ending his speech in a manner that mimics his first address to the people in 1987 (Ben Ali, 2011). In addition, there are few references to non-democratic factors of legitimacy, such as the ruling bargain and related socio-economic measures of Political Legitimacy, as discussed by Peter (2016). Examining Ben Ali's last speech through Searle's theory of Speech Acts, it can be argued that Ben Ali establishes the preparatory conditions of his address by highlighting social unrest and also by switching to the Tunisian dialect to "[...] speak to you in the language of Tunisians" (ibid.). As a preparatory condition is defined as a speaker's starting point, providing appropriate historical, cultural or political context for the speech, this latter aspect echoes Searle's discussions of communication being done through mutually comprehensive rules (Searle, 1965, p. 3). In other words, by communicating in the local Tunisian dialect as opposed to the colonial era French or formal *Fusha*, Ben Ali's address should be understood and his instructions also comprehended (ibid.).

Immediately after referring to social unrest, Ben Ali admits that "[...] the situation demands deep change" (Ben Ali, 2011) before plunging into promises. It is possible to consider Ben Ali's promises as being part of the preparatory condition, as they are stated early on (Ben Ali, 2011). Moreover, a closer examination of his promises reveals their political nature. "I have understood everyone", the President pleads, "the unemployed, the needy, the politician and those demanding more freedoms" (ibid.). The latter element of "those demanding more freedoms" implies that Ben Ali's promise of listening to such demands will require a change in the (apolitical) relationship between ruler and subjects (ibid.). This implication has consequences for how Ben Ali can justify his Political Legitimacy through non-democratic factors, which is reflected in his weak references to non-democratic criteria.

Returning to Peter's Political Legitimacy, a non-democratic regime may be considered legitimate if it can prove that it provides benefits to its citizens (Beneficial Consequences), often of a socio-economic nature (Peter, 2016). Ben Ali engages in a list of personal accomplishments that can be considered preparatory conditions before reiterating his instructions for protests to come to a halt (Ben Ali, 2011). "I have spent more than fifty years of my life in service to Tunisia", he explains. "[F]rom the National Army to various other responsibilities, and twenty-three years as head of state. Every day of my life has been and continues to be in the service of the country" (ibid.). In this passage, Ben Ali attempts to justify his rule as providing Beneficial Consequences. His reference to positions in the National Army certainly connects with later references to security and stability, which could be considered a non-democratic benefit and one that has been espoused in the speeches of other Arab leaders such as Bahrain's King Hamad (Peter, 2016; Bahrain Independent Commission of Inquiry, 2011). In addition to security being part of Ben Ali's ruling bargain, he also suggests that education is another Beneficial Consequence of his rule, explaining that because of unrest "[...] children today have stayed home and did not go to school" (Ben Ali, 2011). Further, Ben Ali promises that he will "[...] reduce the prices of basic commodities and foodstuffs", reflecting the economic core of the ruling bargain through subsidies, as discussed in Chapter 3.

However, Ben Ali's attempts to draw on non-democratic legitimacy (including security, subsidies and education as part of a ruling bargain) are overshadowed by his constant promises for political reform and contradictory messages regarding Tunisia's security. For although Ben Ali attempts to construct security as a legitimate provision by the state and hence part of a ruling bargain, he contrasts this position with assertions that ordinary Tunisians are responsible for security and stability. In reference to unrest, Ben Ali insists that "[...] each one of [you] is responsible, from their positions, for restoring [Tunisia's] security" and that rather than the state responding to "[...] gangs who have robbed and looted and assaulted people" it is "[...] [the] citizens, all citizens [who] must stand up to them" (ibid.).

It is possible to regard Ben Ali's speech as circular; preparatory conditions and promises are given before the essential condition is (re)iterated and further preparatory conditions issued to emphasize the same essential condition: unrest and all forms of protest should come to an end. Again, from the perspective of non-democratic legitimacy, Ben Ali's address is weak as it does not attempt to systemically defend non-democratic factors of his legitimacy. Instead, Ben Ali continually promises political reforms "[...] for freedom of political expression" and an independent investigation into corruption and violence against protestors (ibid.). Such promises imply that Ben Ali's non-democratic legitimacy was always weak; shifting the responsibility of security to citizens implies that Ben Ali's regime can no longer provide this Beneficial Consequence, and if promises of political reform overshadow claims of other non-democratic Beneficial Consequences, then according to Peter, the non-democratic ruling bargain is no longer valid because Ben Ali's regime is unable to evidence benefits of its non-democratic rule for its populace (Peter, 2016).

Ben Ali's promises of political reform and investigation into corruption in exchange for an end to protests may have worked against him. By making such promises, Ben Ali was indirectly admitting that he was aware of corruption and aware that there was an unmet desire by his people for democratic involvement (Ben Ali, 2011). At the same time, mass reaction to his address reveals a populace that saw his promises as anything but sincere. Ben Ali's final speech was given January 10, 2011. Within days, increased unrest in defiance of security crackdowns pressured Ben Ali into leaving Tunisia for exile in Saudi Arabia (BBC, 2011, "Tunisia: President Zine al-Abidine Ben Ali forced out"). Amid his hasty exit, soldiers were stripping portraits of Ben Ali from all government buildings, expunging him from public view (ibid.).

Had Ben Ali's promises been believed and regarded as sincere, it is unlikely that protestors would have continued with their resistance to the point of compelling Ben Ali to flee (ibid.). Further, the lack of religious references and greater promises of political reform (in essence canceling an apolitical ruling bargain) than assertion of non-democratic accomplishments or Beneficial Consequences cannot be ignored. Ben Ali's non-democratic credentials are weak against the tacit or indirect admission that he was aware of corruption and violence toward protestors (BBC, 2011, "Tunisia: President Zine el-Abidine Ben Ali forced out"; Joyce and Dreisbach, 2014). The fact that he ends his final address as an almost verbatim copy of the end of his 1987 speech shows a man out of touch with the reality that any ruling bargain can be forced to change, as discussed earlier in Chapter 2. Ben Ali was overthrown by "[...] the unemployed, the needy" and the youth of Tunisia's future who saw him as their past (Ben Ali, 2011).

Detailed analysis of speeches given in response to unrest across Tunisia, Egypt, Jordan and Bahrain allow for a structured focus on the nature of political rule in the MENA region within the context of the Arab Spring and the main assumption of this book: that republics will emphasize the socio-economic ruling bargain as the main source of their non-democratic legitimacy in response to the Arab Spring, due to most republics being the result of coups rather than established familial rule. Hence, many republican rulers have weaker ties to traditional (religious) institutes and popular support and rely on a ruling bargain to maintain legitimacy. Monarchs, on the other hand, will draw on Religious Legitimacy more than the ruling bargain due to their longevity and ties to traditional institutions and accepted socio-cultural norms.

Tunisia's Ben Ali gave few religious references and did acknowledge subsidies and their importance, a link to the socio-economic ruling bargain. Security was a further theme shared by monarch and republican alike, which Ben Ali also mentioned in his address. However, his desperate promises of political reform overshadow attempts to justify non-democratic legitimacy through Beneficial Consequences, and Tunisian reactions to such promises strongly imply they were insincere. Hence, while the hypothesis of republicans relying on the ruling bargain rather than religion is partially confirmed, Ben Ali's non-democratic credentials are weak and the turn to last-minute political reforms illustrates that he was unable to maintain a ruling bargain.

Egypt's Mubarak, on the other hand, placed greater emphasis on security and external threats, much as Hamad of Bahrain would end up doing. Linked to security was Mubarak's brief reference to maintaining stable territory for Muslims and Christians, a link to the concept of *Dar al-Islam* as discussed in Chapter 2. Mubarak uses paternalism as a springboard to highlight his non-democratic achievements and related factors, including security and Democratic Approval through constitutional amendments. Democratic Approval is used as a preparatory condition to build to the same essential condition as Ben Ali: protestors should stop protesting. As Mubarak is overseeing and implementing such reforms, his Democratic Approval becomes a circular method to validate his rule. Mubarak's emphasis on these factors and vague discussion of political promises with his "children" resulted in his resignation shortly after his final address, implying that his promises were not regarded as sincere and did not meet the political expectations of Egyptians. Interestingly, subsidies are not mentioned once in his address, a historically central pillar of former

Egyptian rulers. Mubarak's address hence does not conform to the assumption that republicans draw more heavily on ruling bargains than monarchs. Egypt's President does not draw heavily on a socio-economic ruling bargain (though perhaps he should have) and even makes tacit references to the religious concept of *Dar al-Islam*, a domain the book assumed would be exclusive to monarchs. On the other hand, security is emphasized as a Beneficial Consequence of his rule, presented within the context of paternalism that infantilized his subjects. This attempt to create "a father's dialogue with his sons and daughters" did not end well for Mubarak and is a reminder that the ruling bargain is not static and may need to coexist alongside political elements, especially if socio-economic welfare can no longer be provided by a non-democratic regime. Such a situation is better explored by Bahrain's compensation for the Arab Spring atop existing welfare.

Bahrain's Hamad is a monarch ruling a sectarian kingdom. Hence, sparse religious references are no surprise. As with Mubarak and Abdullah, Hamad engages in Democratic Approval through the mention of ongoing reforms. And as with Mubarak, Hamad creates an external threat, also mimicking his fellow monarch by painting a picture of regional insecurity. However, while Abdullah draws on religion to legitimize his rule and de-legitimize opposition in the face of neighboring insecurity, Hamad pushes religious divides, playing on Bahrain's sectarianism and regional fears of Shia'a Iran. In a sense, Hamad does use or manipulate religion but rather than drawing on religion for unity between monarch and masses as the book assumes, Hamad draws on religion to sow division and prevent united unrest against his throne. By building on sectarian fears, Hamad sells security as a Beneficial Consequence to his domestic audience while also creating an essential condition for regional leaderships: fellow Sunni monarchies must continue to support the al-Khalifa crown.

Security is the strongest theme in Hamad's speech and more conspicuous when compared to other case studies. Indeed, reforms mentioned are less about political openness than correcting security violations and enforcing security as part of the ruling bargain. Hamad's speech focuses on reinforcing the ruling bargain through security and compensation, a reminder of the socio-economic aspect of the ruling bargain. Hamad seeks to keep the social contract apolitical and hence uses security, external threats and socio-economic payouts as preparatory conditions that build to Bahrainis continuing to accept (apolitical) rule by the al-Khalifa monarchy. Compared to Abdullah's address, this aspect is markedly different. While both monarchs create security as a Beneficial Consequence, Jordan's Abdullah invites citizens to political participation. Hamad, on the other hand, seeks to enforce an apolitical social contract.

A further difference between Hamad and the remaining case studies is Bahrain's focus on a regional and international audience. By mentioning the Peninsula Shield Force and how Bahrain is a lynchpin for stability across the GCC, Hamad draws on international legitimacy or Peter's Political Cosmopolitanism, which is further emphasized by Hamad's references to the UN and Bahrain's eventual election to the Human Rights Council. Indeed, given Jordan's reliance on external aid and Western relations, it is interesting that Abdullah's address did not appeal to the international community but seemed structured for a domestic audience.

The result of Hamad's address seems to be that Bahrainis accepted compensation, reinforcing the ruling bargain and with a seat on the Human Rights Council as of 2018, Bahrain continues to enjoy international support under the al-Khalifas. It must be noted that sporadic protests continued to occur after Hamad's address, with larger protests in Bahrain's capital also used to mark the anniversary of the original 2011 unrest (Regencia, 2018). Yet, intervention by the Saudi-led GCC even before Hamad's speech emphasizes that the al-Khalifa family maintains regional legitimacy in the face of sectarianism.

It is interesting to consider that republican discourse from Tunisia's Ben Ali and Egypt's Mubarak does not engage in a long-term view that espouses democratic elements. Instead, analysis of select speeches has revealed that the monarchies of Jordan and Bahrain are able to discuss long-term political themes that are commonly associated with democratic discourse, including reforms and elections. In both Abdullah's speech and Hamad's speech, reforms are mentioned as being part of ongoing programs as opposed to last-minute plea bargains, as issued by Ben Ali. This finding links back to the book's assumption: republicans have weaker ties to institutions and are often the result of coups rather than familial rule. Hence, any use of democratic discourse may act as an unwanted reminder that such republicans did not become presidents-for-life through democratic means. Monarchies, on the other hand, enjoy longevity and familial rule, including ties to traditional institutions and accepted socio-cultural norms. As such, stronger institutional ties and socio-political legitimacy provide monarchies with the ability to consider long-term political views as theirs is a long-term familial rule rather than a one-man rule (Magen, 2013, p. 27).

Furthermore, as discussed in Chapter 3 monarchies historically faced political threats at a time when republics were overthrowing kings across the Arab world (Cavendish). Abdullah of Jordan no doubt remembers the coup attempt against his father that was inspired by republican President Nasser of Egypt (ibid.). Within such an historical context, monarchies in the Middle East may go through periods of "defensive democratization", during which democratic elements are carefully introduced to the ruling bargain in a regime-controlled process (Robinson, 1998, p. 389).

Finally, Jordan's Abdullah draws heavily on Religious Legitimacy and the image of family, feeding into the assumption of monarchical reliance on traditionalism and faith. His links to the Prophet Muhammad allow for him to frame the Hashemite dynasty as "martyrs" for the nation and effectively weave Quranic language into his address. The use of religion is apparent from the start of his speech. Rather than talk to Jordanians through the mutual language of colloquial Arabic, as Ben Ali attempted, Abdullah opens the speech with an Islamic blessing understood by all. Hence, religion can be regarded as the mutually comprehended rule Searle discusses in his Speech Acts. The consistent use of religion also allows Abdullah to paint some opposition as immoral or going against Islam by engaging in *fitna* through their resistance to a pious monarch. Further, religion is weaved into references to Beneficial Consequences such as security.

At the same time, Abdullah's address is, unlike Mubarak's, not paternalistic but does draw on familial language. Referring to his subjects as "Jordanian brothers and sisters" creates an atmosphere of greater equality, which can be linked to how his address focuses on ongoing political reforms. These reforms reveal a limited ruling bargain and Abdullah's essential condition: unlike Ben Ali and Mubarak, who simply want protests to cease, Abdullah invites Jordanians to take part in the election process. It should be noted that religion is not reserved for only non-democratic factors. When encouraging voters, Abdullah refers to the dome of parliament, conjuring images of the mosque and hence equating his essential condition with being a good Muslim (Abdullah II, October 2012). Although both Mubarak and Abdullah seem to use Democratic Approval through the offer of amendments, Abdullah's focus on elections differs from his republican counterparts. Again, Abdullah recognizes that Jordan's ruling bargain relies on external aid and that in times of economic difficulty, citizens may expect to take part in political decisions as economic privileges are curtailed or taxes applied.

However, Democratic Approval is also used by Abdullah to push blame for political and socio-economic improvements upon (successive) elected governments and away from his throne. The use of Democratic Approval is a reminder of the limits to any democratic legitimacy the King may claim. Although election turnout after his address was just above half of registered voters, observers claimed that elections were influenced by traditional tribalism and, more conspicuously, fears of instability. The notion of insecurity can be linked to Abdullah's mention of *fitna*, pairing the risk of chaos with certain elements of the opposition. Insecurity is a shared factor across all four case studies; however, it is Bahrain's Hamad and Jordan's Abdullah who emphasize the fear of (regional) instability the most and only Abdullah who links security as a Beneficial Consequence with Islamic concepts.

In the case of Jordan's Abdullah, the Hashemite monarch draws far more on Religious Legitimacy than his republican counterparts. Further, the ruling bargain is actually de-emphasized in Abdullah's address, with the King mentioning Jordan's fiscal problems and Jordan having a history of the social contract being politicized during periods of socio-economic turmoil. At the same time, religion is used as a tool to emphasize fear of instability and security as a Beneficial Consequence, while Abdullah's image of brothers and sisters ties monarch and citizens in a social contract that may not be paternal but still emphasizes a (traditional) familial image. Jordan as a case study hence presents a confirmation of the assumption that monarchies draw more on religion and traditionalism than their republican counterparts.

The Arab world illustrates a context of republican anti-monarchical nationalism and a history of monarchies in the Middle East providing carefully balanced democratic elements in their ruling bargains. It is hence no surprise that when kings saw their republican counterparts shying away from democratic discourse during the Arab Spring, they took the chance to discuss political reforms and democratic processes (albeit those of proceduralism) and to remind their citizens that, unlike their republican opposites, such reforms were not split-second plea bargains but part of an ongoing process that began before the Arab Spring.

While such democratic discourse can be linked back to parts of the book's assumption with regards to monarchies and their ties to traditionalism encouraging such discourse and "defensive democratization", it must be remembered that there is a difference between democratic discourse and democratic practice. The analysis of this chapter has also considered the fact that Jordan's parliamentary elections did not necessarily reflect democratic openness but the ability of the Hashemites to play on fears of instability while enforcing tribalism and loyalist voting lines. Likewise, Bahrain's Hamad made promises of reform that must be put into the context of non-democratic practices: establishing a compensation fund to enforce the socio-economic aspect of the ruling bargain and of course Saudi Arabia's military intervention that ensured serious opposition to the ruling al-Khalifa family was crushed.

Moreover, promised reforms by both monarchs may be considered apolitical and not truly enforcing democratic practice. Abdullah's invitation for Jordanians to vote can be considered a form of democratic proceduralism, while Hamad's reforms emphasize restoring security as a Beneficial Consequence. Returning to Chapter 3's discussions of legitimation theory, it is interesting to consider Weber's sources of legitimacy: tradition, charisma and legality. To reiterate, tradition is a form of legitimacy through "[...] ancient recognition and habitual orientation", charisma is a form of political recognition that rests on "[...] the authority of the extraordinary and personal gift of grace" and legality is defined as the belief in the "validity of legal statute and functional "competence" based on rationally created rules" (Weber & Gerth, 2009, pp. 78–79). Within the context of Weber's sources of legitimacy, analysis of select speeches by kings and republicans reveals a pattern. Monarchies may typically be considered to draw on Weber's tradition due to their longevity and ties to traditional institutions. However, with speeches that emphasize reform, it would seem that the Arab Spring has encouraged them to draw more from Weber's legality. This is certainly the case with Hamad of Bahrain, who complements reform with international recognition by the UN and draws on international legitimacy. Abdullah of Jordan not only presents reforms, thus also covering Weber's legality aspect of legitimacy but emphasizes his links to Islam and Prophet Muhammad, hence also drawing on charisma and of course Religious Legitimacy (ibid.).

Republicans, on the other hand, appear to follow Weber's legitimacy but from the path of charisma to legality (as opposed to tradition to legality). As discussed in Chapters 2 and 3, most republicans gained power in coups or inherited governments that were the result of military revolutions (as with Mubarak). Therefore, many such leaders would have started their rule by pushing Weber's charisma as a form of recognition to make them distinct from previous rulers and previous forms of governance. Mubarak, for example, introduced himself to Egypt as distinct from his predecessors. "I am neither Gamal Abdel Nasser nor Anwar el Sadat," he insisted shortly after inauguration. "'My name is Hosni Mubarak'" (Nagarajan, 2013, p. 28). However, the Arab Spring saw such republicans turning to Weber's legal definition of legitimacy through their promises of reform. While kings have kept their thrones after similar discourse, for republicans it was too little too late as their discourse on reforms did not address political demands and in some cases omitted socio-economic ones as well. Further, reform promises by republicans were last-minute rather than part of a long-term context that monarchies seemed to consider. Perhaps when comparing presidents and monarchs, it's still good to be king.

However, it is oil rather than traditionalism that determines if welfare will be emphasized over religious credentials. In the case of monarchies, analyzed discourse strongly supports a ruling bargain under Hamad's hydrocarbon House of al-Khalifa, while Jordan's Abdullah draws heavily on religion rather than a socio-economic ruling bargain to justify his rule. In other words, Religious Legitimacy is emphasized over welfare. Nonetheless, as previously discussed ruling bargains are not static and may be politicized in a form of defensive democratization. Jordan's Abdullah seems to recognize this, though Bahrain's Hamad less so with the ability to provide financial sweeteners. Republicans, however, reveal discourse that fails to uphold a ruling bargain and that draws on Democratic Approval that does not recognize the political and socio-economic nature of unrest (Mubarak) or that desperately offers political reform, which indirectly acts as an admission of corruption and an inability to uphold the ruling bargain (Ben Ali).

As Chapter 4 has provided discourse analysis of select speeches to understand non-democratic rule and Religious Legitimacy, Chapter 5 will augment Chapter 4's findings by considering non-democratic and democratic factors formalized in each case study's constitutions and to what extent such constitutional aspects were drawn on by each leader to justify their rule in the face of the Arab Spring. Understanding the link between constitutional legitimacy and non-democratic rule will explain to what extent non-democratic political rule can be justified through discourse and formal means.

References

Primary Data

Abdullah II, H. M. (2012, October). *Remarks by His Majesty King Abdullah II During a Gathering with National Public Figures, Amman, Jordan*. Available at: http://kingabdullah.jo/index.php/en_US/speeches/view/id/507/videoDisplay/0.html (accessed 21 October 2016. Inaccessible since 2021, saved as a pdf by author).

Al Jazeera. (2011). نص خطاب مبارك للشعب المصري. Available at: https://www.aljazeera.net/news/arabic/2011/2/11/%D9%86%D8%B5-%D8%AE%D8%B7%D8%A7%D8%A8-%D9%85%D8%A8%D8%A7%D8%B1%D9%83-%D9%84%D9%84%D8%B4%D8%B9%D8%A8-%D8%A7%D9%84%D9%85%D8%B5%D8%B1%D9%8A (accessed 13 January 2022).

Bahrain Independent Commission of Inquiry. (2011). *Speech of HM King Hamad bin Isa Al Khalifa on 23rd November*. Available at: http://www.bici.org.bh/indexc971.html?news=speech-of-hm-king-hamad-bin-isa-al-khalifa-on-23rd-november (accessed 12 January 2022).

BBC. (2011). *Bahrain Independent Commission of Inquiry Excerpts*. Available at: https://www.bbc.co.uk/news/world-middle-east-15861353 (accessed 16 January 2022).

Ben Ali, Z. (2011). *The Last Official Address by Tunisian President Zine el-Abidine Ben Ali* (T. Badran, Trans.). Available at: https://msmunatunagb.wikispaces.com/file/view/The+Last+Official+Address+of+Ben+Ali.pdf (accessed 20 November 2017. Inaccessible since 2021, saved as a pdf by author).

British Broadcasting Corporation. (2011). *Egypt Unrest: Full Text of Hosni Mubarak's Speech*. Available at: http://www.bbc.co.uk/news/world-middle-east-12427091 (accessed 12 October 2021).

Kingdom of Bahrain: Ministry of Foreign Affairs. (2012). *HM King Hamad: Bahrain Will Always Remain a Nation Where the Culture of Tolerance*. Available at: https://www.mofa.gov.bh/Default.aspx?tabid=7824&language=en-US&ItemId=2203 (accessed 26 January 2022).

Secondary Data

Academic Reports/Papers

Ahram, A. I., & Lust, E. (2016). The Decline and Fall of the Arab State. *Survival, 58*(2), 7–34.

Ayoob, M. (2004). Political Islam: Image and Reality. *World Policy Journal, 21*(3), 1–14.

Culcasi, K. (2016). Warm Nationalism: Mapping and Imagining the Jordanian Nation. *Political Geography, 54*, 7–20.

Grupico, T. (2011). *The Dome in Christian and Islamic Sacred Architecture.* Available at: https://go.gale.com/ps/i.do?id=GALE%7CA317588296&sid=googleScholar&v=2.1&it=r&linkaccess=abs&issn=1556763X&p=AONE&sw=w&userGroupName=anon%7Ef04e77#:~:text=The%20architects%20of%20Christian%20and,more%20directly%20from%20each%20other.&text=In%20the%20Islamic%20as%20much,articulation%20of%20a%20spiritual%20journey (accessed 10 January 2022).

Hawkins, S. (2011). Who Wears *Hijab* with the President: Constructing a Modern Islam in Tunisia. *Journal of Religion in Africa, 41*, 35–58.

Korany, B. (2014). A Microcosm of the Arab Spring: Sociology of Tahrir Square. In B. Korany (Ed.) *Beyond the Arab Spring: The Evolving Ruling Bargain in the Middle East* (pp. 249–276). New York: Oxford University Press.

Liden, G. (2014). Theories of Dictatorships: Sub-Types and Explanations. *Studies of Transition States and Societies, 6*(1), 50–67.

Milton-Edwards, B. (2017). *Jordan's Troubles in Its Own Backyard.* Available at: https://www.brookings.edu/blog/markaz/2017/02/22/jordans-troubles-in-its-own-backyard/ (accessed 11 January 2022).

Nagarajan, K. V. (2013). Egypt's Political Economy and the Downfall of the Mubarak Regime. *International Journal of Humanities and Social Science, 3* (10), 22–39.

Obaid, N. (2014). *A Saudi Arabian Defense Doctrine:Mapping the Extended Force Structure the Kingdom needs to lead the Arab World, Stabilize the Region, and Meet its Global Responsibilities.* Cambridge, Massachusetts: Belfer Centre for Science and International Affairs. Available at:http://www.belfercenter.org/sites/default/files/legacy/files/Saudi%20Strategic%20Doctrine%20-%20web.pdf (accessed 8 June 2017).

Peter, F. (2016). *Political Legitimacy.* Available at: http://plato.stanford.edu/entries/legitimacy/ (accessed 18 January 2022).

Pin, A. (2016). *The Arab Road to Dignity: The Goal of the "Arab Spring"* (Working Paper #408). Kellogg Institute for International Studies.

Robinson, G. E. (1998). Defensive Democratization in Jordan. *International Journal of Middle East Studies, 30*(3), 387–410.

Vajda, G. (2012). Ahl al-Kitab. Bearman, P. et al., *Encyclopedia of Islam.* Available at: https://referenceworks.brillonline.com/entries/encyclopaedia-of-islam-2/ahl-al-kitab-SIM_0383 (accessed 5 January 2022).

Weber, M., & Gerth, H. H. (Eds.). (2009). *From Max Weber: Essays in Sociology.* Routledge Classics in Sociology. Routledge.

Media Reports

Arab News. (2018). *Bahrain Elected Among 18 Countries to Join the Human Rights Council by UN General Assembly*. Available at: http://www.arabnews.com/node/1387296/middle-east (accessed 19 January 2022).

BBC. (2018). *Bahrain Country Profile*. Available at: https://www.bbc.co.uk/news/world-middle-east-14540571 (accessed 18 January 2022).

Butler, W. (2011). *Saudi Arabian Intervention in Bahrain Driven by Visceral Sunni Fear of Shias*. Available at: https://www.theguardian.com/world/2011/mar/20/bahrain-saudi-arabia-rebellion (accessed 19 January 2022).

Dickinson, E. (2013). *Bahrain Selected as HQ of Arab Court for Human Rights*. Available at: https://www.thenational.ae/world/mena/bahrain-selected-as-hq-of-arab-court-for-human-rights-1.330101 (accessed 19 January 2022).

Driesbach, T., & Joyce, R. (2014, March 27). Revealing Tunisia's Corruption Under Ben Ali. *Al Jazeera*. Available at: http://www.aljazeera.com/indepth/features/2014/03/revealing-tunisia-corruption-under-ben-ali-201432785825560542.html (accessed 03 January 2022).

Gambrell, J. (2018). *Kuwait, Saudi Arabia and UAE Pledge $10B for Bahrain*. Available at: https://www.apnews.com/211c7399b9d843a6a808364fe5fd50d6 (accessed 19 January 2022).

Greenfield, D. (2013). *Optimism After Jordan's Election*. Available at: https://foreignpolicy.com/2013/01/25/optimism-after-jordans-election/ (accessed 15 January 2022).

Lower, M. (2013). *Abdullah Appears Not to Have Taken to the Crown the Way His Father Did*. Available at: https://yourmiddleeast.com/2013/08/01/abdullah-appears-not-to-have-taken-to-the-crown-the-way-his-father-did/ (accessed 9 January 2022).

Luck, T., & Warrick, J. (2012). Jordan Hit with More Protests, Work Stoppages Over Fuel Price Hikes. *Washington Post*. Available online at: https://www.washingtonpost.com/world/middle_east/jordan-hit-with-more-protests-work-stoppages-over-fuel-price-hikes/2012/11/14/7adc28ce-2e63-11e2-beb2-4b4cf5087636_story.html (accessed 9 September 2022).

Regencia, T. (2018). *Clashes Mark Anniversary of Bahrain's 2011 Uprising*. Available at: https://www.aljazeera.com/news/2018/02/clashes-mark-anniversary-bahrain-2011-uprising-180214075612644.html (accessed 23 January 2022).

Reuters. (2011). *Bahrain Announces Fund to Pay Crackdown Victims*. Available at: https://english.ahram.org.eg/NewsContentP/2/21922/World/Bahrain-announces-fund-to-pay-crackdown-victims.aspx (accessed 19 January 2022).

Saab, B. Y. (2018). *Relocating the Fifth Fleet?* Available at: https://www.the-american-interest.com/2018/08/22/relocating-the-fifth-fleet/ (accessed 18 January 2022).

Trade Arabia. (2012). *Bahrain Creates $26.5 Billion Fund for Unrest Victims.* Available at: http://www.tradearabia.com/news/law_214192.html (accessed 19 January 2022).

Printed/Online Books

Brown, L. C. (2000). *Religion and State: The Muslim Approach to Politics.* Columbia University Press.

Searle, J. (1965). What Is a Speech Act? In M. Black (Ed.), *Philosophy in America* (pp. 221–239). Allen and Unwin.

Shahrur, M. (2009). Chapter One: Al-Islam and Al-Iman. In D. F. Eickelman (Ed.), *The Qur'an, Morality and Critical Reason: The Essential Muhammad Shahrur* (pp. 21–71). Brill.

International Organization Reports

Amnesty International. (2020). *Bahrain 2020.* Available at: https://www.amnesty.org/en/countries/middle-east-and-north-africa/bahrain/report-bahrain/ (accessed 19 January 2022).

El-Sherif, A. (2014). *Egypt's Post-Mubarak Predicament.* Available at: https://carnegieendowment.org/files/post_mubarak_predicament.pdf (accessed 6 January 2022).

Hawthorne, E. (2016). *The Strangely Stable Kingdom of Jordan.* Available at: https://worldview.stratfor.com/article/strangely-stable-kingdom-jordan (accessed 15 January 2022).

Mabon, S. (2012). *The Battle for Bahrain: Iranian-Saudi Rivalry.* Available at: http://www.mepc.org/battle-bahrain-iranian-saudi-rivalry (accessed 8 January 2022).

Magen, A. (2013). *The Crisis of Governance in the Middle East: Implications for Democracy, Development and Security.* International Institute for Counter-Terrorism (ICT).

Wahba, M. M. (2017). *GCC: A Force for Regional Stability.* Available at: https://agsiw.org/gcc-force-regional-stability/ (accessed 18 January 2022).

CHAPTER 5

Tyranny and the Constitution: Formalizing Dictatorship During the Arab Spring

5.1 Introduction

Analysis of speeches from each case study has used Searle's Speech Acts as a framework for understanding said speeches as the formal issuing of instructions from speaker to listeners (the essential condition). As such, there is a parallel between speeches and related (modern) constitutions as formal communication and the issuing of instructions. Both modern constitutions and the analyzed speeches can be regarded as political speech acts. The Arab Spring has provided a contemporary context for the analysis of speeches, which were the discourse responses of each leadership to unrest. This chapter's investigation into constitutions will analyze to what extent political factors of said speeches (democratic, non-democratic and religious) are present in the modern constitutions of each case study. Such analysis identifies the relevant political factors of each speech. Analysis will then compare such factors with their respective constitutions to examine whether leaders drew on any constitutional elements to emphasize their essential conditions or instructions to protestors. In such cases, political elements of each constitution that match the political factors of each respective speech will serve as preparatory conditions that augment the essential conditions of each speech. Discourse analysis of speeches across all four case studies has revealed a certain emphasis on Democratic Approval. Hence, comparing such discourse with written formalities will augment understanding to what extent Arab leaders can further justify their

N. Due-Gundersen, *Non-Democratic Legitimacy During the Arab Spring*,
https://doi.org/10.1007/978-3-031-11882-1_5

legitimacy by drawing on constitutional elements in their public discourse addressing their rule within the context of the Arab Spring.

Furthermore, Chapters 2 and 4 have discussed Weber's sources of legitimacy and to what extent monarchs and republicans may have started their respective rules through charisma (extraordinary personal traits that can influence others) or tradition (authority that has always existed) and are now drawing far more on Weber's legality (acceptance of rules) and Peter's Democratic Approval. In other words, there is the prospect that Arab rulers relied on their personal status and the notion of being respected as authority figures early in their rule but are now replacing this form of non-democratic legitimacy with proceduralism. Therefore, filtering constitutional factors through Weber's sources of legitimacy and discussing to what extent constitutional elements are present in the speeches of each case study will allow deeper understanding of the link between dictatorship and constitutionalism.

5.2 Constitutions, Speeches and the Arab Spring

5.2.1 Constitution of the Hashemite Kingdom of Jordan

> We [...] the [...] King of the Hashemite Kingdom of Jordan, in accordance with Article 25 of the Constitution, and in pursuance of the decision of the Senate and the House of Representatives, hereby approve the following amended Constitution and decree its promulgation. (Constitute Project, 2011)

Jordan's Constitution was first enacted in 1952. From that time up until 2011, no major amendments took place (Muasher, 2011). While 2011 amendments proposed limiting the political involvement of the *mukhabarat* or state intelligence services, monarchical authority was not curbed in any way (ibid.). This fact illustrates that, as with republican counterparts, centralized authority around a head of state would not be compromised, with Jordan's Constitution granting its kings sweeping powers from the beginning (ibid.). This is no surprise as the Constitution was drawn up not by the people of Jordan but by the ruling Hashemites (*Jordan* Times, 2018).

By September of 2011, King Abdullah had approved certain constitutional amendments. These included independent monitoring of elections and the establishment of a constitutional court (Haaretz, 2011). Such measures targeted electoral reform and political party involvement in such elections, but royal authority went untouched, along with *mukhabarat* involvement in political affairs (ibid.). As discourse analysis for Jordan in Chapter 4 examined King speech in response to unrest, it is the 2011 edition of Jordan's 1952 Constitution (with the latest amendments as of 2012) that forms the basis of analyzing the political factors of Abdullah's discourse and whether such factors are present in the Constitution.

Tunisia's preamble mentions Islam specifically as a value that is protected in the Constitution (Official Printing Office of the Republic of Tunisia, 2010b). In contrast, the preamble to Egypt's Constitution contains vaguer references to national objectives being blessed "[...] in the name of God" (Palataurus Center, 2007). Jordan's Constitution takes after its Tunisian counterpart. While featuring only a one sentence preamble, the Constitution's first chapter on "[...] The State and its Ruling Regime" immediately declares that "[...] Islam is the religion of the state" (Constitute Project, 2011). This declaration links both to Bulliet's Religious Legitimacy and Jordan's history as discussed in Chapter 3, especially the lineage of the Hashemites to the Prophet Muhammad (Bulliet, 2013, p. 17). By formalizing Islam as the state's religion, the Constitution creates a written social contract between the Hashemites and Jordanian citizens, solidifying the concept of *Dar al-Islam* and confirming the expectation that a pious ruler must protect Islamic law and customs.

In addition, the constitutional guarantee of Islam as a protected state religion allows a strengthening of Abdullah's speech in the face of unrest. Returning to Searle, it is possible to consider that Article Two of Jordan's Constitution hence acts as a preparatory condition that strengthens Abdullah's religious references in his address. As Article Two formalizes the state protection of Islam, it allows Abdullah to draw on Democratic Approval and constitutional legitimacy more so than his republican counterparts. Analysis of Abdullah's speech reveals far more references to Islam than those of Ben Ali or Mubarak (Abdullah II, 2012a). Placing such references within the context of Jordan's Constitution and its mention of Islam, Abdullah can be seen as drawing on constitutional legitimacy as a preparatory condition that augments the other religious references in his speech, especially his "[...] honour of being a descendant of our forefather Prophet Mohammad" (ibid.).

The use of Democratic Approval by connecting the Constitution as a preparatory condition with his speech helps augment Abdullah's essential condition: not only to participate in elections but to remember that a state that protects Islam and is run by those of Muslim heritage is legitimate, and that to go from acceptable protest to chanting "[...] 'overthrow the regime'" is hence religiously unacceptable and a form of inciting "[...] *fitna* (chaos) [that should be] rejected by Jordanians" (ibid).

While the Constitution may strengthen Abdullah's Religious Legitimacy, it also outlines the social contract between the Hashemites and Jordanian citizens (Constitute Project, 2011). It is interesting to note, however, that the relevant chapter is entitled "[...] Rights and Duties of Jordanians", implying that the state controls the social contract between the monarchy and its citizens (ibid.). On the one hand, this fact parallels discussion of Jordan's history in Chapter 3 and the fact that the political nature of Jordan's ruling bargain with its citizens has always been a top-down process rather than a transparent framework that includes citizens as stakeholders. On the other hand, this chapter of Jordan's Constitution, emphasizing citizen obligations to the state and government control augments Democratic Approval as a political strategy. Further, the chapter cannot help but create irony in Abdullah's speech, where he consistently portrays an equal partnership between himself and citizens, his "[...] Jordanian brothers and sisters" (Abdullah II, October 2012a). As discussed in Chapter 3, the top-down process of "defensive democratization" can illustrate an unequal rather than equal contract between state and citizens. However, another aspect of Jordan's historical ruling bargain has been tribal privilege in exchange for monarchical loyalty. This defining feature of Jordan's ruling bargain is not formalized by the Constitution, limiting Abdullah's ability to draw on constitutional legitimacy to augment tribal loyalty as a key theme of Jordan's social contract, which is not referred to in his speech.

Yet, the Constitution's chapter on Rights and Duties of Jordanians still provides the Hashemites with further constitutional legitimacy that feeds into regime security and Jordan's history under their rule. It is arresting that the first article in this chapter proclaims that the state has the right to define Jordanian nationality (Constitute Project, 2011). Returning to Chapter 3, Jordan's geostrategic location has resulted in the influx of refugees at several key points of regional conflict. The Constitution's emphasis on a state definition of citizenship acts as a reminder that refugees are not part of the ruling bargain and that Palestinians granted Jordanian citizenship may not enjoy the full benefits of being a Jordanian national (as Hussein's purge of Palestinians from the public sector implied). This constitutional stipulation of state-defined citizenship can again connect with Abdullah's speech and insistence that Jordan is only "[...] the home of all Jordanians" (Abdullah, II, 2012). Abdullah's indirect remark that the ruling bargain will prioritize Jordanian citizens—and of those, citizens loyal to monarchy and of East Bank origin thus gain augmentation through constitutional legitimacy/Democratic Approval.

Building on citizenship is the Constitution's insistence that all Jordanians must serve in the military (Constitute Project, 2011). The specific statement declares that "[...] the defence of the country, its territory; the unity of its people and the preservation of social peace are a *sacred* duty of every Jordanian" (ibid., emphasis added). In this statement, the duty to effectively provide security (typically a Beneficial Consequence) is intriguing, especially when compared to Ben Ali's speech. Chapter 4's discourse analysis of Ben Ali's speech has argued that pushing security upon citizens as a factor they must provide for themselves may be regarded as a violation of the ruling bargain (Ben Ali, 2011). However, there are different factors to consider in Jordan's case. The use of the word "sacred" gives religious connotation to "[...] the unity of [...] people and the preservation of social peace" (ibid.). Such connotations can thus be linked to Abdullah's mention of *fitna* in his address to Jordanians, as *fitna* can be regarded as social unrest against a pious ruler (Brown, 2000, p. 67). Again, Abdullah is able to use constitutional legitimacy to augment his speech and non-democratic factors of his rule.

The same article that outlines the duties of Jordanians to the state also completes this social contract by mentioning state obligations to citizens, touching upon the ruling bargain (Constitute Project, 2011). Again, the article's wording appears to link directly to Jordan's political history and divide between East and West Bank. The state promises "[...] work and education within the limits of its possibilities, and [to] ensure tranquility and equal opportunities to all Jordanians" (Constitute Project, 2011). Work and education can be regarded as Beneficial Consequences. Education was certainly pushed under Bourguiba and Ben Ali in Tunisia, including in Ben Ali's final speech (albeit indirectly) (Ben Ali, 2011). In Jordan's case, unemployment and related socio-economic woes have been key factors in protests since 2011 (Tobin). On the other hand, education became a source of tension between Jordan's ruling Hashemites and Palestinian militias. As discussed in Chapter 3, while Mubarak may have contended with the Muslim Brotherhood's ability to provide public services, Hussein found that Palestinian militias offered education to buy loyalty from nearby residents (Culcasi, p. 13). Hence, formalizing the state's duty to provide education (and thus centralize its role as political administrator over non-state actors) is unsurprising (ibid.). However, these Beneficial Consequences are not categorically guaranteed by the Constitution; rather, the state should provide education and employment "[...] within the limits of its possibilities" (Constitute Project, 2011). For a kingdom without oil wealth, this stipulation is significant in how Abdullah can discuss the ruling bargain in his speech addressing protests.

In a sense, the constitutional cap on what the state should provide allows Abdullah to defend unemployment and related socio-economic problems by indirectly arguing that these problems extend beyond the limits of the state's possibilities. In his address, he reminds Jordanians that the "[...] increase in deficit and public debt [is no longer] within reasonable ranges" while also emphasizing that despite these limits, the state continues to "[...] raise salaries and pensions to protect the purchasing power of our citizens" and maintains "[...] subsidies for some basic commodities, and invest[s] in improving education and health services as well as infrastructure" (Abdullah II, October 2012a). Again, it is possible to regard the Constitution's element on state duty to provide work and education as a preparatory condition. Because the state should provide employment and schooling "[...] within the limits of its possibilities", Abdullah can draw on this restriction to augment his discourse. By discussing Jordan's socio-economic struggles and how the state continues to invest in subsidies and education, he can once more draw on constitutional legitimacy to present a subtle message or essential condition: accept that the state is doing what it can, within the limits of (socio-economic) possibilities (ibid.).

Such a cap on socio-economic responsibilities and Abdullah's political immunity (Article Thirty, ibid., p. 9) must be considered within the context of the ruling bargain. On the one hand, political immunity can be understood as a defining feature of non-democratic political legitimacy. As discussed through Peter's Political Legitimacy and in previous chapters, the socio-economic nature of the ruling bargain replaces political involvement of citizens and hence democratic accountability of leaders with Beneficial Consequences or material benefits that act as tangible proof of a leader's ability to maximize citizen (fiscal) well-being (Peter, 2016). Because such an approach emphasizes the utilitarian core of non-democratic legitimacy, Abdullah's immunity can be regarded as formalizing the apolitical nature of the ruling bargain.

On the other hand, such immunity must be placed within the context of the Constitution's limits on state responsibilities to citizens. If immunity is acceptable as part of the ruling bargain, this is due to the non-democratic and utilitarian nature of such a social contract (Peter, 2016). However, a state cap on Beneficial Consequences can be regarded as going against the material and utilitarian nature of the ruling bargain. The balance between apolitical benefits and political participation implies tension between sovereign immunity and limits on state benefits. As detailed in Chapter 3, Jordan's patronage network has not been immune to financial strain and it is during such times that nationals have expected greater political participation if Beneficial Consequences are limited. From a historical perspective, there is hence a parallel between the Constitution's immunity versus state caps on benefits and the citizen demand for political participation when state benefits are limited. This parallel/tension also feeds into Abdullah's speech and his explanation of Jordan's fiscal woes due to proximate unrest (Abdullah II, October 2012a). Abdullah does not invoke his constitutional immunity during his address but acknowledges benefit limitations and the need for citizens' political participation through elections (ibid.).

As Mubarak partially draws on constitutional rhetoric to address the masses (British Broadcasting Corporation, 2011), so too does Jordan's King Abdullah II. Article Six describes the right of all Jordanians to found a family, arguing that family "[...] is the basis of society, the core of which shall be religion, morals and patriotism" (Constitute Project, 2011). The notion of the state defining family is significant, as it allows the Hashemites to define a good family as being pious and loyal to monarchy (ibid.). Returning to Chapter 3, equating patriotism with loyalty to Hashemite rule has been a defining feature of Abdullah II. The 2002 Jordan First campaign was regarded by some critics not as a promotion of equal citizenship but as a tool to brand criticism of the monarchy as unpatriotic (Ryan, 2004, pp. 55–56). Within such a context, the notion of family takes on a very politicized image. Abdullah's speech refers to "[...] brothers and sisters [...] of the one Jordanian family" (Abdullah II, October 2012a). While discourse analysis may regard such language as emphasizing equality between ruler and subjects, a different tone is apparent when filtering such references through constitutional legitimacy. If the state can formally define "the Jordanian family", then Abdullah's references to family are not necessarily creating an atmosphere of equality. Rather, these frequent references draw on Democratic Approval to remind Jordanians that as family members, they must be religiously pious and accept the rule of "[...]

a descendant of our forefather, Prophet Mohammad" and not "[...] incite chaos and *fitna* (sedition)" (ibid.). For to do so would be constitutionally unpatriotic (Constitute Project, 2011).

A last note on Jordan's Constitution must be that of how Democratic Approval enforces Abdullah's tactic of pushing blame for socio-economic struggles away from himself and unto successive governments (Tobin, 2012). Under Article Thirty of the Constitution, King Abdullah II enjoys what is termed "[...] Head of state immunity" (Constitute Project, 2011). A most specific clause, the article in question asserts that "The King is Head of State and is immune from every liability and responsibility" (ibid.). In addition to allowing Abdullah to draw on Democratic Approval when pushing blame for unrest upon a revolving door of government officials, such a clause also extends to Abdullah's speech, creating a further connection between his address and constitutional legitimacy (Abdullah II, October 2012a). In his speech, Abdullah emphasizes the constitutional nature of his monarchy and his aloof relationship with the political framework of constitutional legitimacy. "My responsibility", Abdullah explains, "under our constitutional monarchy system, is to be committed to the outcomes that achieved consensus through our constitutional process" (ibid.). Again, Abdullah draws on Democratic Approval, as previously discussed in Chapter 4's main analysis of Abdullah's speech. However, when filtering such discourse through Jordan's Constitution, such Democratic Approval and even aloofness from political responsibility is augmented and granted constitutional legitimacy, as Abdullah can draw on constitutionally approved immunity from "[...] every liability and responsibility", ensuring that he can make political decisions and draw on Democratic Approval without formally absorbing blame for unpopular results of those decisions (ibid.). As previously noted, Abdullah does not draw on constitutional immunity during his speech. Hence, although Article Thirty's immunity does not augment his speech, it is still worth noting as providing constitutional legitimacy for the Hashemite strategy of blaming successive governments, as discussed in Chapter 3.

Returning to Weber's legality and the notion that contemporary Arab rulers have transitioned from reliance on charisma to reliance on legality, Jordan's Abdullah proves more successful than his republican counterparts. Like Mubarak, Abdullah engages heavily in Democratic Approval. However, a key difference is that Abdullah does not make last-minute amendments to augment such Democratic Approval and enjoys immunity as head of state under Jordan's Constitution, providing aloofness from political tension between citizens and successive government figures. A further difference between Abdullah and republicans is the use of religion and even how religion is manipulated through discourse to augment a state-defined version of human dignity (Abdullah II, October 2012a).

The notion that religion and human dignity are linked has been discussed in Chapter 2. There was a historic expectation that Islamic law would protect human dignity in the Muslim world (Pin, p. 3). Indeed, Islam has been regarded by some as espousing a specific form of social justice or *ʿadl* (Ibrahim, 2006, p. 7). Jordan's Constitution contains clauses specifying Islam as the state religion and the necessity of its protection (Constitute Project, 2011). Hence, Abdullah's references in his address to Hashemite links to "our forefather Prophet Mohammad" and his mention of the "martyrs" the Hashemites have offered to protect Jordan and Islam augment the constitutional legitimacy of religion as a state-protected right (Abdullah II, October 2012a).

However, when placing such Democratic Approval within the context of dignity and religion being linked, Abdullah's speech creates a nuance from republican attempts to cling to power. This nuance is due to the fact that Abdullah builds his discourse on political reform by referring to ongoing promises of augmenting citizen rights and political participation, with such reforms initiated before the Arab Spring. Republicans, on the other hand, promised last-minute reforms as a direct response to unrest. The non-existence during their rule of reform no doubt damaged the credulity of such promises. Hence, filtering Hashemite religious credentials through Jordan's Constitution augments Abdullah's constitutional legitimacy (without the King resorting to last-minute amendments that could risk creating specious Democratic Approval à la Mubarak). However, Abdullah also draws on images of family in his address (ibid.). As discussed in this analysis, constitutional definitions of family tie religion and dignity (morals) to Hashemite loyalty (Constitute Project, 2011). This link between monarchy and family confirms aspects of the hypothesis: that monarchs emphasize longevity and ties to traditional institutions, the image of family easier to manipulate in discourse due to their established familial rule.

Here lies a key difference between Abdullah and North Africa's fallen presidents. Through constitutional legitimacy, the Hashemites tie religion and human dignity together as part of "the good Jordanian family". In other words, while Ben Ali and Mubarak were disconnected from protestors' demands for dignity, the Hashemites draw on Democratic Approval or constitutional legitimacy to augment their Religious Legitimacy while also using the state-defined understanding of family to tie religion and dignity together under the umbrella of Hashemite loyalty (ibid.). Through a careful balancing act, Abdullah draws on constitutional legitimacy and religious credentials to create preparatory conditions that augment his speech's underlying essential condition to Jordanians: not simply to "[…] work from under the dome of Parliament and through the ballot boxes" but to also be good "brothers and sisters" (ibid.). A good family maintains religious dignity, as defined by the Constitution (Constitute Project, 2011). A good family remembers that they are ruled by a king who holds "the honour of being a descendant of our forefather Prophet Mohammad" and therefore the good Jordanian family avoids inciting "chaos and *fitna* (sedition), [which] are rejected by Jordanians" (ibid.).

5.2.2 *Constitution of the Kingdom of Bahrain*

> In the name of God on high, and with His blessing, and with His help, we Hamad bin Isa Al Khalifa, Sovereign of the Kingdom of Bahrain, in line with our determination, certainty, faith, and awareness of our national, pan-Arab and international responsibilities; and in acknowledgment of our obligations to God, our obligations to the homeland and the citizens, and our commitment to fundamental principles and our responsibility to Mankind. (Constitute Project, 2002)

Bahrain's current 2002 Constitution redefined the nation as a constitutional monarchy, with said Constitution being drafted and approved by the current King Hamad (Borgognone & Furlow, 2018). Although, as discussed in Chapter 3, the 2002 Constitution was based on the 2001 National Action Charter, under which Bahrainis voted for the transition to a constitutional monarchy, 2002 was the year in which many freedoms under the Charter were rolled back by Hamad (Wehrey, p. 119). As with Jordan's Constitution and the constitutions of analyzed republics, significant power is formalized in Bahrain's Constitution for the country's ruling regime (Freedom House, 2021). Hamad retains key constitutional authority over executive, legislative and judicial branches (ibid.). As with Jordan's Constitution, Bahrain's own Constitution was drafted by the nation's monarchy rather than its citizens (Khalaf, 2008). This fact can be linked back to earlier discussion in Chapter 4 of how monarchs may be using Weber's legality or the "validity of legal statute and functional 'competence' based on rationally created rules" that can be formalized in a legal document (Weber, pp. 78–79). As the 2002 edition of the Constitution is the latest edition, this version has been used in analyzing the political factors of Hamad's 2011 address and to what extent such factors are bolstered by said Constitution.

The theme of religion is continued by Abdullah's counterpart in the al-Khalifa monarchy of Bahrain. The Constitution's preamble emphasizes religion by assuming that the Constitution's values and amendments are formalized "[...] [i]n the name of God on high, and with His blessing, and with His help" (ibid.). At the same time, King Hamad is introduced not as "His Majesty" or "King" but as "[...] Sovereign of the Kingdom of Bahrain" (ibid.). The notion of sovereignty has been discussed in Chapter 2. Peter highlights that concepts of sovereignty are significant when addressing Political Cosmopolitanism. To reiterate, Political Cosmopolitanism outlines how globalization has created a need for international legitimacy or the recognition of states by global actors (Peter, 2016). Peter discusses how Political Cosmopolitanism can emphasize individual rights within communities that are globally connected but also balances such recognition with recognition of international relations being principally among states (Peter, 2016). Hence, sovereignty within the latter context is significant as it emphasizes national boundaries and non-interference of international actors on the global stage (Peter, 2016). Further, such an argument that globalization must be balanced with state-centricism links back to Ahram and Lust's assertion that the Arab Spring was inevitable because state sovereignty has always been an artificial construct (Ahram & Lust, 2016, p. 7). Consequently, as the Arab Spring blossomed, states would turn to the international system and seek world recognition by global political actors to emphasize international legitimacy, another form of Political Cosmopolitanism (ibid.). This assumption is a significant factor in analyzing both Hamad's address and Bahrain's Constitution (ibid.).

Sovereignty and stability are key themes underlined in Hamad's address. In it, Hamad insists that Iran "[...] not only directly challenges the stability and sovereignty of [Bahrain] but also poses a threat to the security and stability of the GCC" (Bahrain Independent Commission of Inquiry, 2011). Previous analysis of this speech has discussed how Hamad presents security as a Beneficial Consequence and ties Bahrain to the GCC as a form of regional/international legitimacy. This key theme in Hamad's address can be regarded as a form of Democratic Approval and constitutional legitimacy. In Bahrain's Constitution, the preface acts as a declaration of Bahrain's "[…] affiliation to the great Arab nation, and their association with the Gulf Cooperation Council" (Constitute Project, 2002). This stipulation creates a form of constitutional legitimacy when Hamad refers to the GCC. Such legitimacy not only bolsters Hamad's attempts at regional legitimacy and emphasis that Bahrain's security is vital to the survival of the GCC but also indirectly augments the Saudi-led intervention against protestors, referred to by Hamad as protection of "[…] key installations by […] the Peninsula Shield Force, without any confrontation with civilians" (Bahrain Independent Commission of Inquiry, 2011). Because Bahrain's political identity is tied to regional legitimacy and closeness to the GCC, it would seem that Hamad's speech and elements highlighting security, regional legitimacy and Bahrain-GCC links are augmented (ibid.). Hence, the Constitution's mention of the GCC can be regarded as a preparatory condition that augments Hamad's essential condition in his speech: that Bahrain has regional legitimacy due to its GCC membership and that fellow (Sunni) monarchs must come to its aid as it plays a lynchpin role in regional stability (Constitute Project, 2002). As discussed earlier, the fact that protests were countered by a Saudi-led intervention illustrates that Hamad's essential conditions aimed at fellow monarchies were indeed met.

At the same time, it must be noted that Hamad's presentation of GCC intervention "without any confrontation with civilians" is indirectly false. While some commentators confirmed that Peninsula Shield Force members did not directly engage with Bahraini protestors, their presence freed up domestic soldiers to do just that (Whitaker, 2011). Therefore, Hamad's ability to draw on constitutional legitimacy or Democratic Approval within the context of providing security as a Beneficial Consequence and as a form of regional legitimacy through linkage with the Peninsula Shield Force is limited. Association with the GCC may be constitutionally approved, augmenting regional legitimacy but this does not include regional legitimacy through military alliances or the intervention of external actors to restore national security (Constitute Project, 2002). Indeed, nowhere in the Constitution is the Peninsula Shield Force even mentioned (ibid.). From this perspective, there is an interesting parallel between how ordinary Bahrainis rejected Peninsula Shield interference as illegitimate and the Constitution's non-recognition of said Force. Indeed, protestors in the street chanted against not only the al-Khalifa monarchy but against the Peninsula Shield force, shouting "[...] Bahrain is free, [Peninsula] Shield out" (Shehabi, 2013).

Chapter 3 has discussed Bahrain's ruling bargain and the luxury of oil benefits. Within such a context, it is interesting to note that the preface to Bahrain's Constitution expresses that the document is an "[...] implementation of the popular will [...] [borne] out of our desire to complete the requirements of the democratic system of government" (Constitute Project, 2002). The notion of popular will implies a political ruling bargain with democratic legitimacy. However, Hamad does not mention popular will in his address (Bahrain Independent Commission of Inquiry, 2011). The constitutional assumption of a democratic system can be regarded as a form of Democratic Approval. Indeed, Chapter 2 briefly addressed the image of the Arab *majlis* or parliament as espousing a system of democratic decision-making but in reality, providing merely Democratic Approval by acting as a rubber stamp for non-democratic rulers (Whrey, 2014, p. 322). In addition, Chapter 3 has discussed Bahrain's parliamentary system in detail, emphasizing how the National Action Charter presented parliament as a method of deepening citizen involvement with political decision-making (Wehrey, p. 118).

However, as discussed in Chapter 3, parliament served as a vehicle for fixed elections that weakened opposition groups and emphasized sectarianism in order to dilute the political clout of non-royalists (al-Rawi, pp. 119–120). Thus, any attempt to draw on Democratic Approval through the Constitution must be balanced with the reality of a ruling bargain and parliamentary manipulation (ibid.). It is hence no surprise that Hamad's speech does not mention popular will or any democratic institutions and instead focuses on what may be considered non-democratic factors such as compensation and security (Bahrain Independent Commission of Inquiry, 2011).

Returning to Beneficial Consequences, Bahrain's Constitution guarantees state pursuit of specific values on behalf of citizens. These values include "[...] greater welfare, [...] stability and prosperity" (Constitute Project, 2002). As previously discussed, Beneficial Consequences are often regarded as utilitarian rather than moral; hence, (material) improvement in the lives of citizens justifies non-democratic rule (Peter, 2016). As discussed in Chapter 3, welfare through subsidy of diverse goods has been a common expenditure from oil profits, consistently prioritized in Bahrain over investment or savings. Furthermore, Hamad's speech draws on both security and financial welfare as Beneficial Consequences (Bahrain Independent Commission of Inquiry, 2011). Again, Bahrain is mentioned within the context of being a lynchpin state in the Gulf and its stability being essential to the GCC, highlighting regional security (ibid.). For his fellow (Sunni) Gulf monarchs, Hamad can be regarded as drawing on constitutional legitimacy and its guarantee of security as a preparatory condition to again augment his essential condition that the GCC should protect the al-Khalifa Bahrain in times of need (ibid.).

However, Hamad's emphasis on security within the framework of international legitimacy may not be successfully augmented by Bahrain's Constitution. As discussed in Chapter 4, Hamad appears to draw heavily on international legitimacy. The Constitution's guarantee of security is intended to be a form of "[…] popular will [for] […] the citizen" (ibid.). In other words, provision of security should be guaranteed for nationals and cannot therefore be used by the state as an instrument of regional (rather than national) stability intended to bolster external intervention on behalf of the regime (ibid.). Hence, any attempt to bolster international legitimacy through Democratic Approval is weak at best (Constitute Project, 2002).

Returning to welfare, Hamad's speech does draw on this constitutional guarantee for Bahrainis. Hamad emphasizes material welfare and within the context of unrest promises "[…] a range of remedies, including the newly established Victims Compensation Fund" (Bahrain Independent Commission of Inquiry, 2011). Hamad's offer to effectively buy off protestors is arresting for two reasons. Like Ben Ali's last-minute (political) offers, Hamad's Victims Compensation Fund is a strategy specifically established in response to the Arab Spring and aimed at curbing unrest, albeit as a financial rather than political instrument (ibid.). On the surface, the ability of Hamad to draw on constitutional legitimacy for welfare provision would seem limited if such provision was not consistent. Returning to Ben Ali, the President's offers of last-minute reform failed as they were a tacit admission of corruption and hence ironically emphasized that Ben Ali's rule had not exactly maintained the Tunisian Constitution's values of "[…] human dignity, justice and liberty" (Official Printing Office of the Republic of Tunisia). However, the key difference between Hamad and Ben Ali is that although both offer last-minute remedies, Hamad's Victims Compensation Fund comes atop already existing welfare arrangements (Bahrain Independent Commission of Inquiry, 2011).

As discussed in Chapter 3, oil wealth has consistently allowed the government to provide total or partial subsidies for:

- Commercial petrol
- Basic foodstuffs, including fresh meat
- All utilities
- Prescription medicine (Epstein and Miller, p. 29)

In other words, Hamad's rule has consistently provided welfare, with the Victims Compensation Fund being an additional welfare channel and another Beneficial Consequence. Because al-Khalifa rule has consistently provided welfare (as guaranteed by Bahrain's Constitution), it is possible for Hamad to use the Constitution's preface to augment his address's reference to welfare. The Constitution's mention of welfare acts as a preparatory condition so that Hamad can draw on Democratic Approval to emphasize welfare provision in his address and the creation of the Victims Compensation Fund as a further form of welfare (Bahrain Independent Commission of Inquiry, 2011). In turn, such constitutional legitimacy allows Hamad to augment the essential condition or instruction of his address to Bahrainis: cease protest and accept the Victims Compensation Fund as an additional welfare outlet and a reminder of a successful ruling bargain (ibid.).

Finally, the place of Islam in Bahrain's Constitution must be addressed, especially within the context of not only Hamad's speech but Bahrain's history of sectarianism, as discussed in Chapter 3. Within its preface, the Constitution declares that Bahrainis and their ruler(s) are united through "[...] their adherence to Islam as a faith, a code of laws and a way of life" (Constitute Project, 2002). Returning to Bulliet and Religious Legitimacy, the mention of Islam as a religion of unity certainly ties into Bulliet's discussions of Islam as a "[...] religious-political community" that is headed by a pious ruler (Bulliet, p. 4). Further, such a connection enshrined in the Constitution without a hierarchical framework emphasizes Bulliet's argument that Islamic law is universal and applies to all, with the state acting as an enforcer of Islamic law to maintain legitimacy (ibid., p. 12). A further religious concept highlighted by the wording of Bahrain's Constitution is *Dar al-Islam*. As discussed in Chapter 2, the rule of territory often allowed a regime to use Islamic titles as a form of Religious Legitimacy over defined borders (ibid., p. 5). Under *Dar al-Islam*, a pious ruler must allow freedom of religion and protection of the Islamic faith (Ayoob, p. 9).

Bahrain's Constitution does not mention *Dar al-Islam* specifically. Instead, there is an arresting form of semantics. Unity through Islam is defined under Bahrain's Constitution as one of "[...] the lofty values and great human principles" of Bahrain (Bahrain Independent Commission of Inquiry, 2011). Directly following Islamic unity is Bahrain's "[...] association with the Gulf Cooperation Council now and in the future" (ibid.). Mentioning the GCC immediately after a lengthy paragraph on Islamic unity allows the GCC to be indirectly included in such a religious union (ibid.). This concept plays with the notion of *Dar al-Islam* by emphasizing regional unity among Gulf Muslims (but without mentioning Sunni-Shia'a strains). Such an interpretation of Bahrain's Constitution, under which the GCC is part of Islamic unity and *Dar al-Islam* feeds Religious Legitimacy via Democratic Approval into Hamad's speech.

As already discussed, a central theme of Hamad's address was regional unity and international legitimacy (Bahrain Independent Commission of Inquiry, 2011). Further, Hamad emphasized Bahrain's role in maintaining this regional *Dar al-Islam* by insisting that unrest in Bahrain "[...] not only directly challenges the stability and sovereignty of our country, but also poses a threat to the security and stability of the GCC" (ibid.). Hence, the Constitution's preface and its marriage of Islam and the GCC act as a preparatory condition. Hamad draws on Democratic Approval to augment his essential condition via Religious Legitimacy: Bahrain acts as a lynchpin for a stable *Dar al-Islam*, the community of (Sunni) believers that also acts as a regional security buttress under the GCC and that hence, the GCC is obligated to intervene to keep Bahrain stable under the al-Khalifas (Bahrain Independent Commission of Inquiry, 2011).

As previously addressed in Chapters 3 and 4, the GCC agreed to this essential condition and did indeed intervene through the Peninsula Shield Force. Although the Constitution's preface conveniently describes Islamic unity without reference to sectarianism, it is worth noting that any Religious Legitimacy Hamad drew on via Democratic Approval in his address was laced with sectarian fears that fed into GCC concerns over a so-called "Shia'a Crescent" or Shia'a domination of regional politics (Black, 2007). Given the fact that the Constitution mentions only Islamic unity and does not even address Sunni or Shia'a branches, it is possible to conclude that Hamad's use of Religious Legitimacy through Democratic Approval is weakened by references to divisive sectarianism (Constitute Project, 2002). Perhaps, this was why his regional audience, the GCC intervened but local Bahrainis chanted against the Peninsula Shield Force (Shehabi).

An analysis of Bahrain's Constitution reveals elements of the ruling bargain through promises of welfare, which can be regarded as a Beneficial Consequence (Peter, 2016). Of further note is the formalizing of religion and GCC relations in the same paragraph, conjuring the notion of regional legitimacy and *Dar al-Islam* intertwined (Constitute Project, 2002). When filtering Hamad's speech through such constitutional elements, Hamad's mention of the Victims Compensation Fund can be regarded as an element of welfare provisions covered by the Constitution (Bahrain Independent Commission of Inquiry, 2011). Hence, Hamad's address draws on Democratic Approval to emphasize the socio-economic nature of the ruling bargain, a key element of the oil state as explained in Chapter 3.

On the other hand, the dominant theme of Hamad's speech is international legitimacy. Filtering this element of Hamad's speech through Bahrain's Constitution reveals weaker Democratic Approval for international legitimacy, religion and security. Returning to the Constitution's preface, stability is promised alongside welfare not as a regional guarantee but an individual right for "[...] the homeland and the citizen" (Constitute Project, 2002). In other words, security is for domestic citizens (ibid.). Therefore, when Hamad uses his address to target the GCC and international legitimacy by emphasizing Bahrain's lynchpin status (akin to Jordan's own geopolitics), he is not able to draw on Democratic Approval and any constitutional legitimacy between security and regional recognition is weak (Bahrain Independent Commission of Inquiry, 2011). Hence, while the GCC may have warmed to Hamad's caution of Bahrain's stability and the dangers of a "Shia'a Crescent", domestic citizens, who are the beneficiaries of stability according to the Constitution, were less than impressed and ordered the Peninsula Shield Force out (Whitaker).

At the same time, the Constitution constructs an association between Bahrain and the Gulf Cooperation Council "[...] now and in the future" in the interests of maintaining "[...] justice, good and peace" (Constitute Project, 2002). Again, there is the notion of Hamad drawing on Democratic Approval for regional legitimacy and Bahrain's connections to the GCC, were such connections for regional "justice, good and peace" (ibid.). However, Hamad's flaw when compared to discussing welfare is that the GCC is not consistently mentioned as a partner of peace but rather referenced once within the context of the Peninsula Shield Force's intervention (Bahrain Independent Commission of Inquiry, 2011). Again, merging recognition of the GCC with regional security (at the expense of domestic security, a constitutional guarantee) dilutes attempts at Democratic Approval (ibid.).

Lastly, constitutional references to religion go against Bahrain's sectarian history, as discussed in Chapters 3 and 4. It is no surprise that Hamad minimizes references to religion but instead feeds the fear of sectarianism and Iran to goad his fellow Sunni monarchs into protecting the al-Khalifa throne (ibid.). Ironically, the divisive references to sectarianism contradict the Constitution's message of Islamic unity, preventing Hamad from augmenting the image of *Dar al-Islam* and any Religious Legitimacy (ibid.).

Within the context of Weber's legality, Hamad's use of Democratic Approval is consistent on one point: welfare. As welfare is a constitutional guarantee and has been consistently provided by the state, Hamad's announcement of buying off protestors through the Victims Compensation Fund comes atop existing subsidies and other socio-economic sweeteners that serve as Beneficial Consequences. As previously addressed, most nationals accepted the offered money, proving that welfare remains the key element of Bahrain's ruling bargain as an oil state (Kingdom of Bahrain, 2012). In a sense, Hamad is the opposite of Jordan's Abdullah. Abdullah draws heavily on Religious Legitimacy and uses his links to the Prophet Muhammad to strengthen state definition of Jordanian citizens as pious royalists. Hamad, on the other hand, cannot pass such a test of faith against the backdrop of sectarianism. Instead, he resorts to a luxury that Jordan lacks: generous welfare drawn from oil wealth. It is through maintaining welfare that Hamad augments constitutional legitimacy and Democratic Approval, proving that the ruling bargain remains an apolitical pillar if the state coffers can afford to buy off citizens (ibid.).

5.2.3 *Constitution of the Arab Republic of Egypt*

> We, the people who in addition to preserving the legacy of history, bear the responsibility of great present and future objectives whose seeds are embedded in the long and arduous struggle, with which the banners of liberty, socialism and unity have been hoisted along the great march of the Arab Nation. (Palataurus Center of Studies, 2007)

During Mubarak's administration, Egypt operated under the Constitution of 1971 (Brown, 2011). This period is significant, as the 1971 Constitution was introduced by President Sadat at a time when military rule was firmly entrenched after the anti-monarchical Nasser period (ibid.). As with Tunisia's 1959 Constitution, Egypt's 1971 document strengthened presidential powers (ibid.). Sadat amended the Constitution to allow some liberalism for political parties and religion (while balancing such openness with further executive authority). Mubarak, however, oversaw a reversal in such amendments. By 2007, his regime was supervising elections, controlling electoral candidates and barring the Muslim Brotherhood from eligibility while augmenting presidential powers further through so-called emergency measures (ibid.). Such a backdrop to understanding Mubarak's final address within the context of the 1971 Constitution no doubt feeds into Mubarak's circular Democratic Approval and why Mubarak's attempts to use this form of non-democratic legitimacy failed within the context of a Constitution that was already seen as unpopular after 2007 (ibid.). For these reasons, it is the 2007 edition of the 1971 text that is analyzed.

While Tunisia's Constitution is established by "the representatives of the Tunisian people" (Official Printing Office of the Republic of Tunisia), Egypt's Constitution features wording that creates the image of it being established by the people directly (ibid.). Indeed, the Constitution's preamble asserts the will, values and (political) objectives of "[...] [w]e, the people of Egypt" throughout, emphasizing the image of the Constitution's creation through the direct involvement of Egyptians (ibid.). While such discourse may clash with the reality of military influence behind the 1971 Constitution, this wording is significant when considering how Mubarak addressed protestors through paternalism. While Ashraf El-Sherif may argue that Egypt's social history encouraged "authoritarian guardianship" in response to an apolitical populace, the wording of Egypt's Constitution challenges such an assumption (El-Sherif, p. 6; ibid.). Mubarak may have well seen his subjects as unassertive children, yet the Constitution's wording and popular activism linked to it contrasts his belief. After all, an apolitical populace would not have connected with the Constitution's discourse as "the people of Egypt" and before Mubarak's 2007 amendments, Egyptian activists had faith in the popular will of the Constitution, as evidenced by attempts to revive liberal promises from the 1971 text (Brown, 2011). If Egyptians could not make their political will known or did not have a political will, they would not have lobbied to preserve a

Constitution that included objectives as precise as world peace, (Arab) unity, human dignity (again a key driver of the Arab Spring) and socio-economic development (ibid.).

Nonetheless, certain linguistic elements of the Constitution are drawn upon in Mubarak's final speech. The people of Egypt are mentioned in the preamble as having "[...] the honour of defending this land" and that Egypt is a nation of "[...] immortal heritage" (ibid.). Mubarak attempted to tap into such patriotic discourse when claiming that he "[...] spent a lifetime defending [Egypt's] soil and sovereignty" and that he can continue to play a part in maintaining Egypt's "[...] immortal identity" (British Broadcasting Corporation, 2011). While not a form of Democratic Approval per se, it is still arresting that Mubarak mimics constitutional language, again reflecting an attempt to emphasize Weber's legality by connecting his speech's discourse with that of the Constitution (ibid.).

From a historical perspective, the mention of socialism and unity is a reminder of Nasserism, as discussed in Chapter 3. Gamal Abdel Nasser had birthed Egypt as a socialist republic, which was defined by Nasser as a state that would provide subsidies and related benefits to increase living standards (Nagarajan, p. 24). Hence, while subsidies are not specifically mentioned in the preamble, it is apparent from Egypt's republican history that subsidies and related welfare were expected and even a constitutional right, listed under Article 122 of the Constitution (Palataurus Center of Studies, 2007). There is a certain irony, then that Mubarak partially lifted constitutional language in his final speech but failed to address socialism and subsidies, despite their presence in the same Constitution that he formally ruled through.

The role of socialism also appears to come before that of religion. Mention of Egypt's socialist nature comes before that of God. However, it is worth noting that the Constitution outlines the objectives of the people and their political values as goals that can only be achieved "[...] in the name of God and with his assistance" (Palataurus Center of Studies, 2007). The assumption that God must "bless" the efforts of Egyptians returns discussion to Chapter 2 and Brown's Political Quietism or the belief in fatalism that means Muslims balance efforts to realize (socio-political) goals with the notion that God more than human exertions shapes significant events (Brown, 2000, p. 3).

At the same time, invoking Political Quietism also acts as an indirect reminder that Egypt will only accept a pious ruler who protects Islamic customs and law (ibid., p. 67). The notion of a pious ruler being legitimate if protecting Muslim territory (*Dar al-Islam*) is hence indirectly referenced in Egypt's Constitution, partially augmenting Mubarak's own references to religion in his final address. Mubarak's emphasis on defending the sovereignty of a nation with Muslims and Christians highlights Bulliet's Religious Legitimacy. Bulliet's discussion of a ruler maintaining Islamic laws is emphasized by Mubarak reminding listeners that the protection of Muslims and Christians is a Quranic obligation (Vajda). From this perspective, Mubarak's address can be regarded as drawing (indirectly) on Religious Legitimacy through constitutional references that highlight Peter's Democratic Approval and Weber's legality, more so than any constitutional references by his counterpart, Ben Ali.

When reviewing the political objectives set out in Egypt's Constitution, there are references to be found to drivers of the Arab Spring. World peace or "[...] [p]eace to our world" is the first objective enshrined in the Constitution, with emphasis on such an objective being achieved through social justice and the prevention of exploitation, "[...] whatever its form" (Palataurus Center of Studies, 2007). Justice is not mentioned directly in Mubarak's final address. Rather, Mubarak discusses constitutional amendments that will be led by himself but advised by a committee of "[...] justice system and law experts that I have set up" (ibid.). As previously discussed, Mubarak's amendments serve as a form of Democratic Approval. With the Constitution demanding justice and Mubarak arguing that his reforms are led by justice specialists, there is an indirect form of constitutional legitimacy. However, as Mubarak is leading said reforms and makes no direct reference to justice (as outlined in the Constitution), this aspect of Democratic Approval does not draw on Egypt's Constitution but rather engages in a circular argument that he has legitimacy through Democratic Approval but is amending the Constitution in response to the Arab Spring (British Broadcasting Corporation, 2011). Under Weber's legality, such an argument is weak. Had Mubarak drawn on constitutional elements more consistently, especially the political objectives outlined in the Constitution (and his ability to uphold them), an argument through Democratic Approval may have been strengthened.

Moreover, the prevention of exploitation is a constitutional element that was certainly not upheld by Mubarak's regime. Exploitation and corruption are never even addressed in Mubarak's last plea (unlike Ben Ali's final speech). Indeed, Chapter 3 has already explained how Mubarak's Egypt exploited economic resources and international aid and credit to placate the military elite and other political friends at the expense of Egyptian citizens, widening the wealth gap and creating the conditions of his overthrow. Mubarak certainly did not uphold the Constitution's demands for exploitation prevention, which forms a part of the Constitution's understanding of justice. No wonder that justice went unmentioned in his final address.

At the same time, Mubarak's exploitation of economic resources maintained a ruling bargain with the military elite. The importance and sacrosanct status of the Armed Forces is significant when examining the Constitution, which praises their role in "[...] the July 23rd Revolution [against the monarchy]" (Palataurus Center of Studies, 2007). The mention of the Armed Forces in the Constitution is a reminder of the real authors behind it but also the fact that the military elite have historically enjoyed a privileged position, which Mubarak maintained through his separate ruling bargain with them (at the expense of the people), as discussed in Chapter 3. However, this brief mention of the Armed Forces must be balanced against the Constitution's lengthier references to social justice (ibid.).

Further emphasizing Mubarak's failure to maintain constitutional legitimacy is the Constitution's focus on "[...] Freedom for the Humanity of [...] Egyptian(s)" (ibid.). This passage asserts that Egypt's progress is dependent on the individual's "[...] humanity and dignity", as the "[...] dignity of every individual is [a] natural reflection of the dignity of his nation" (ibid.). Such a detailed passage enshrining individual dignity is most ironic. While Mubarak mentions "[...] Egypt's dignity" in passing during his final speech, he fails to mention the dignity of the Egyptian and the context of individual dignity guaranteed by the Constitution (British Broadcasting Corporation, 2011). Mubarak's focus on nationhood and territory combined with religion may connect with *Dar al-Islam* but the failure to provide the individualistic context of "Egypt's dignity" again limits Mubarak's ability to meaningfully connect his discourse with constitutional legitimacy (ibid.). Moreover, such a failure cannot but emphasize Mubarak's disconnect with the political nature of the protests against him and the fact that they were motivated by the need for dignity and respect.

This latter aspect is paramount in illustrating Mubarak's failure to successfully draw on Democratic Approval and constitutional legitimacy as defined by Weber. Egypt's Constitution asserts that sovereign law as a basis for legitimacy is constitutionally sound if such laws and constitutional practices act as "[...] a guarantee for the freedom of the individual"

(Palataurus Center of Studies, 2007). Again, Chapter 3 clearly illustrates that Mubarak, like Ben Ali did not prioritize maintaining the dignity of his citizens but allowed corruption and the wealth gap to grow. If discussing why Mubarak's speech engages heavily in Democratic Approval, it is worth noting that the Constitution does state that constitutional legitimacy is "[...] the sole basis for the legality of authority". Hence, Mubarak could have drawn on constitutional elements as preparatory conditions and connected them with essential conditions or instructions related to constitutional legitimacy. However, Mubarak's attempts to rely on Democratic Approval fall short as he fails to create preparatory conditions that could have created acceptable essential conditions related to constitutional legitimacy. This failure mirrors his regime's inability to draw on the strongest elements of the Constitution, namely justice and dignity. Instead, Mubarak resorted to self-serving amendments that did not connect with key constitutional elements, and he could not save his throne after all (ibid.).

5.2.4 Constitution of the Republic of Tunisia

> In the name of God, the Merciful, the Compassionate, We, the representatives of the Tunisian people, meeting as members of the Constituent National Assembly, Proclaim the will of our people, who freed themselves from foreign domination thanks to their strong cohesion and their fight against tyranny, exploitation and regression. (Official Printing Office of the Republic of Tunisia, p. 5)

At the time of Ben Ali's final address, his regime operated under Tunisia's Constitution of 1959, which was formally drawn up by his predecessor, Habib Bourguiba (Vandewalle, 1980, p. 154). Of note was Bourguiba's delay in formalizing Tunisia's Constitution until he was confident that he could limit its scope to ensure presidential domination over parliamentary processes, a reality later reflected by Ben Ali's democratic window-dressing (ibid.). Moreover, the 1959 Constitution was amended further to augment presidential powers even more by Bourguiba and later by Ben Ali himself (The Carter Center, 2014, p. 4). The last of these amendments was affixed to the 1959 Constitution on July 28th, 2008, two years before Ben Ali's overthrow (Printing Office of the Republic of Tunisia, p. 13). The latest edition of the 1959 Constitution from 2010 is used for Chapter 5's investigation as it reflects these amendments and is the final edition of the 1959 Constitution still printed in the last year of Ben Ali's rule (ibid.).

Unlike Ben Ali's final speech, the Tunisian Constitution immediately references Islam, declaring "[i]n the name of God, the Merciful, the Compassionate", indicating that religion and politics are intertwined in a constitution written by "[...] the representatives of the Tunisian people" (ibid.). The wording in such a sentence alludes to a social contract that is politicized and even democratic; if Tunisia is to be led by "representatives of the Tunisian people", it can be assumed that any leader should represent the popular will of Tunisians rather than offer an apolitical ruling bargain (ibid.). On the other hand, such a preamble can be regarded as a condition to formalize Democratic Approval (Peter, 2016). Peter argues that the existence of any constitution that is supposedly endorsed by most citizens means political legitimacy is automatically granted to the ruling regime. In other words, if the Constitution is written by those representing popular will ("the people"), then it can be assumed that the Constitution itself is accepted by the same popular will, opening up the path for Democratic Approval and mere proceduralism (ibid.).

As previously discussed, Ben Ali's address does not mention democracy or popular will, avoiding what may have been an unwanted reminder that Ben Ali did not gain power through democratic means (Ben Ali, 2011). However, one commonality between the Tunisian Constitution and Ben Ali's last speech is the element of external threats and security. The Constitution declares that it represents "[...] the will of our people, who freed themselves from foreign domination" (Official Printing Office of the Republic of Tunisia, p. 5). The Constitution's highlighting of foreign intervention is arresting. Returning to Chapter 3, it should be recalled that modern Tunisia was founded on anti-colonialist nationalism under Bourguiba and so a constitutional reference to refusing foreign domination is not surprising (ibid.). At the same time, such a reference can be regarded as a preparatory condition for Ben Ali's portrayal of protest as vandalism that has been incited by foreign or external influence. "[The] events currently taking place in our country are not part of us", he insists. "Vandalism is not part of the customs of Tunisians" (Ben Ali, 2011). Ben Ali, unlike Mubarak, does not directly refer to such "vandalism" as foreign interference and hence the implication is weak at best. At the same time, this tenuous connection allows him to build his credentials on the Beneficial Consequence of security from external threats, with references to his various security and military positions "[...] in the service of the country", albeit all in vain (ibid.).

The preamble of Tunisia's Constitution also includes values of social justice that the "representatives of the Tunisian people" are expected to maintain (Printing Office of the Republic of Tunisia, p. 5). These values include "[...] human dignity, justice and liberty" (*ibid*). The notion of human dignity and justice links back to one of the strongest drivers of the Arab Spring: the simple desire for respect, as discussed in Chapter 2 (Fukuyama, 2012). Further, the mention of justice under the faith of Islam returns discussion to *'adl* or the concept of social justice specific to Islamic law (Ibrahim, 2006, pp. 6–7). None of these values are mentioned in Ben Ali's final speech. Ironically, they form part of his first address in 1987. During his "inauguration" so many decades ago, he promised that "[...] the liberation and development of Tunisia [will be] countless" and that "[...] the law [will be] correctly enforced in a way that will proscribe any kind of iniquity or injustice" (Ben Ali, 2015).

A younger Ben Ali drew on constitutional elements that guaranteed justice and dignity; yet his final speech did not mirror these (broken) promises. Given the fact that he was popularly ousted, this irony was not lost on bitter Tunisians (Driesbach and Joyce).

Perhaps most contradictory with the realities of Ben Ali's rule is the Constitution's instructions "[...] to establish a democracy founded on the sovereignty of the people, and characterized by a stable political system based on separation of powers" (Official Printing Office of the Republic of Tunisia, p. 5). Again, such a stipulation can be filtered through Peter's Democratic Approval, as democratic elements can exist as mere proceduralism. However, the mention of a democratic system goes against the apolitical ruling bargain discussed across this book. Ben Ali's final address does not mention any democratic elements of his regime and his rule was more corrupt than democratic, as discussed in Chapter 3. However, Ben Ali's last speech does mention reform and promises to acknowledge popular political demands while also promising to investigate "[...] corruption, bribery, and the mistakes of officials" (Ben Ali, 2011). Returning to the initial discourse analysis and setting aside Ben Ali's attempts to appear blameless, there is an interesting interpretation of connecting the Constitution's instructions with Ben Ali's "mistakes". Just as Ben Ali's admission of corruption indirectly implies that he was aware of its existence, any attempt to offer reforms or investigations that return Tunisia to a democratic rule augments such guilt even further. Given the fact that the

Tunisian Constitution was first published in 1959, Ben Ali cannot draw on democratic elements of the Constitution for legitimacy without revealing that his rule has not upheld the (democratic) values of the Constitution, illustrating a failure to draw on Weber's legality and even Democratic Approval as he has not upheld the political procedures of the Constitution.

Finally, the preamble of the Tunisian Constitution ends with a declaration of what the republican regime should constitute. This paragraph is tantamount to proclaiming the political nature of the regime, which feeds directly into this book's discussions of the apolitical ruling bargain and its links to Democratic Approval, Beneficial Consequences and constitutional legitimacy as discussed by Weber's legality (Weber, pp. 78–79). This passage defines the Tunisian regime as constituting:

- Respect for human rights and equality among citizens
- Guaranteeing economic development by using Tunisia's resources for the benefit of the people
- Ensuring citizens' right to work, health care and education (Printing Office of the Republic of Tunisia, pp. 5–6).

These factors present a mix of elements that can be considered political but also socio-economic. Unsurprisingly, Ben Ali does not mention human rights or citizen equality in his last address, nor in his first address for that matter. However, it is worth noting that two out of three of these factors are socio-economic rather than political or focused on human rights (ibid.). The final requirement that the state must ensure citizens have access to health care, employment and education is arresting. As discussed in Chapter 3, education and employment are typical promises of Beneficial Consequences delivered under the ruling bargain. At the same time, Tunisia became known for its emphasis on providing education (but not employment). Indeed, in Ben Ali's final speech, Ben Ali implies that education is a part of his ruling bargain and that protests and unrest have prevented the state from fulfilling this obligation ("[...] children today have stayed home and did not go to school") (Ben Ali, 2011).

The concept of education as a Beneficial Consequence is implied and hence augmented by its constitutional guarantee. In this respect, Ben Ali is partially resorting to legality. However, it is doubtful that Ben Ali is actively drawing on the Constitution given the indirect and single reference to education rather than a consistent approach (ibid.). Further, his mention of education as a Beneficial Consequence must be measured against what he does not mention in his final address: human rights, equal citizenship and the use of Tunisia's resources for economic development that will benefit nationals (Printing Office of the Republic of Tunisia, pp. 5–6). Again, as discussed in Chapter 3, Ben Ali did not use Tunisia's resources for sound economic development but plundered said resources, tailoring economic laws to benefit himself and his inner circle.

When comparing the Tunisian Constitution with Ben Ali's final address, there are few instances in which Ben Ali draws on any elements of the Constitution as preparatory conditions to further augment his essential conditions through Democratic Approval. Perhaps this is no surprise, given that discourse analysis has revealed that Ben Ali's last-minute reforms and tacit admission to (knowledge of) corruption reveal that his regime is unable to justify a non-democratic ruling bargain when many Beneficial Consequences were not delivered. Returning to Weber's legality, Ben Ali does not augment his legitimacy through Democratic Approval, as he fails to reflect any constitutional elements in his address, the exception being an indirect reference to education. Returning to Ben Ali's promises of subsidies, a key element of typical ruling bargains, the Tunisian Constitution contains no references to state provision of subsidies (ibid.). Instead, the Constitution contains elements reflecting popular will, which can be interpreted as allowing Democratic Approval, as discussed by Peter (ibid.).

While it is true that Ben Ali engaged in democratic window-dressing, as discussed in Chapter 3, there are no references to democratic procedures in his final speech. Further, the key elements of Tunisia's Constitution include human rights, equal citizenship, social justice and sound economic development for the benefit of the people (ibid.). None of these factors are covered by Ben Ali's final speech, illustrating that even constitutional legitimacy of his regime was lacking. The irony of Ben Ali's fall is the contrast it presented to his beginnings and the discourse of his first address, which did reflect key elements of the Constitution, promising equality, justice and even emphasizing that "[...] there will be no more favoritism or indifference where the squandering of the country's wealth is concerned" (Ben Ali, 2015).

After twenty-three years in power, such irony had morphed into tragedy. A comparison between Tunisia's Constitution and the last words of President Ben Ali only emphasizes his failure to meet the political and socio-economic demands of Tunisians and his failure to employ Weber's legality as a republican who could not draw on tradition or rely on what so many dictators claim in their first years of power: charisma.

Filtering each case's speech through the respective country's constitution deepens the discourse analysis of this project and its original knowledge contribution by examining if democratic and non-democratic factors of legitimacy (including religion) have any constitutional basis and to what extent such a constitutional basis is drawn upon in each related address. Further, filtering each speech through its respective constitution allows a deeper examination of Democratic Approval as an instrument of non-democratic legitimacy.

Tunisia's Ben Ali does not draw much on constitutional legitimacy. There is a thin link between the Constitution's mention of Tunisia's people freeing themselves "[…] from foreign domination" (Official Printing Office of the Republic of Tunisia, p. 5) and Ben Ali's emphasis on his military record and other political posts "[…] in the service of the country" (Ben Ali, 2011). However, such a link and Ben Ali's claim to serve Tunisians are countered by evidence of corruption and the other constitutional factors that his regime did not uphold, including liberty, justice and human dignity. There is a sad irony that such forms of social justice were promised in Ben Ali's "inauguration" speech of 1987 (Ben Ali, 2015). Indeed, as expressed in Chapter 2, the need for human dignity was a driving force behind the Arab Spring (Fukuyama).

Ben Ali could not draw on Democratic Approval from the Constitution without indirectly reminding Tunisians of his failure to consistently uphold most of these values. This is especially true when considering the Constitution's existence since 1959 from before Ben Ali's 1987 beginnings until his overthrow in 2010. Hence, when filtering Ben Ali's address through Weber's legality, a comparison between Tunisia's Constitution and said speech augments Ben Ali's failure to draw on the Constitution for Democratic Approval by highlighting the full obligations between the state and Tunisians and Ben Ali's failure to fulfill all his constitutional obligations.

The book assumes that republican presidents-for-life will draw primarily on the socio-economic ruling bargain as the main source of their non-democratic legitimacy. However, when analyzing the political factors of Ben Ali's speech and comparing them with related political factors of Tunisia's 1959 Constitution, it is clear that non-democratic factors are not bolstered by said Constitution. Very few constitutional guarantees are drawn on in Ben Ali's address. Only security, free education, employment and economic development can be regarded as socio-economic and non-democratic factors of legitimacy. Ben Ali's address mentions education and subsidies but these constitutional guarantees are overshadowed both by his history of corruption and the democratic guarantees of the Constitution, including separation of powers and social justice that Ben Ali did not maintain. Because of this failure, a comparison of his address with Tunisia's Constitution does not buttress the hypothesis that republicans will rely on a socio-economic ruling bargain, as Tunisia's Constitution makes it clear that the social contract was intended to include political elements and not to support a purely utilitarian ruling bargain.

Understanding Ben Ali's failure to uphold the political elements of the Constitution and maintain a material ruling bargain (instead of indulging in corruption) can feed into and expand the book's hypothesis. The original hypothesis outlines that republics will emphasize the socio-economic ruling bargain as the main source of their non-democratic legitimacy in response to the Arab Spring, due to most republics being the result of coups rather than established familial rule. However, Ben Ali's inability to justify his non-democratic ruling bargain, as illustrated by tacit admission of corruption, failure to provide both education and employment and the political nature of protests against him beg the question of whether republicans who are challenged by unrest can successfully justify their rule if they recognize the need to politicize the ruling bargain (McClatchy Newspapers, 2011).

In other words, an extended hypothesis for further investigation may be: republics will emphasize the socio-economic ruling bargain as the main source of their non-democratic legitimacy in response to the Arab Spring, due to most republics being the result of coups rather than established familial rule. However, failure to justify non-democratic rule through tangible Beneficial Consequences should encourage such regimes to politicize the ruling bargain in a step-by-step manner, perhaps akin to Jordan's "defensive democratization" rather than offer last-minute reforms that emphasize a regime's weakness and knowledge of corruption (Ben Ali, 2011). In Tunisia after Ben Ali, 2018 protests have emphasized socio-economic grievances but not a desire to overthrow new governments (International Crisis Group, 2018). At the same time, political analysts have noted that opposition and rival political actors have attempted to inject such unrest with their own agenda and that any central government must address not only socio-economic gaps but politicize the social contract to prevent a return to dictatorship (ibid.). It would be interesting to apply the aforementioned extended hypothesis to regimes that replaced overthrown republics after the Arab Spring and determine if a politicization of the ruling bargain has allowed new regimes to survive ongoing unrest, though this approach is outside the scope of this book.

Egypt's Mubarak reveals a more complex relationship with Democratic Approval when his discourse is filtered through Egypt's Constitution. Mubarak draws on constitutional discourse (which is not the same as constitutional legitimacy), echoing the Constitution's praise of the Egyptian people's "[…] honour of defending this land" (Palataurus Center of Studies, 2007) with his own sentiments that he holds the honor of spending "[…] a lifetime defending [Egypt's] soil and sovereignty" (British Broadcasting Corporation, 2011). His reference to "[…] Muslims and Christians" (ibid.) echoes the concept of *Dar al-Islam* and the Constitution's assertion that Egypt's territory exists "[…] in the name of God and with His assistance" (Palataurus Center of Studies, 2007).

However, Mubarak's paternalism, linked to the notion of "authoritarian guardianship" contrasts with the notion that Egypt's Constitution is written not by representatives of the people (as in Tunisia) but "[w]e, the people of Egypt" (ibid.). Moreover, Mubarak's indulgence in Democratic Approval is circular, with promises of constitutional amendments that will ultimately be overseen by himself (British Broadcasting Corporation, 2011). Mubarak does not draw on existing constitutional factors in his speech (ibid.). Like Ben Ali, this means that he avoids constitutional references to social justice and preventing exploitation (corruption), the latter being a hallmark of his own regime as much as Ben Ali's, as discussed in Chapter 3. Again, reflecting Ben Ali's mistake and the fuel of the Arab Spring's fire, Mubarak does not address the notion of human dignity, augmented by Egypt's Constitution as an individual right because "[…] the dignity of every individual is [a] natural reflection of the dignity of his nation" (Palataurus Center of Studies, 2007).

As with Ben Ali, Mubarak's dismissal of the political nature of protests and the simple desire for respect proved fatal. Both Ben Ali and Mubarak could not draw on the political and human values of their respective constitutions, severely limiting the use of Democratic Approval and illustrating a failure to successfully conform to Weber's legality. The (limited) use of religion contrasts somewhat with the hypothesis that republicans will rely solely on the ruling bargain. However, Chapter 3 has discussed the importance of subsidies for North African regimes, especially in Egypt. Mubarak's failure to acknowledge the importance of subsidies in his final speech is arresting, especially when compared to Ben Ali's promises of subsidized food prices (Ben Ali, 2011). In other words, there is the implication that Mubarak's failure to recognize the socio-economic nature of unrest means that, like Ben Ali, he had maintained a weak ruling bargain, again illustrated by corruption and a growing wealth gap addressed in Chapter 3. Nonetheless, subsidies formed only one factor for Mubarak's overthrow and the inability to provide dignity and social justice, related drivers of the Arab Spring, is reflected in weak constitutional legitimacy that again fails to successfully draw on Weber's legality.

A comparison of political factors in Mubarak's speech with any similar factors from Egypt's Constitution reveals a weak link between the two and hence a disconnect from the assumption that the ruling bargain can be sanctioned by Egypt's Constitution as a form of non-democratic legitimacy. This disconnect is evident from the fact that Mubarak engages in circular Democratic Approval rather than drawing on the Constitution, despite his 2007 amendments that restricted previous liberties and strengthened his presidential authority. On the one hand, the Constitution's mention of subsidies could have been built upon by Mubarak in his speech to emphasize the utilitarian ruling bargain. On the other hand, Mubarak shared Ben Ali's history of corruption and faced politicized protests, while technically still operating under a Constitution that guaranteed political and moral freedoms, including social justice, human dignity and the prevention of exploitation. It is curious that his 2007 amendments did not remove such politicized values from a Constitution that was intended to empower his regime. Despite their political nature, perhaps Mubarak recognized the popularity of such values, as evidenced by 2007 activism and faith in the 1971 Constitution's original liberties. In retrospect, comparing the Constitution with Mubarak's actions augments his failure to maintain expected political values, revealing that Egypt's Constitution cannot bolster the assumption that the republican President could gain constitutional legitimacy for an apolitical ruling bargain. Finally, the Constitution's protection of Islam as the state religion is drawn upon in Mubarak's discourse and the concept of *Dar al-Islam*. This link between Constitution and discourse contrasts with the assumption that religion would be a non-democratic factor exclusively manipulated by monarchs. However, the few political factors Mubarak's speech could augment through the Constitution were not enough to save him or formally support a non-democratic social contract, in the light of protestors' political demands that were constitutionally guaranteed (such as dignity) and Mubarak's corruption, which went against constitutional promises of combating exploitation.

From Mubarak to monarchs, Hamad of Bahrain presents a strong example of the socio-economic ruling bargain when his address is filtered through constitutional factors. While Hamad's speech makes few religious references, constitutional references to Bahrain's unity with the Gulf Cooperation Council are arresting. The wording within Bahrain's Constitution ostensibly holds Islamic unity and identification with the GCC as equal values, conjuring images of *Dar al-Islam* as a regional concept. The notion of regional legitimacy and international legitimacy are central themes in Hamad's address and the GCC is a conspicuous element of the Constitution's preface. There is therefore the prospect of Hamad augmenting regional and international legitimacy through Democratic Approval linked to Bahrain's Constitution. Indeed, Hamad's speech plays to more than one audience, not only Bahrainis but the international community and the Gulf's Sunni monarchs. Though Hamad's essential conditions aimed at the global community and the GCC appear successful, the Constitution does not serve as a preparatory condition for Hamad's international legitimacy.

Hamad's address presents security as a regional affair; Bahrain is a lynchpin that keeps the GCC stable and thus grants it regional legitimacy (Bahrain Independent Commission of Inquiry, 2011). This notion returns to Ahram and Lusts's thoughts on international legitimacy and Peter's Political Cosmopolitanism or the belief that there can be an international legitimacy that is state-based and that states will cooperate in an international system that prioritizes the stability of sovereign states over the rights of citizens of individual states (Peter, 2016). However, Bahrain's Constitution guarantees security as an individual right for Bahrainis, not as a regional right to allow Bahrain to be a lynchpin in the security of the GCC (Constitute Project, 2002). The same goes for the concept of *Dar al-Islam*. If the Constitution defines security as an individual right exclusive to Bahrainis, not a regional right, then the concept of Islamic unity in the Constitution is separate from (domestic) security (ibid.).

Therefore, any attempts by Hamad to draw on constitutional legitimacy as a form of Democratic Approval to augment regional legitimacy and *Dar al-Islam* through GCC stability would be weak. This weakness is evidenced by the chants of Bahrainis who wanted the swiftest departure from Bahrain of the GCC's military arm, the Peninsula Shield Force, a militia not recognized by Bahrain's Constitution (ibid.).

As with his republican counterparts, Hamad has not enforced (social) "[...] justice, good and peace" for Bahrainis, as evidenced by crackdowns on unrest and GCC military intervention (ibid.). However, Hamad has maintained consistent provision of welfare, augmented by the Victims Compensation Fund and by the constitutional guarantee of welfare provision for Bahrainis (ibid.). From this perspective, Hamad can be regarded as conforming to Weber's legality but only through welfare provision. He lacks the extensive Democratic Approval of his Jordanian counterpart but boasts the one luxury Jordan lacks: oil wealth. In a sense, Hamad represents a reverse of this book's hypothesis for monarchies: that they draw on Religious Legitimacy more than the ruling bargain due to their longevity and ties to traditional institutions and accepted socio-cultural norms. In Bahrain's case, the ruling bargain remains the defining feature of al-Khalifa non-democratic legitimacy, with nationals accepting such an arrangement, as illustrated by their claiming of compensation from the Victims Compensation Fund (Kingdom of Bahrain, 2012). For Bahrain, money talks.

For Jordan, it's still good to be king. Returning to the heart of the Levant, discourse analysis of constitutional elements in Abdullah's speech has revealed the ability of Abdullah II to survive through Democratic Approval that draws on constitutional legitimacy far more successfully than his republican counterparts. The Hashemite Abdullah is not afraid to remind Jordanians of his direct links to the Prophet Muhammad and the fact that descendants of his throne have "[...] offered many martyrs" (Abdullah II, October 2012a). Religious Legitimacy and religious discourse are augmented by Jordan's Constitution. Article Two formalizes Islam as the state religion and Abdullah successfully uses Democratic Approval within the confines of the existing Constitution to argue against unrest from the religious context of *fitna* rather than resort to last-minute political pleas or self-serving constitutional amendments. While previous analysis in this chapter and Chapter 4 has argued that Ben Ali failed to provide security as a Beneficial Consequence by telling citizens to fend for themselves, Abdullah can draw on the Constitution and its statement that Jordanians have a duty to defend the homeland, while also presenting this duty as a pious commitment to prevent *fitna*. Abdullah thus transforms security from a Beneficial Consequence into a patriotic and religious duty of Jordanians and does so through constitutional legitimacy. Hence, security as an element of the utilitarian ruling bargain is bolstered by the Constitution, partially contrasting the assumption that republicans rather than monarchs will rely on the ruling bargain as a (main) source of non-democratic legitimacy. On the other hand, presenting security as a sacred duty of Jordanians to prevent *fitna* merges security with religion, the latter of which has been assumed by our assumptions as a strong factor of non-democratic legitimacy for monarchs.

A blessing for Abdullah no doubt must be the Constitution's cap on the ruling bargain, with Beneficial Consequences to be provided to citizens by the state "[…] within the limits of [the state's] possibilities" (ibid.). This cap on the ruling bargain allows Abdullah to use his address as a lengthy explanation of Jordan's socio-economic woes linked to regional turmoil, defending lack of employment and limited welfare (Abdullah II, October 2012a). Therefore, the Constitution acts as a preparatory condition to deliver Abdullah's essential condition: Jordanians must accept a limited ruling bargain in exchange for (limited) political involvement (ibid.).

While such involvement may seem political and go against the assumption of monarchies drawing on religion via traditional institutions as part of non-democratic legitimacy, there are two factors to consider. First, Abdullah's language during his discourse transforms elections into a religious symbol, with voting taking place "under the dome of Parliament" (Abdullah II, October 2012a). Hence, what appears to be a political invitation now has religious connotations. Second, Chapter 3 has discussed Jordan's history of tribal voting alongside "defensive democratization", with Chapter 2 describing the Arab *majlis* as a rubber stamp institution that serves as a forum for democratic window-dressing. Therefore, Jordan's Parliament can be regarded as a traditional institution, with Abdullah drawing on religion and traditionalism, bolstered by Abdullah's reliance on the Constitution for Democratic Approval as a method of deflecting blame (Tobin, 2012). From such a perspective, Abdullah's invitation to vote actually maintains the assumption that monarchs will rely on traditional institutions for non-democratic legitimacy. This interpretation is augmented by the Constitution's immunity for Jordan's head of state, emphasizing that Abdullah's revolving door of elected politicians is constitutionally sanctioned while providing him aloofness from democratic accountability. This is a key difference between Mubarak and Ben Ali: while both may blame external factors for unrest and avoid constitutional references, Abdullah can augment his inculpability through constitutional legitimacy as it guarantees him an immunity his republican counterparts do not enjoy.

Mubarak's paternalism was apparent in Chapter 4. However, Abdullah's references to family and equal "brothers and sisters" take an ominous tone when filtered through Jordan's Constitution. If family is defined by the

Constitution as loyalty to the Hashemites and piety, then Abdullah's references to his family can be regarded as less equal than paternal. The state defines family and Abdullah's address draws on this constitutional definition to remind his brothers and sisters that good Jordanians recognize his religious credentials and are loyal to monarchy, avoiding *fitna* by not spreading unrest. This protracted image of family in Abdullah's discourse is matched by constitutional definitions of family, strengthening the assumption that monarchs will rely on ties to traditional institutions to bolster their rule. In Abdullah's speech and the Constitution, religion is intertwined with concepts of family and the socio-cultural norm in Jordan of familial rule under the Hashemites.

Ben Ali and Mubarak failed to address human dignity, the driver of the Arab Spring. Jordan's monarch avoids this pitfall through a Constitution that defines what dignity is. Dignity is a pious family loyal to the Hashemites (Constitute Project, 2011). As defined by the state, dignity and religion are part of "the good Jordanian family" along with patriotism. Any good Jordanian cannot maintain their religion and dignity by going against a descendant of their Prophet (Abdullah II, October 2012a).

As a monarchical case study, Abdullah conforms strongly to the assumption that royals will draw on Religious Legitimacy more than the ruling bargain due to their longevity and ties to traditional institutions and accepted socio-cultural norms. What is interesting about Abdullah is that he draws on constitutional legitimacy to both augment Religious Legitimacy but also to minimize the ruling bargain, resorting to the "defensive democratization" Jordan is known for. As a political leader who draws on Democratic Approval via the existing Constitution rather than self-approved amendments, Abdullah presents a successful case of Weber's legality. At the same time, his success in drawing on constitutional legitimacy is aided by constitutional immunity from "[...] every liability and responsibility", a luxury his republican counterparts do not share (Constitute Project, 2011). Such immunity exists amid a backdrop of strong religious credentials and fears of regional instability that encourage the status quo.

An overview of the four case studies and their speeches, understood within the context of each respective Constitution illustrates that only one out of the four case studies strongly upholds the book's assumptions. Jordan's Constitution and Abdullah's discourse confirm the notion that Religious Legitimacy and traditional ties are heavily drawn upon by monarchs when defending non-democratic legitimacy. However, the same cannot be said for Bahrain, in which the socio-economic ruling bargain defines non-democratic legitimacy. Welfare is drawn upon by Hamad in discourse responding to the Arab Spring and is a constitutional right, augmenting the ruling bargain more so than Religious Legitimacy and traditional ties. While this result contrasts with the assumption that Religious Legitimacy and traditionalism is drawn upon heavily by monarchs when justifying non-democratic rule, it comes as no surprise in the context of Bahrain's oil wealth. Finally, the republican case studies of Tunisia and Egypt reveal weak ties between discourse and Constitutions. Tunisia's Ben Ali could not draw heavily upon political factors from Tunisia's Constitution without revealing that he had not maintained the overwhelming political values of the Constitution such as social justice and equality. Tunisia's Constitution hence does not augment the assumption that republicans will rely on a socio-economic and apolitical ruling bargain as their main source of non-democratic legitimacy, as the Constitution contains democratic and related political elements, including a separation of powers. The political nature of Tunisia's Constitution is also reflected in Egypt's Constitution, which guarantees individual human dignity and freedom from exploitation for citizens. Again, Mubarak's ability to draw on political factors from the Constitution in his discourse during unrest was limited, as Egypt's Constitution does not formally support a socio-economic ruling bargain. The Constitution's brief reference to subsidies was not echoed by Mubarak in his speech, a reminder that, as with Ben Ali, protests were politicized amid a backdrop of corruption.

Chapter 5's analysis of constitutional factors in select speeches has expanded on Chapter 4's discourse analysis to explore how non-democratic legitimacy may be formalized and to what extent such factors are drawn on by Arab leaders in discourse justifying non-democratic rule in the face of the Arab Spring. The result: understanding that constitutional legitimacy can augment the socio-economic ruling bargain and Religious Legitimacy for Bahrain's Hamad and Jordan's Abdullah, respectively, but fails to strengthen non-democratic justifications of republicans, who resorted to tacitly admitting corruption and avoiding references to a Constitution that formalized democratic factors (Ben Ali) or attempting to use Democratic Approval to push constitutional amendments (Mubarak). The fact that non-democratic factors are often lacking in republican constitutions illustrates that republicans struggle more than monarchs to draw on Weber's legality and may have little to no constitutional basis for upholding an apolitical ruling bargain. Although Egypt's 1971 Constitution mentions subsidies, Mubarak's failure to draw on this factor and reliance on Democratic Approval through constitutional amendments coupled with Ben Ali's desperate political offers, tacit admission of corruption and inability to refer to Tunisia's Constitution for his right to rule illustrates that for republicans, non-democratic legitimacy through constitutional factors is weak. From such a perspective, the hypothesis that monarchies will draw on Religious Legitimacy, tradition and Weber's legality while republicans draw on a socio-economic ruling bargain and Weber's legality has been partially disproved. Monarchies seem able to employ constitutional legitimacy with greater success in their discourse than republican counterparts, using Weber's legality to bolster Religious Legitimacy and traditionalism (Jordan's Abdullah) but also the ruling bargain (Bahrain's Hamad), the latter aspect assumed to be exclusive to republicans. However, as discussed in Chapter 4, republicans failed to uphold ruling bargains during their rule, leading to weak arguments when forced to defend non-democratic legitimacy and limited ability to draw on constitutional factors.

Chapter 6 concludes the book and summarizes how successfully we have addressed our core assumption: that republics will emphasize the socio-economic ruling bargain as the main source of their non-democratic legitimacy in response to the Arab Spring, due to most republics being the result of coups rather than established familial rule. Hence, many republican rulers have weaker ties to traditional (religious) institutes and popular support and rely on a ruling bargain to maintain legitimacy. Monarchs, on the other hand, will draw on Religious Legitimacy more than the ruling bargain due to their longevity and ties to traditional institutions and accepted socio-cultural norms. Chapter 6 also addresses how successfully this book has answered: What are the factors Arab leaders use in discourse justifying their rule within the context of the Arab Spring? To what extent does this discourse support a (socio-economic) ruling bargain and Religious Legitimacy? Chapter 6 draws on the analysis of Chapters 4 and 5, discussing these findings within the context of the book's assumption and questions being addressed.

References

Primary Data

Abdullah II, H. M. (2012a, October). *Remarks by His Majesty King Abdullah II During a Gathering with National Public Figures, Amman, Jordan*. Available at: http://kingabdullah.jo/index.php/en_US/speeches/view/id/507/videoDisplay/0.html (accessed 21 October 2016. Inaccessible since 2021, saved as a pdf by author).

Abdullah II, H. M. (2012b, December). *Remarks by His Majesty King Abdullah II on the Occasion of the University of Jordan's 50th Anniversary*. Available at: https://kingabdullah.jo/en/speeches/occasion-university-jordan%E2%80%99s-50th-anniversary (accessed 24 January 2022).

Bahrain Independent Commission of Inquiry. (2011). *Speech of HM King Hamad bin Isa Al Khalifa on 23rd November*. Available at: http://www.bici.org.bh/indexc971.html?news=speech-of-hm-king-hamad-bin-isa-al-khalifa-on-23rd-november (accessed 12 January 2022).

Ben Ali, Z. (2011) *The Last Official Address by Tunisian President Zine el-Abidine Ben Ali* (T. Badran, Trans.) Available at: https://msmunatunagb.wikispaces.com/file/view/The+Last+Official+Address+of+Ben+Ali.pdf (accessed 20 November 2017. Inaccessible since 2021, saved as a pdf by author)

Ben Ali, Z. (2015). *Speech to the Tunisian Parliament by Zine el Abidine Ben Ali on 7 November 1987 After President Bourguiba Was Declared Unfit to Govern*. Available at: http://al-bab.com/albab-orig/albab/arab/docs/tunisia/declaration_07111987.htm (accessed 11 November 2021).

British Broadcasting Corporation. (2011). *Egypt Unrest: Full Text of Hosni Mubarak's Speech*. Available at: http://www.bbc.co.uk/news/world-middle-east-12427091 (accessed 12 October 2021).

Constitute Project. (2002). *Bahrain's Constitution of 2002*. Available at: https://www.constituteproject.org/constitution/Bahrain_2002.pdf (accessed 3 December 2021).

Constitute Project. (2011). دستور الأردن الصادر عام 1952 شاملا تعديلاته لغاية عام 2011. Available at: https://www.constituteproject.org/constitution/Jordan_2011.pdf?lang=ar (accessed 14 January 2022).

Official Printing Office of the Republic of Tunisia. (2010a). دستور الجمهورية التونسية, 1959. Publications of the Official Printing Office of the Republic of Tunisia.

Official Printing Office of the Republic of Tunisia. (2010b). *Constitution of the Republic of Tunisia*. Available at: http://www.tunisie-constitution.org/sites/all/downloads/constitution-tunisienne-anglais.pdf (accessed 3 January 2022).

Palataurus Center of Studies. (2007). *Constitution of the Arab Republic of Egypt, 1971*. Available at: http://constitutions.albasio.eu/constitution/?id=19 (accessed 26 November 2021).

Secondary Data

Academic Reports/Papers

Ahram, A. I., & Lust, E. (2016). The Decline and Fall of the Arab State. *Survival, 58*(2), 7–34.

Bulliet, R. W. (2013). *Religion and the State in Islam: From Medieval Caliphate to the Muslim Brotherhood* (Occasional Paper Series, Paper No. 2). Center for Middle East Series, University of Denver.

Ibrahim, A. (2006). *Universal Values and Muslim Democracy*. Available at: https://www.journalofdemocracy.org/articles/universal-values-and-muslim-democracy/ (accessed 13 January 2022).

Muasher, M. (2011). *Jordan's Proposed Constitutional Amendments—A First Step in the Right Direction*. Available at: https://carnegieendowment.org/2011/08/17/jordan-s-proposed-constitutional-amendments-first-step-in-right-direction-pub-45366 (accessed 11 January 2022).

Peter, F. (2016) *Political Legitimacy*. Available at: http://plato.stanford.edu/entries/legitimacy/ (accessed 18 January 2022)

Ryan, C. R. (2004). "Jordan First": Jordan's Inter-Arab Relations and Foreign Policy Under King Abdullah II. *Arab Studies Quarterly, 26*(3), 43–62.

Tobin, S. A. (2012). 'Jordan's Arab Spring: The Middle Class and Anti-Revolution. *Middle East Policy, 19*(1), 96–109.

Vandewalle, D. (1980). Bourguiba, Charismatic Leadership and the Tunisian One Party System. *Middle East Journal, 34*(2), 149–158.

Media Reports

Black, I. (2007). *Fear of a Shia Full Moon*. Available at: https://www.theguardian.com/world/2007/jan/26/worlddispatch.ianblack (accessed 5 December 2021).

Borgognone, S., & Furlow, R. (2018). *The US Must Tell Bahrain's Rulers: It's Time to Reform*. Available at: https://www.defenseone.com/ideas/2018/06/us-must-tell-bahrains-rulers-reform/148984/ (accessed 11 January 2022).

Brown, N. J. (2011). *Egypt's Constitutional Ghosts*. Available at: https://www.foreignaffairs.com/articles/north-africa/2011-02-15/egypts-constitutional-ghosts (accessed 11 January 2022).

Fukuyama, F. (2012, January 12). The Drive for Dignity. *Foreign Policy.* Available at: http://foreignpolicy.com/2012/01/12/the-drive-for-dignity/ (accessed 17 January 2022).

Haaretz. (2011). *Jordan's King Abdullah Approves Constitutional Reforms.* Available at: https://www.haaretz.com/1.5184945 (accessed 11 January 2022).

Jordan Times. (2018). Jordan Marks 72nd Independence Anniversary. Available at: http://www.jordantimes.com/news/local/jordan-marks-72nd-independence-anniversary (accessed 11 January 2022).

Kingdom of Bahrain. (2012). *Bahrain Disburses $2.6 Million from Victim's Compensation Fund in First 17 Cases.* Available at: https://www.prnewswire.com/news-releases/bahrain-disburses-26-million-from-victims-compensation-fund-in-first-17-cases-160404545.html (accessed 19 January 2022).

McClatchy Newspapers. (2011). *Tunisian President Ben Ali Flees Country as Thousands Protest.* Available at: https://www.mcclatchydc.com/news/special-reports/article24607879.html (accessed 10 January 2022).

Shehabi, A. (2013). *Bahrain's Sovereign Hypocrisy.* Available at: https://foreignpolicy.com/2013/08/14/bahrains-sovereign-hypocrisy/ (accessed 3 January 2022).

Whitaker, B. (2011). *Bahrainis Cannot Be Subdued Forever.* Available at: https://www.theguardian.com/commentisfree/2011/mar/17/bahrain-saudi-intervention-sectarian-conflict-protests (accessed 3 January 2022).

Printed/Online Books

Brown, L. C. (2000). *Religion and State: The Muslim Approach to Politics.* Columbia University Press.

Brown, N. J. (2001). *Constitutions in a Nonconstitutional World: Arab Basic Laws and the Prospects for Accountable Government.* SUNY Series in Middle Eastern Studies. State University of New York Press.

Whrey, F. (2014). Bahrain's Decade of Discontent. In L. Diamond & M. F. Plattner (Eds.), *Democratization and Authoritarianism in the Arab World* (pp.315–326, p. 322). Johns Hopkins University Press.

International Organization Reports

Freedom House. (2021). *Bahrain.* Available online at: https://freedomhouse.org/country/bahrain/freedom-world/2021 (accessed 9 September 2022).

Khalaf, A. (2008). *Bahrain's Parliament: The Quest for a Role*. Available at: https://carnegieendowment.org/sada/21282 (accessed 11 January 2022).

The Carter Center. (2014). *The Constitution-Making Process in Tunisia*. Available at: https://www.cartercenter.org/resources/pdfs/news/peace_publications/democracy/tunisia-constitution-making-process.pdf (accessed 11 January 2022).

CHAPTER 6

Conclusion

This book has examined non-democratic legitimacy within the context of the Arab Spring through discourse analysis in the cases of Jordan, Bahrain, Egypt and Tunisia. The purpose of such an approach has been to address the question: What are the factors Arab leaders use in discourse justifying their rule within the context of the Arab Spring? To what extent does this discourse support a (socio-economic) ruling bargain and Religious Legitimacy? The discourse analysis in Chapter 4 reveals that Jordan and Bahrain as monarchical case studies vividly illustrate Religious Legitimacy and a socio-economic ruling bargain, respectively. Discourse from Jordan's Abdullah II in response to protests highlights Jordan's socio-economic struggles as opposed to a socio-economic ruling bargain while drawing heavily on religious imagery, language and Abdullah's links to the Prophet. Conversely, Bahrain's Hamad treads carefully on religion due to Bahrain's sectarianism and instead emphasizes Bahrain's status as a lynchpin state for Gulf stability while reiterating welfare and offering financial compensation through the Victims Compensation Fund. Hamad's discourse hence emphasizes the socio-economic ruling bargain.

Republican discourse does not necessarily justify a socio-economic ruling bargain, with weak references to subsidies from Ben Ali and Mubarak. However, these former presidents-for-life do emphasize Beneficial Consequences such as security and stability, in addition to other material benefits such as education. Nonetheless, in both cases there is a weak argument for a successful socio-economic ruling bargain, as emphasized by Ben Ali's last-minute reforms (implying that his rule must be politicized).

N. Due-Gundersen, *Non-Democratic Legitimacy During the Arab Spring*, https://doi.org/10.1007/978-3-031-11882-1_6

Mubarak, on the other hand, engages heavily in Democratic Approval, with discourse justifying his rule turning to formal proceduralism, as discussed in Chapter 2. Either way, such discourse fails to strongly support a socio-economic ruling bargain. It is ironic, however, that Mubarak's discourse draws on concepts of *Dar al-Islam* and thus partially supports the notion of Religious Legitimacy.

Chapter 5 has analyzed the constitutions of the four cases and their connection to the speeches examined in the respective case study and revealed limited use of constitutional factors to bolster discourse justifying non-democratic rule across most case studies. Ironically, Jordan's Abdullah draws heavily on constitutional authority to enjoy immunity from political accountability as the head of state. Furthermore, he is able to draw on the Constitution's definition of dignity and religion to emphasize his right to rule over his fellow Muslims and to attack those opposing him as engaging in un-Islamic *fitna*. Bahrain's Hamad draws on constitutional endorsement of the socio-economic ruling bargain, as the Victims Compensation Fund can be regarded as coming atop constitutional expectations of welfare. Hamad's attempts to link international legitimacy, religion and (regional) security to Bahrain's Constitution are weak, however, as the Constitution guarantees security and religious unity for Bahrainis and not for the Gulf region.

Egypt's Mubarak engaged heavily in Democratic Approval rather than drawing on constitutional elements to justify non-democratic rule. Brief references to Egypt's dignity in Mubarak's address partially echo the Constitution's mention of dignity. However, Mubarak's speech did not reflect the Constitution's full context of individual dignity and social justice. Like his Tunisian counterpart, Mubarak cannot draw extensively on constitutional elements without reminding the masses of his failure to uphold democratic values rather than impose non-democratic authority. Finally, Tunisia's Ben Ali made few references to Tunisia's Constitution in his address, as doing so may have acted as an indirect reminder of the democratic rather than non-democratic elements Ben Ali failed to uphold.

Our main findings can be split twofold: discussing monarchies, it would seem the ruling bargain and related socio-economic benefits remain central in oil states as a response to the Arab Spring. The Bahrain monarchy did not resort to religion but compensation when faced with unrest, while Abdullah of Jordan did conform strongly to the hypothesis assumption that monarchs would resort to Religious Legitimacy. However, Abdullah's use of religion can be placed within the context of Jordan's oil poverty and reliance on external aid, while Bahrain's sectarianism and moderate oil reserves encouraged financial sweeteners and minimized reference to religion by the ruling Sunni al-Khalifas presiding over a Shia'a majority. Hence, the religious element of this hypothesis has been partially proved to be correct but only if the ability to distribute material benefits is limited.

Analysis of Ben Ali's and Mubarak's speeches may have partially confirmed a link between republicans and the ruling bargain through subsidies. However, Ben Ali's desperate promises of (political) reform and tacit admission to corruption show a weak connection of his regime to a legitimate ruling bargain and further implies, as explored in Chapter 5, that failed ruling bargains may require regimes to politicize their social contracts in order to maintain legitimacy. Mubarak's speech also connected somewhat with the ruling bargain but emphasized external security threats and state protection from those threats as a Beneficial Consequence of his rule. This element can thus be regarded as feeding into the assumption on republicans but allowing the ruling bargain to not be purely socio-economic. Further, Mubarak's use of *Dar al-Islam* partially contrasts the assumption that drawing on religion is the exclusive domain of monarchs.

Examining each case study's speech within the context of constitutional factors shows that monarchies can draw on such factors to augment Religious Legitimacy and traditionalism when welfare distribution is limited, while the ruling bargain may actually be constitutionally guaranteed for oil states. This fact contrasts the book's assumption that the ruling bargain would be reserved for republicans while also confirming that Religious Legitimacy is tied to monarchy (when material resources are limited). On the other hand, constitutional factors in republican case studies were lacking in analyzed speeches due to Tunisia's and Egypt's respective Constitutions formalizing democratic as opposed to non-democratic elements. The focus of both Constitutions on social justice, exploitation prevention and dignity prevented republicans from augmenting their (weak) justifications of non-democratic rule with constitutional legitimacy, contrasting with the hypothesis that republicans will rely on the ruling bargain.

At the same time, some limitations must be acknowledged. First, it is conspicuous that Syria is not addressed. This absence is noticeable no doubt due to Syria's ongoing civil war as of writing. In addition, it is worth noting that, unlike his fellow republicans or monarchical counterparts, Assad used the term "Arab Spring" directly in a 2014 "inauguration" address. Referring to the apparent voter turnout, Assad insisted that the resilience of his supporters "[...] constituted the official obituary of what was falsely called the Arab Spring" (Voltaire Network, 2014). Nonetheless, this book selected four specific case studies to understand whether non-democratic legitimacy was used in discourse by leaderships responding to the Arab Spring, with the intent of addressing the hypothesis of republicans relying on ruling bargains and monarchs relying on Religious Legitimacy. These four case studies constitute an even split between republican and monarchical case studies. Further, main analysis examines two case studies of overthrown republicans and two case studies of monarchs who have kept their thrones. Hence, the addition of Syria would have affected the parity of analyzed case studies and also created an anomaly, as Syria's Assad has not been officially overthrown but remains entrenched in a protracted civil war.

Another limitation has been the analysis of English rather than Arabic texts. Our aim has been to understand justification of non-democratic legitimacy through public discourse by specific Arab leaderships in response to the Arab Spring. The select speeches and constitutions are hence primary sources. However, such discourse has been analyzed in translated English editions rather than the original Arabic. For Arabic editions, the analyzed speech by Jordan's Abdullah II is available in its original Arabic as a video issued by official government sources (RHC JO, 2012). Finally, the address of Bahrain's Hamad is also available as an Arabic transcript from the same source as its English counterpart (Bahrain Independent Commission of Inquiry, 2011). It is worth mentioning that three out of four Arabic transcripts or videos hail from official or otherwise objective sources or from sources that match their English counterparts: Mubarak's Arabic address is available as a transcript from BBC Arabic, with the English translation also from the BBC. Hamad's Arabic speech is available as a text from the same source as the English translation, while Abdullah's Arabic speech is available from the Royal Hashemite Court as a video, with the analyzed English translation also released by the Royal Hashemite Court. Returning to republics, this author has found one video source of Ben Ali's speech (LyanOran, 2011) and one transcript source of said speech (Babnet, 2011). There is also an audio recording of Ben Ali's final address in the original Arabic (Abdulsalam, 2011). For Mubarak's final address, this author has identified several video sources (Mubarak TV, 2014; Omonoganees, 2011) and two transcript sources (Al Jazeera, 2011, BBC Arabic, 2011). The fact that these Arabic sources are from the same outlets as their English counterparts strengthens the validity and likely accuracy of the analyzed English translations.

Although Ben Ali's original Arabic transcript is not from an official government source, this is unsurprising as he was overthrown. However, this author has read the Arabic transcript and listened to the video and audio sources to ensure that these sources match the analyzed English translation by ensuring that key phrases in the English transcript are found in the same passages of the Arabic address. As discussed in Chapter 4, Tunisia's Ben Ali attempted to use his final speech to quell unrest by speaking to the masses "in the language of Tunisians" (Ben Ali, 2011). This passage is a reference to Ben Ali's speech being in the local Tunisian dialect rather than the formal Arabic known as *Fusha*. Hence, analyzing the linguistic elements of Ben Ali's speech being delivered in the Tunisian dialect (with the speeches of other case studies in *Fusha*) may have strengthened our understanding of non-democratic legitimacy. However, the diversity of Arabic dialects and the lack of a structured writing system for such dialects presents a challenge for a non-native speaker to measure select speeches at the advanced linguistic level required for discourse analysis. In addition, because constitutions are written in *Fusha* while related speeches may have been given in a specific dialect, for reasons of parity analysis has been conducted using English translations of speeches and constitutions.

Moreover, it would be most interesting to have attempted to understand if such public discourse matched what the analyzed leaderships truly thought of the Arab Spring and non-democratic legitimacy. However, such an approach would require direct access to each respective leader. Such access for interviews would have enhanced our understanding of dictatorship but would be unrealistic due to access limitations.

As with the speeches of each case study, constitutions of each case study were also analyzed in English in order to facilitate in-depth analysis. The author has attempted to ensure that the original Arabic versions of all constitutions exist and match their English counterparts. Jordan's 1952 Constitution with 2011 amendments was used as an English translation for Chapter 5's investigation. An Arabic edition has been located from the same publisher (Constitute Project, 2011), also based on the 1952 Constitution of Jordan with amendments up to 2011. Again, there is a direct match between the English and Arabic versions. Bahrain's 2002 Constitution in English was used for the Bahrain case study in Chapter 5's investigation of constitutional factors of legitimacy. An Arabic edition has been located from a governmental source (Kingdom of Bahrain Shura Council, 2002). Despite the different sources, the Arabic edition is also from the same year as the English edition. Given that neither the English nor Arabic edition have any amendments and the fact that the author has searched the Arabic edition's preamble for matching phrases from the English edition, it is safe to assume that the analyzed English edition of the Constitution matches its Arabic counterpart.

For Tunisia's Constitution, the English edition is a 2010 publication that acted as the final edition of the original 1959 Constitution, including amendments up to 2008. A matching Arabic edition has been found, also as a 2010 edition and released by the same publisher as the English edition (Official Printing Office of the Republic of Tunisia, 2010). Lastly, for the Egyptian Constitution case study, the 1971 English edition of the Constitution was used, reflecting amendments up to 2007. The Arabic edition of this Constitution has also been located, matching the inception year of 1971 and the final amendments of 2007 (Al Jazeera, 2019). It is worth noting that the publisher of the Arabic edition (Al Jazeera) differs from the publisher of the English edition (Palataurus Center of Studies). However, both texts are copies of the 1971 Constitution with amendments up to 2007 and hence match.

Finally, as the Arab Spring can be regarded as an ongoing event that is now pressuring newly elected or created governments in, inter alia, Tunisia and Egypt, it is worth mentioning that this book addresses a limited period of the Arab Spring, namely 2010–13 and has not analyzed political events related to the Arab Spring beyond this timeline. This limitation can be linked back to the specific case studies and the attempt to understand non-democratic legitimacy in the face of unrest that peaked with the overthrow of decades-long governments (Tunisia's Ben Ali and Mubarak's Egypt) or that saw protests diminish at a time when it was expected that the Arab Spring would spread through a domino effect (Jordan's Abdullah and Bahrain's Hamad). This approach of a limited timeline again feeds into the book's focus on monarchies surviving through traditionalism and Religious Legitimacy and republicans emphasizing the ruling bargain. The need for parity in analyzing overthrown republics and surviving monarchies within the same time frame explains why governments that were formed after the end of republicans-for-life have not been analyzed. Further and as mentioned in Chapter 5, as some new governments may be regarded as politicizing the ruling bargain, using newly formed regimes as case studies would not connect with the main aim of this book, which is to examine non-democratic legitimacy and the success of dictatorship within the context of the Arab Spring.

As discussed in Chapter 5, findings from the main analysis have led to the prospect of an extended hypothesis: republics will emphasize the socio-economic ruling bargain as the main source of their non-democratic legitimacy in response to the Arab Spring, due to most republics being the result of coups rather than established familial rule. However, failure to justify non-democratic rule through tangible Beneficial Consequences should encourage such regimes to politicize the ruling bargain in a step-by-step manner, perhaps akin to Jordan's "defensive democratization" rather than offer last-minute reforms that emphasize a regime's weakness and knowledge of corruption. The focus of this book on understanding dictatorship has prevented such an extended investigation into post-Arab Spring governments. However, future works can consider the political legitimacy of governments that have replaced regimes overthrown during the Arab Spring. Such an approach could examine unrest during the era of post-Arab Spring governments and official discourse from such leaderships as a response to unrest, with the aim of understanding to what extent political legitimacy has become more politicized.

References

Abdulsalam, A. (2011). خطاب زين العابدين بن علي 13 جانفي 2011 [audio]. Available at: https://soundcloud.com/lr5qtaoy0ycg/13-2011 (accessed 13 January 2022).

Al Jazeera. (2019). دستور مصر 1971. Available at: https://www.aljazeera.net/encyclopedia/events/2015/12/7/%D8%AF%D8%B3%D8%AA%D9%88%D8%B1-%D9%85%D8%B5%D8%B1-1971 (accessed 14 January 2022).

Al Jazeera. (2011). نص خطاب مبارك للشعب المصري. Available at: https://www.aljazeera.net/news/arabic/2011/2/11/%D9%86%D8%B5-%D8%AE%D8%B7%D8%A7%D8%A8-%D9%85%D8%A8%D8%A7%D8%B1%D9%83-%D9%84%D9%84%D8%B4%D8%B9%D8%A8-%D8%A7%D9%84%D9%85%D8%B5%D8%B1%D9%8A (accessed 13 January 2022).

Babnet. (2011). زين العابدين بن علي: أنا فهمتكم. Available at: https://www.babnet.net/cadredetail-31940.asp (accessed 13 January 2022).

Bahrain Independent Commission of Inquiry. (2011). *Speech of HM King Hamad bin Isa Al Khalifa on 23rd November*. Available at: http://www.bici.org.bh/indexc971.html?news=speech-of-hm-king-hamad-bin-isa-al-khalifa-on-23rd-november (accessed 12 January 2022).

BBC Arabic. (2011). مبارك يتنحى عن منصبه والجيش يتولى ادارة البلاد. Available at: http://www.bbc.com/arabic/middleeast/2011/02/110211_egypt_protests_mubarak_army.shtml (accessed 13 March 2019).

Ben Ali, Z. (2011). *The Last Official Address by Tunisian President Zine el-Abidine Ben Ali* (T. Badran, Trans.). Available at: https://msmunatunagb.wikispaces.com/file/view/The+Last+Official+Address+of+Ben+Ali.pdf (accessed 20 November 2017. Inaccessible since 2021, saved as a pdf by author).

Constitute Project. (2011). دستور الأردن الصادر عام 1952 شاملا تعديلاته لغاية عام 2011. Available at: https://www.constituteproject.org/constitution/Jordan_2011.pdf?lang=ar (accessed 14 January 2022).

Kingdom of Bahrain Shura Council. (2002). دستور مملكة البحرين. Available at: http://www.shura.bh/ar/legislativeresource/constitution/pages/default.aspx (accessed 14 January 2022).

LyanOran. (2011). خطاب زين العابدين بن علي 13 جانفي 2011 [film]. Available at: https://www.youtube.com/watch?v=2AQm45CGcHo (accessed 13 January 2022).

Mubarak TV. (2014). خطاب الرئيس مبارك يوم 10 فبراير 2011 [video]. Available at: https://www.youtube.com/watch?v=ySQp73bZA6o (accessed 13 March 2019).

Official Printing Office of the Republic of Tunisia. (2010). دستور الجمهورية التونسية, 1959. Publications of the Official Printing Office of the Republic of Tunisia.

Omonoganees. (2011). خطاب حسنى مبارك 10 فبراير 2011 الجزء الأول [video]. Available at: https://www.youtube.com/watch?v=JBBLWSXRCWs&t=1s (accessed 9 September 2022).

RHC JO. (2012). *His Majesty King Abdullah II Remarks During a Gathering with National Public Figures at the Royal Hashemite Court on 23 October 2012* [video]. Available at: https://www.youtube.com/watch?v=Bf60Ft2B6HQ (accessed 14 February 2022).

Voltaire Network. (2014). *Inaugural Speech of President Assad*. Available at: https://www.voltairenet.org/article184784.html (accessed 22 January 2022).

APPENDICES

APPENDIX 1: REMARKS BY HIS MAJESTY DURING A GATHERING WITH NATIONAL PUBLIC FIGURES

In the name of God, the Most Merciful, the Compassionate

My brothers and sisters,

I would like to welcome you all to your home, the home of all Jordanians.

I wanted to meet with you today for a sincere talk at this particular stage in our beloved country's history, in order to highlight our reform roadmap.

I fully realise, my brothers and sisters, that every modernisation and change initiative is accompanied by anxiety and uncertainty. This is natural. Popular demands over the last year and a half have focused on enhancing citizens' rights to participate effectively in the decisions that impact them and their future, and I am committed to guaranteeing this right for all.

The trajectory of the political reform roadmap under which this phase was launched was agreed upon a year and a half ago. It included constitutional reforms to make the people a true partner in the political process, and its most notable components were the Constitutional Court, the Independent Elections Commission, laws governing political life such as the Elections and Political Parties Laws, in addition to holding early elections, which will bring a new Parliament and pave the way to piloting parliamentary government.

Here, I would like to assure you that our country is on the right track towards the reform we aspire to, and I would like to reiterate that we will have a new Parliament by the new year, following parliamentary elections that will be conducted with the highest degree of integrity and transparency.

N. Due-Gundersen, *Non-Democratic Legitimacy During the Arab Spring*,
https://doi.org/10.1007/978-3-031-11882-1

And as I stated before, my message to you and to all political parties and forces is this: If you want to change Jordan for the better, there is a chance, and that chance is through the upcoming elections, and there is a way, and that way is through the next Parliament.

As for those who want additional reforms or want to develop the Elections Law, they can work from under the dome of Parliament and through the ballot boxes, which are the true representative of the will of the people.

My brothers and sisters,

My responsibility, under our constitutional monarchy system, is to be committed to the outcomes that achieved consensus through our constitutional process and to respect the opinion of the majority, as I am for all segments of society, be it the "herak," the opposition, or the silent majority, and I regard them all as working in the service of our country.

It is citizens' vote in this election that will determine the make-up of the next Parliament and the next parliamentary government, thus determining the policies and decisions that will affect the life of every citizen. Therefore, citizens must not allow anyone to deprive them of their right to vote and affect change.

Political parties and lists should organise themselves as quickly as possible, build their electoral platforms for the next four years and explain to voters what policies and additional reforms they seek. To cite a few examples:

How will candidates, political parties, and lists address the challenges of poverty and unemployment? How will they tackle the challenges of debt and budget deficit?
What is the best tax reform?
How will they further develop the voting system?
How will they meet the water and energy challenges of Jordan?
How can the quality of services such as health, education and transport be improved?

For citizens have the right to get clear answers to these and many other questions, through practical programmes that are realistic and not just theoretical, so that voters can make the best choice at the ballot boxes. For the larger the participation, the greater will the change be.

The next Parliament is the gate to comprehensive reform. It is the institution constitutionally mandated to continue achieving true change and overcoming national challenges, by consolidating a democratic approach, the culture of dialogue and the highest standards of constructive debate.

My brothers and sisters,

It has become necessary to distinguish between national constructive opposition and positive "herak", on the one hand, and negative opposition and "herak", on the other hand, which do not serve the reform path, nor the country's future.

Constructive opposition and positive "herak" play a legitimate and needed role, while negative "herak", with empty slogans and attempts to incite chaos and fitna (sedition) are rejected by Jordanians. We should always remember that catchy slogans are not the solution, and backward and radical intolerant mentalities cannot be trusted with the future of our children.

Let us pause and think of the slogans that have been raised against corruption. I agree with you on the need to counter corruption. Enormous efforts are being exerted to uproot and deter corruption, and cases are currently before the courts and the AntiCorruption Commission. These institutions must be allowed enough time for justice to take its course.

But, regrettably, there is another category of such slogans, based on personalisation, defamation, slander, and prejudgment, which results into trial by public opinion at the expense of justice.

As for the budget deficit and public debt, let us remember that we used to receive oil from Iraq at subsidised prices until 2003, at less than US $30/barrel. Today, we buy oil at over US$100/barrel.

The increase in deficit and public debt was previously within reasonable ranges, rising annually as a result of steady rises in oil and food prices, the state's initiatives to raise salaries and pensions to protect the purchasing power of our citizens, continue subsidies for some basic commodities, and invest in improving education and health services as well as infrastructure. These all contributed to a reasonable increase of debt in absolute terms.

But, in addition to all this, and over the past two years particularly, there was an unprecedented increase in debt and deficit due to disruptions in the supply of Egyptian gas, which cost us till now around US$4 billion in additional annual deficit and debt for the past two years. Even the support from our brothers in Saudi Arabia during the last year—and we are extremely grateful to them—barely covered the additional deficit resulting from the disruption in Egyptian gas supply in 2011.

Therefore, we have to be objective and uphold the truth when we interpret things, and be honest in our words.

We believe in the opposition's right to be an active and genuine partner in the political process, steering away from opportunism and empty slogans, and from manipulating economic hardships and people's sentiments. But no group is allowed to claim that they hold a monopoly over the truth and that they represent all Jordanians.

The opposition's role, as I envisage it, is to have a vision and practical programmes, to participate in Parliament, so that it can carry out its legislative mandate and oversight role in monitoring parliamentary governments.

My brothers and sisters,

A small group of those in top decisionmaking posts, responsible for policies, programmes and temporary laws, some of whom have even benefitted from providing consultancy and legal services, we see them today criticise policies and decisions and defend their experiences and performances, although they are the ones who formulated, at their complete discretion, these same programmes, policies and laws that they are today criticising. So does this mean that when they are in a position of responsibility, everything is alright and rosy, but when they are out of these positions, everything becomes wrong and bleak?

Let us speak frankly today about some slogans raised by a limited number of protesters—"overthrow the regime"—and it is regrettable that some very limited number of the "herak" protestors have raised this slogan. Let us pause and cross the t's and dot the i's.

First, what is the "regime"? The regime is the state in all its institutions and agencies, under the umbrella of the Constitution. The regime is the values and the principles these institutions and agencies are founded upon. The regime is also the cadres who operate such institutions, which actually encompass all segments and components of our Jordanian society. No one has a monopoly over the components of the state. The regime is the organisations and citizens. Every individual in this society is part of the regime. This country, which only relies on its people and their determination, has managed to overcome the impossible through unforgettable sacrifices. This Jordanian state is not the accomplishment of a single individual, or a single entity or party—it is the cumulative achievement of every Jordanian across generations.

If the intention behind these slogans was to undermine the Hashemite umbrella of this country, then let me be absolutely clear: Governing for us

Hashemites was never at any point a gain that we sought, but rather a responsibility, a duty and a sacrifice that we have been carrying out in the service of this nation and in defence of its causes and interests—a cause to which we have offered many martyrs. Moreover, governing was never for us about holding a monopoly over authority, nor about power and its tools, but about supporting state institutions run by Jordanians from all segments of society, according to the provisions of our Constitution.

This is the path we have adhered to since the time of our greatgrand-father, the founder of the nation, and to this very day.

As for me, personally, Abdullah ibn Al Hussein, I will continue true to this path. Being king to me is not a gain I seek, it is a responsibility, "for only to Allah belongs all dominion." What I cherish the most is the honour of being a descendant of our forefather Prophet Mohammad (PBUH). After this honourable lineage and what it entails in terms of commitments, I am honoured to be a Jordanian and to share with this noble and genuine people their stances and great sacrifices. After this, comes my duty to shoulder my responsibilities and foster the interests of my people and my beloved country. Al Hussein, may God bless his soul, taught me and taught us all that pleasing God and serving this country are our sole purpose in this life. You all know that I am the son of the Jordan Armed Forces and the Arab Army this Army that is made of all elements of our Jordanian society. In this Army, I have spent my youth, between Zarqa, Qatraneh, the Badia, and every other place in Jordan. Hence, I know my people, I have lived amongst them like one of them, I know their concerns, their ambitions and since the first day that I was honoured to serve in the Arab Army, I have dedicated myself to the service of my country, which deserves the best from each of us, and all that we can give.

My brothers and sisters,

Sons and daughters of the one large Jordanian family,

I call on you all to take part in the upcoming elections, so that we can achieve the desired change and reform, and to stand united in the face of those who try to undermine the achievements of the Jordanian state or threaten its unity, or thwart its progress, or jeopardise the country's security and stability.

The path is open in front of all, including those in the opposition, to be in the next Parliament. The path of political participation remains open to all segments of society, to all those who are truly concerned about Jordan's interests, in deeds and not only in words. I'm certain that the future that we seek for our people and future generations will be bright, God willing.

My brothers and sisters,

As we are about to celebrate Eid Al Adha, I would like to congratulate you, the sons and daughters of our beloved Jordan, on this blessed occasion.

Kullu 'am wantum bikheir.

God's peace and mercy be upon you.

Source: *Remarks by His Majesty King Abdullah II During a Gathering with National Public Figures, Amman, Jordan*. Available at: http://kingabdullah.jo/index.php/en_US/speeches/view/id/507/videoDisplay/0.html (accessed 21 October 2016. Inaccessible since 2021, saved as a pdf by author).

Appendix 2: Speech of HM King Hamad bin Isa Al Khalifa on 23rd November

Your Highnesses, Excellencies,

Professor Mahmoud Cherif Bassiouni, Chair of the Commission,

Distinguished Commissioners,

Ladies and Gentlemen,

Distinguished Guests,

Having heard the important speech of the Chair of the Independent Commission of Inquiry, we extend our sincere thanks to the Chair and the Commissioners, as well as their staff, for their remarkable efforts. You merit our deep appreciation. Your Report is of profound value to us. By taking to heart your findings and recommendations, the people of Bahrain can make this day one that will be remembered in the history of this nation.

Your Report deals with controversial matters of importance. You have sought to establish the true facts of a period of painful unrest which has affected all of us. You have understood the unprecedented challenges faced by our authorities as they confronted relentless provocation, from hostile sources both inside and outside the country. You have recognised the need for our authorities re-establish public order in the face of violence and intimidation against ordinary people as well as against the essential institutions of this nation. At the same time, you have also identified serious shortcomings on the part of some organs of our Government, particularly in failing to prevent instances of excessive force and of the mistreatment of persons placed under arrest.

Some may wonder why we asked a commission of foreign experts to examine the events of February and March 2011 and their subsequent ramifications. The answer is that any Government which has a sincere desire for reform and progress understands the benefit of objective and constructive criticism.

There are many examples of this around the world. For example, in Europe, we see that the leading national governments are routinely criticised by external institutions which they have themselves created. The European Court of Human Rights frequently sanctions European States for violations of human rights. Leading European powers, notwithstanding their long traditions of human rights, have been condemned in literally hundreds of cases for denial of justice, and for the torture and ill treatment of detainees.

And yet the governments of these countries do not denounce the European Court. They do not protest or boycott the judges who have criticised them. To the contrary, they are grateful to the Court for having identified the ways in which they must improve if they are to be in harmony with international law and morality. Nor does the international community conclude that these are oppressive governments. They are seen to follow a path of wisdom, acknowledging that they benefit from neutral investigations and from trusting their own capacity to use criticism constructively in the interest of their people.

The question is then, Members of the Commission: what will we do with your Report, so that we derive maximum benefit from it?

The answer is that we are determined, God willing, to ensure that the painful events our beloved nation has just experienced are not repeated, but that we learn from them, and use our new insights as a catalyst for positive change.

We do not want, ever again, to see our country paralysed by intimidation and sabotage. We do not want, ever again, to learn that our expatriate work-force, which makes such valuable contributions to the development of our nation, has been repeatedly terrorised by racist gangs. We do not want, ever again, to see civilians tried anywhere else but in the ordinary courts. We do not want, ever again, to experience the murder of policemen and the persecution of their families for the work they do in protecting us all; nor do we want, ever again, to discover that any of our law enforcement personnel have mistreated anyone.

Therefore, we must reform our laws so that they are consistent with international standards to which Bahrain is committed by treaties. Even before receiving your Report, we have introduced proposals to amend our laws to give greater protection to the valuable right of free speech; and to expand the definition of "torture" to ensure that all forms of ill treatment are sanctioned by our criminal laws. Both of these proposals would place our laws in full conformity with international human rights standards. We have addressed issues of due process in criminal trials, in particular for the medical professionals who are now being re-tried in ordinary courts. We have reviewed, and are continuing to review, the circumstances of job dismissals and expulsions from educational institutions. In addition to retrials and reinstatement, affected persons have access to a range of remedies, including the newly established Victims Compensation Fund.

And of course, as I said on the day your Commission was established, we do not tolerate the mistreatment of detainees and prisoners. We are dismayed to find that it has occurred, as your Report has found, and we will not accept any excuse based on national exceptionalism.

Distinguished Members of the Commission,

Your Report is lengthy and detailed. We must study it with the care it deserves. As a first step, a working group of members of the Government will immediately be asked to conduct an in-depth reflection on your findings and recommendations. This working group will then urgently propose concrete responses to your recommendations. We intend to waste no time in benefitting from your work. Your Report provides an historic opportunity for Bahrain to deal with matters that are both serious and urgent. Officials who have not been up to their task must be held accountable, and be replaced. Above all, we must conceive and implement reforms that satisfy all segments of our population. That is the only way to achieve reconciliation, to heal the fractures in our society. In order to ensure that there is no return to unacceptable practices once the Commission has left Bahrain, we have decided to engage international organizations and eminent individuals to assist and advise our law enforcement agencies, and to improve their procedures.

We trust that all will understand that this day, this day which turns a new page of history, has been made possible by the grace of God and because we have had the confidence to resort to an objective and impartial body. To repeat: the nations of Europe are routinely held accountable before the European Court in Strasbourg. That Court, through its hundreds of judgments, has set the standards for modern international human rights. The same is true of the Inter-American Court of Human Rights in Costa Rica. The whole world benefits from the jurisprudence of these Courts.

Surely, this shows us that there is something missing. Surely, the Arab nations, with our ancient transitions of fairness and justice, also have something to contribute. Surely, we too need to show that our officials are subject to a higher law, and that we can be proud of our traditions of respect for human rights.

Bahrain was an immediate supporter of the Arab Charter of Human Rights 15 years ago, but in truth this text has not created a system like those of Europe and the Americas. I will propose to our fellow Arab states that we now move concretely toward the creation of an Arab Court of Human Rights to take its proper place on the international stage.

The Kingdom of Bahrain assumes its international responsibilities seriously. Indeed, it has taken the initiative to contribute to collective international action by providing facilities for multilateral organisations. In 2009, during the visit of Mr. Ban Ki-moon, Secretary-General of the United Nations, we dedicated a significant plot of land in our Capital, Manama, to serve the community of the United Nations; it now houses a regional office of the UN Development Programme. We would welcome other UN agencies, perhaps, for example, by the establishment of a regional office of the UN Office on Drugs and Crime.

Such international cooperation will of course not replace national initiatives. Just the day before yesterday, we announced that the National Institution for Human Rights is henceforth established as an independent body possessing its own organic law, to operate in accordance with the Paris Principles, which embody international human-rights standards relevant to the functioning of national institutions.

As for the Government's responses to the findings and recommendations of your Report, I say again that they involve fundamental issues, and must be dealt with urgently.

All of this being said, we cannot fail to extend our gratitude to our armed forces and law enforcement agencies who restored public order in the face of intimidation and violence; to our GCC allies who participated in protecting key installations by deploying the Peninsula Shield Force, without any confrontation with civilians; and to the multitude of ordinary Bahrainis who took a stand against the forces of violence and sectarian division.

We have every sympathy for those who sincerely and peacefully seek reforms within a pluralistic society where the rights of all are respected, but not for those who seek to impose totalitarian rule. Our desire for liberal reform goes hand in hand with our deep disappointment, after having extended so many times a hand of friendship toward the Islamic Republic of Iran, by the around-the-clock broadcasts in the Arabic language by Iranian state-controlled radio and television stations, inciting our population to engage in acts of violence, sabotage, and insurrection. Iran's propaganda fuelled the flames of sectarian strife—an intolerable interference in our internal affairs from which Bahrain has suffered greatly. As you have just correctly said, Chair of the Commission, the Government of Bahrain was not in a position to provide evidence of links between Iran and specific events in our country this year. But this propaganda, an objective fact to be observed by all who have eyes and ears and comprehend Arabic, not only directly challenges the stability and sovereignty of our country, but also poses a threat to the security and stability of the GCC countries. We hope that the Iranian leadership will reflect, and abandon this policy of enmity and discord.

We affirm our commitment to ensuring the safety and security of our nation and its people, and our commitment to reform, and to the rectification of errors in all transparency. We urge all our people to reflect upon their own attitude and intentions, to address their mistakes, and to do their civic duty to contribute to national unity within a community characterised by tolerance. Our highest objective, after pleasing God, is to promote brotherhood, harmony, and tolerance among all our people, within the environment of a pluralistic, cohesive, and prosperous society; a society that guarantees the rule of law and human rights; a society that ensures the tranquil pursuit of opportunities and fulfillment for everyone.

We thank you all for joining us here on this historic day for our beloved nation.

Source: http://www.bici.org.bh/indexc971.html?news=speech-of-hm-king-hamad-bin-isa-al-khalifa-on-23rd-november.

Appendix 3: Egypt Unrest: Full Text of Hosni Mubarak's Speech

I am addressing the youth of Egypt today in Tahrir Square and across the country. I am addressing you all from the heart, a father's dialogue with his sons and daughters.

I am proud of you as the new Egyptian generation calling for a change to the better, dreaming and making the future.

First and foremost, I am telling you that the blood of your martyrs and injured will not go in vain. I assure you that I will not relent in harshly punishing those responsible. I will hold those who persecuted our youth accountable with the maximum deterrent sentences.

I tell the families of those innocent victims that I suffered plenty for them, as much as they did. My heart was in pain because of what happened to them, as much as it pained their hearts.

I am telling you that heeding to your voice, your message and demands is an irretraceable commitment.

I am determined to live up to my promises with all firmness and honesty and I am totally determined to implement (them), without hesitation or reconsideration.

This commitment springs from a strong conviction that your intentions are honest and pure and your action. Your demands are just and legitimate demands.

The mistakes can be made in any political system and in any state. But, the most important is to recognise them and correct them as soon as possible and bring to account those who have committed them.

I am telling you that as a president I find no shame in listening to my country's youth and interacting with them.

The big shame and embarrassment, which I have not done and never will do, would be listening to foreign dictations whatever may be the source or pretext.

'Defined Vision'

My sons, the youth of Egypt, brother citizens, I have unequivocally declared that I will not run for president in the next elections, satisfied with what I've offered my country in over 60 years during war and peace.

I declared my commitment to that, as well as my equal commitment to carrying out my responsibility in protecting the constitution and the people's interests until power and responsibility are handed over to whoever is elected in next September, following free and candid elections with guarantees of freedom and candour.

This is the oath I took before God and my country and one which I will keep until we take Egypt and its people to a safe harbour.

I have set a defined vision to come out of this crisis and to carry out what the citizens and the youth have called for in a way which would respect the constitutional legitimacy and not undermine it.

It will be carried out in a way that would bring stability to our society and achieve the demands of its youth, and, at the same time, propose an agreedupon framework for a peaceful transfer of power through responsible dialogue with all factions of society and with utmost sincerity and transparency.

I presented this vision, committed to my responsibility in getting the nation out of these difficult times and continuing to achieve it first, hour by hour, anticipating the support and assistance of all those who are concerned about Egypt and its people, so that we succeed in transforming it (the vision) into to a tangible reality, according to a broad and national agreement with a large base, with the courageous military forces guaranteeing its implementation.

We have started indeed building a constructive national dialogue, including the Egyptian youths who led the calls for change, and all political forces. This dialogue has resulted in a tentative agreement of opinions and positions, putting our feet at the start of the right track to get out of the crisis and must continue to take it from the broad lines on what has been agreed upon to a clear road map and with a fixed agenda.

From now to next September, day after day, we'll see the peaceful transition of power.

'Constitutional Reforms'

This national dialogue has focused on the setting up of a constitutional committee that will look into the required amendments of the constitution and the needed legislative reforms.

It (the dialogue) also met about the setting up of a followup committee expected to follow up the sincere implementation of the promises that I have made before the people.

I have made sure that the composition of the two committees is made of Egyptian figures that are known for their independence and experience, experts in constitutional law and judges.

In addition to that, the loss of the martyrs of the sons of Egypt in sad and tragic events has hurt our hearts and shaken the homeland's conscience.

I immediately issued my instructions to complete the investigation about last week's events (the clashes between pro and antiMubarak demonstrators) and submit its results immediately to the general prosecutor for him to take the necessary legal deterrent measures.

Yesterday, I got the first report on the top priority constitutional amendments proposed by the committee of justice system and law experts and that I have set up to look into the required constitutional and legislative amendments.

In response to the proposals in the committee's report, and in compliance with the prerogatives of the president of the republic, in conformity with Article 189 of the constitution, I have submitted a request today asking for the amendment of six constitutional clauses: 76, 77, 88, 93 and 189, in addition to the annulment of clause 179.

Moreover, I am asserting my readiness to submit, at a later time, an (additional) request to change any other clauses referred to me by the constitutional committee, according to the needs and justifications it sees fit.

These toppriority amendments aim to ease the conditions for presidential nominations, and the fixing of limited terms of presidency to ensure the rotation of power, and the strengthening of the regulations of elections oversight to guarantee their freedom and fairness.

It is in the judiciary's prerogative to decide about the validity and membership of MPs and amend the conditions and measures on the amendment of the constitution.

The proposal to delete Article 179 from the constitution aims to achieve the required balance between the protection of the nation from the dangers of terrorism and safeguarding the civil rights and freedoms of the citizens which opens the door to the lifting of the emergency law following the return of calm and stability and the presence of suitable conditions to lift the state of emergency.

'In One Trench'

Brother citizens, the priority now is to bring back trust between Egyptians, trust in our economy and our international reputation, and trust in protecting the change and movement that we have started from turning back or retreating.

Egypt is going through difficult times which it is not right for us to allow continuing, as it will continue to cause us and our economy harm and losses, day after day, which will end in circumstances which those youths who called for change and reform will become the first to be harmed by.

The current moment is not to do with myself, it is not to do with Hosni Mubarak, but is to do with Egypt, its present and the future of its children.

All Egyptians are in one trench now, and it is on us to continue the national dialogue which we have started, with a team spirit, not one of division, and far from disagreement and infighting so that we can get Egypt past its current crisis, and to restore trust in our economy, and tranquillity and peace to our citizens, and return the Egyptian street to its normal everyday life.

I was as young as Egypt's youth today, when I learned the Egyptian military honour, allegiance and sacrifice for my country.

I have spent a lifetime defending its soil and sovereignty. I witnessed its wars, with its defeats and victories.

I lived the days of defeat and occupation, I also lived the days of the (Suez) crossing, victory and liberation.

It was the happiest day of my life when I raised the flag of Egypt over Sinai.

I faced death many times as a pilot, in Addis Ababa, and numerous other times. I never succumbed to foreign pressure or dictations.

I kept the peace. I worked towards the stability and security of Egypt. I worked hard for its revival and for its people.

I never sought power or fake popularity. I trust that the overwhelming majority of the people know who Hosni Mubarak is. It pains me to see how some of my countrymen are treating me today.

'Immortal Identity'

In any case, I am completely aware of the seriousness of the current hard turn of events as I am convinced that Egypt is crossing a landmark point in its history which imposes on all to weigh in the higher interests of our country and to put Egypt first above any and all considerations.

I saw fit to delegate presidential jurisdictions to the vicepresident as defined by the constitution. I am certain that Egypt will overcome its crisis.

The will of its people will not break. It will be back on its feet with the honesty and loyalty of its people, all its people.

It will return the machinations and glee of those who were gleeful and machinated against it.

We, Egyptians, will prove our ability to achieve the demands of the people with civilised and mature dialogue.

We will prove that we are noone's servants, that we do not take instructions from anyone, and that only the demands of the citizens and the pulse of the street take our decisions.

We will prove all this with the spirit and tenacity of Egyptians, through the unity and cohesion of the people, and through our commitment to Egypt's dignity as well as its unique and immortal identity, for it is the essence and the base of our presence for more than 7,000 years.

This spirit will continue to live within us for as long as Egypt and its people are present. It will live in every one of our peasants, workers and intellectuals. It will remain in the hearts of our old men, our youth and our children, Muslims and Christians. It will remain in the minds and conscience of all those yet unborn.

I say again that I lived for the sake of this country, preserving its responsibility and trust. Egypt will remain above all and above everyone.

It will remain so until I hand over this trust and pole. This is the goal, the objective, the responsibility and the duty. It is the beginning of life, its journey, and its end.

It will remain a country dear to my heart. It will not part with me and I will not part with it until my passing.

Egypt will remain immortal with its dignified people with their heads held high. May God preserve the safety of Egypt and watch over its people.

May peace be upon you.

Source: http://www.bbc.co.uk/news/world-middle-east-12427091.

Appendix 4: The Last Official Address of Ben Ali

People of Tunisia:

I am speaking to you today, everyone, both inside and outside Tunisia. I speak to you in the language of Tunisians. I am speaking to you now because the situation demands deep change. Yes, deep and comprehensive change.

I have understood you. Yes, I have understood you. I have understood everyone: the unemployed, the needy, the politician, and those demanding more freedoms. I have understood you. I have understood you all. However, the events currently taking place in our country are not part of us. Vandalism is not part of the customs of Tunisians—civilized Tunisians, tolerant Tunisians.

Violence is not part of us, nor is it part of our conduct. This trend must stop, with the concerted efforts of everyone: political parties, national organizations, civil society, intellectuals and citizens. Hand in hand, for the sake of our country. Hand in hand for the sake of all our children's security.

The change I am announcing now is in response to your demands, to which we have reacted. We have felt deep pain at what has occurred.

My sadness and pain are great, for I have spent more than fifty years of my life in the service of Tunisia, in different positions: from the National Army to various other responsibilities, and twenty-three years as head of state. Every day of my life has been and continues to be in the service of the country. I have offered sacrifices, which I do not like to recount as you all know them, and I have never accepted, and do not accept still, the shedding of a single drop of Tunisian blood.

We felt pain for the victims who fell and the persons who suffered damage, and I refuse to see more fall as a result of the continuation of violence and looting.

Our children today have stayed home and did not go to school. This is a shame and a disgrace, because we have become fearful for them from the violence perpetrated by gangs who have robbed and looted and assaulted people. This is a crime, not protest. This is abhorrent. The citizens, all citizens, must stand up to them. We have issued instructions, and we rely on everyone's cooperation, to distinguish between these gangs and groups of deviants who are taking advantage of the circumstances, and peaceful, legitimate protests, to which we do not object.

My sadness is very great and very deep. Very profound. Enough with violence! Enough with violence!

I have also issued instructions to the interior minister, and I have repeated, and today I confirm: do not use live ammunition. Live ammunition is not acceptable. It is not justified, unless, God forbid, someone tries to disarm you or attacks you with a firearm, or the like, and forces you to defend yourself.

I ask that the independent commission—I repeat, the independent commission, which will investigate the incidents and the abuses and the regrettable deaths—to delineate the responsibilities of all sides, without exception, in all fairness, integrity and objectivity.

We expect every Tunisian, those who support us and those who do not, to support the efforts to restore calm and to abandon violence, vandalism, and depravation. Reform requires calm. The incidents that we have witnessed were at the outset protests against social conditions, which we had made great efforts to fix, but we still require greater efforts to redress shortcomings. We all have to give ourselves the chance and the time required for all our important measures to materialize.

In addition, I have tasked the government—I called the prime minister —to reduce the prices of basic commodities and foodstuffs—sugar, milk, bread, etc.

As for political demands. I told you that I have understood you. Yes, I told you that I have understood you. And I have decided on full freedom for the media, in all its forms, and not shutting down Internet sites, and rejecting any form of censorship on them, while ensuring the respect of our morals and the principles of the journalistic profession.

As for the commission that I announced two days ago to look into corruption, bribery, and the mistakes of officials, this commission will be independent—yes, independent—and we will ensure its fairness and integrity.

The field is open, from this day onward, for freedom of political expression, including peaceful demonstrations—organized and orderly peaceful demonstrations, civilized demonstrations. That is fine. If a party or an organization wishes to organize a peaceful demonstration, they are welcome. But they should notify [us] of it, set its time and place, and organize it, and cooperate with the responsible parties to preserve its peaceful character.

I would like to assure you that many things did not happen the way I would have liked them to. Especially in the areas of democracy and freedoms. Sometimes, some misled me, by hiding the truth from me, and they will be held accountable. Yes, they will be held accountable.

Therefore, I reiterate to you, in all clarity, that I will work to promote democracy and to put pluralism into effect. Yes, to promote democracy and to put pluralism into effect.

And I will work to preserve and respect the country's constitution. And I'd like to reiterate here, in contrast to what some have claimed, that I have pledged, on November 7, that there would be no presidency for life. No presidency for life. Therefore, I renew thanks to all who have urged me to renominate myself in 2014, but I refuse to violate the age condition for candidacy for the presidency of the republic.

We want to reach the year 2014 in a framework of genuine civil consensus, and an atmosphere of national dialogue, with the participation of all national parties in assuming responsibilities.

Tunisia is the country of all of us. The country of all Tunisians. We love Tunisia and all of her people love her. We must protect her.

Let the will of her people remain in its hands and in the faithful hands that it will choose to continue the journey that began since independence and that we have continued since 1987.

To that end, we will set up a national commission headed by an independent national personality, with credibility among all the social and political parties, in order to review the electoral code, the press code, and the law of associations, etc. The commission will suggest the necessary provisional ideas until the 2014 elections, including the possibility of separating legislative elections and presidential elections.

Tunisia belongs to us all. Let us all preserve her. Her future is in our hands. Let us all safeguard it. Each one of us is responsible, from their position, for restoring her security, her stability, and for healing her wounds, and for ushering her into a new era that would better enable her to have a brighter future.

Long live Tunisia. Long live her people. Long live the republic. May peace and God's grace be upon you.

Source: https://msmunatunagb.wikispaces.com/file/view/The+Last+Official+Address+of+Ben+Ali.pdf (accessed 20 November 2017. Inaccessible since 2021, saved as a pdf by author).

Bibliography

Primary Data

Abdullah II, H. M. (2012a, October). *Remarks by His Majesty King Abdullah II During a Gathering with National Public Figures, Amman, Jordan*. Available at: http://kingabdullah.jo/index.php/en_US/speeches/view/id/507/videoDisplay/0.html (accessed 21 October 2016. Inaccessible since 2021, saved as a pdf by author).

Abdullah II, H. M. (2012b, December). *Remarks by His Majesty King Abdullah II on the Occasion of the University of Jordan's 50th Anniversary*. Available at: https://kingabdullah.jo/en/speeches/occasion-university-jordan%E2%80%99s-50th-anniversary (accessed 24 January 2022).

Abdulsalam, A. (2011). خطاب زين العابدين بن علي 13 جانفي 2011 [audio]. Available at: https://soundcloud.com/lr5qtaoy0ycg/13-2011 (accessed 13 January 2022).

Al Jazeera. (2011). نص خطاب مبارك للشعب المصري. Available at: https://www.aljazeera.net/news/arabic/2011/2/11/%D9%86%D8%B5-%D8%AE%D8%B7%D8%A7%D8%A8-%D9%85%D8%A8%D8%A7%D8%B1%D9%83-%D9%84%D9%84%D8%B4%D8%B9%D8%A8-%D8%A7%D9%84%D9%85%D8%B5%D8%B1%D9%8A (accessed 13 January 2022).

Al Jazeera. (2019). دستور مصر 1971. Available at: https://www.aljazeera.net/encyclopedia/events/2015/12/7/%D8%AF%D8%B3%D8%AA%D9%88%D8%B1-%D9%85%D8%B5%D8%B1-1971 (accessed 14 January 2022).

Babnet. (2011). زين العابدين بن علي: أنا فهمتكم. Available at: https://www.babnet.net/cadredetail-31940.asp (accessed 13 January 2022).

Bahrain Independent Commission of Inquiry. (2011). *Speech of HM King Hamad bin Isa Al Khalifa on 23rd November*. Available at: http://www.bici.org.bh/indexc971.html?news=speech-of-hm-king-hamad-bin-isa-al-khalifa-on-23rd-november (accessed 12 January 2022).

N. Due-Gundersen, *Non-Democratic Legitimacy During the Arab Spring*, https://doi.org/10.1007/978-3-031-11882-1

BBC. (2011). *Bahrain Independent Commission of Inquiry Excerpts*. Available at: https://www.bbc.co.uk/news/world-middle-east-15861353 (accessed 16 January 2022).

BBC Arabic. (2011). مبارك يتنحى عن منصبه والجيش يتولى ادارة البلاد. Available at: http://www.bbc.com/arabic/middleeast/2011/02/110211_egypt_protests_mubarak_army.shtml (accessed 13 March 2019).

Ben Ali, Z. (1987). *Speech to the Tunisian parliament by Zine el Abidine Ben Ali on 7 November 1987 After President Bourguiba Was Declared Unfit to Govern*. Available at: http://al-bab.com/documents-section/tunisia-overthrow-bourguiba (accessed 30 January 2022).

Ben Ali, Z. (2010). *Tunisia: Speech by President Ben Ali*. Available at: http://al-bab.com/documents-section/tunisia-speech-president-ben-ali-0 (accessed 4 April 2017).

Ben Ali, Z. (2011). *The Last Official Address by Tunisian President Zine el-Abidine Ben Ali* (T. Badran, Trans.). Available at: https://msmunatunagb.wikispaces.com/file/view/The+Last+Official+Address+of+Ben+Ali.pdf (accessed 20 November 2017. Inaccessible since 2021, saved as a pdf by author).

Ben Ali, Z. (2015). *Speech to the Tunisian Parliament by Zine el Abidine Ben Ali on 7 November 1987 After President Bourguiba Was Declared Unfit to Govern*. Available at: http://al-bab.com/albab-orig/albab/arab/docs/tunisia/declaration_07111987.htm (accessed 11 November 2021).

British Broadcasting Corporation. (2011). *Egypt Unrest: Full Text of Hosni Mubarak's Speech*. Available at: http://www.bbc.co.uk/news/world-middle-east-12427091 (accessed 12 October 2021).

Constitute Project. (2002). *Bahrain's Constitution of 2002*. Available at: https://www.constituteproject.org/constitution/Bahrain_2002.pdf (accessed 3 December 2021).

Constitute Project. (2011). دستور الأردن الصادر عام 1952 شاملا تعديلاته لغاية عام 2011. Available at: https://www.constituteproject.org/constitution/Jordan_2011.pdf?lang=ar (accessed 14 January 2022).

Constitute Project. (2018). *Jordan's Constitution of 1952 with Amendments Through 2011*. Available at: https://www.constituteproject.org/constitution/Jordan_2011.pdf (accessed 12 October 2021).

Constitution Net. (2016). *The Constitution of the Arab Republic of Egypt, 1971 (as Amended to 2007)*. Available at: http://www.constitutionnet.org/sites/default/files/Egypt%20Constitution.pdf (accessed 3 January 2022).

Facebook. (2017). *Personal Correspondence with Student from University of Jordan* (on file with author).

Food and Agriculture Organization of the United Nations. (2008). *Keynote Speech of H.E. Mrs Suzanne Mubarak on the Occasion of the World Food Day Ceremony. "World Food Security: the Challenges of Climate Change and Bio-energy"*. FAO.

Available at: http://www.fao.org/fileadmin/user_upload/newsroom/docs/mubarak.pdf (accessed 12 October 2021).

Gaddafi, M. (2015). *Communique Number One by Muammar Al Gaddafi, 1969, September 1st*. Available at: http://english.algaddafi.org/4/post/2015/07/communique-number-one-by-muammar-al-gaddafi-1969-september-1st.html (last accessed 11 November 2021).

International Constitutional Law. (2010). *Saudi Arabia—Constitution*. Available at: http://www.servat.unibe.ch/icl/sa00000_.html (accessed 17 January 2022).

International Constitutional Law Countries. (2002). *Bahrain Constitution*. Available at: http://www.servat.unibe.ch/icl/ba00000_.html (accessed 3 January 2022).

Kingdom of Bahrain: Ministry of Foreign Affairs. (2012). *HM King Hamad: Bahrain Will Always Remain a Nation Where the Culture of Tolerance*. Available at: https://www.mofa.gov.bh/Default.aspx?tabid=7824&language=en-US&ItemId=2203 (accessed 26 January 2022).

Kingdom of Bahrain Shura Council. (2002). دستور مملكة البحرين. Available at: http://www.shura.bh/ar/legislativeresource/constitution/pages/default.aspx (accessed 14 January 2022).

LyanOran. (2011). خطاب زين العابدين بن علي 13 جانفي 2011 [film]. Available at: https://www.youtube.com/watch?v=2AQm45CGcHo (accessed 13 January 2022).

Mubarak TV. (2014). خطاب الرئيس مبارك يوم 10 فبراير 2011 [video]. Available at: https://www.youtube.com/watch?v=ySQp73bZA6o (accessed 13 March 2019).

National Media Authority. (2014). خطاب الرئيس مبارك يوم 10 فبراير 2011 [video]. Available at: https://www.youtube.com/watch?v=9_06qCKV3bE (accessed 13 January 2022).

New York Times. (2011, February 11). Text of Omar Suleiman's Address. Available at: http://www.nytimes.com/2011/02/12/world/middleeast/12-suleiman-speech-text.html (accessed 21 January 2022).

Official Printing Office of the Republic of Tunisia. (2010a). دستور الجمهورية التونسية, 1959. Publications of the Official Printing Office of the Republic of Tunisia.

Official Printing Office of the Republic of Tunisia. (2010b). *Constitution of the Republic of Tunisia*. Available at: http://www.tunisie-constitution.org/sites/all/downloads/constitution-tunisienne-anglais.pdf (accessed 3 January 2022).

Omanoganees. (2011). خطاب حسنى مبارك 10 فبراير 2011 الجزء الأول [video]. Available at: https://www.youtube.com/watch?v=JBBLWSXRCWs (accessed 13 January 2022).

Palataurus Center of Studies. (2007). *Constitution of the Arab Republic of Egypt, 1971*. Available at: http://constitutions.albasio.eu/constitution/?id=19 (accessed 26 November 2021).

RHC JO. (2012). *His Majesty King Abdullah II Remarks During a Gathering with National Public Figures at the Royal Hashemite Court on 23 October 2012* [video]. Available at: https://www.youtube.com/watch?v=Bf60Ft2B6HQ (accessed 14 February 2022).

Saleh, Y., & Zayed, D. (2011). *Highlights: Egyptian President Hosni Mubarak's Speech.* Available at: https://www.reuters.com/article/us-egypt-mubarak-speech/highlights-egyptian-president-hosni-mubaraks-speech-idUSTRE70S0SA20110129 (accessed 24 January 2022).

Voltaire Network. (2014). *Inaugural Speech of President Assad.* Available at: https://www.voltairenet.org/article184784.html (accessed 22 January 2022).

Warden, P. (2011). *Gadhafi's Speech Transcript.* Available at: https://petewarden.com/2011/02/26/gadhafis-speech-transcript/ (accessed 12 January 2022).

Secondary Data

Academic Reports/Papers

al-Anani, K., & Mali, M. (2013). Pious Way to Politics: The Rise of Political Salafism in Post- Mubarak Egypt. *DOMES: Digest of Middle East Studies, 22*(1), 57–73.

al-Awadi, H. (2005). Mubarak and the Islamists: Why Did the "Honeymoon" End? *Middle East Journal, 59*(1), 62–80.

al-Jawadi, K. H., & Abdul-Majeed, R. K. (2007). Modification of Searle's Speech Act of Promising in Its Application to Selected Religious and Political Texts. *Journal of College of Education for Women, 18*(1), 287–300.

al-Khawaja, M. (2014). Crackdown: The Harsh Realities of Nonviolent Protests in the Bahraini Civil Conflict. *Journal of International Affairs, 68*(1), 189–201.

al-Majali, W. (2015). Discourse Analysis of the Political Speeches of the Ousted Arab Presidents During the Arab Spring Revolution Using Halliday and Hasan's Framework of Cohesion. *Journal of Education and Practice, 6*(14), 96–108.

al-Rawi, A. K. (2015). Sectarianism and the Arab Spring: Framing the Popular Protests in Bahrain. *Global Media and Communication, II*(I), 25–42.

al-Sowaidi, B., Banda, F., & Mansour, A. (2017). Doing Politics in the Recent Arab Uprisings: Towards a Political Discourse Analysis of the Arab Spring Slogans. *Journal of Asian and African Studies, 52*(5), 621–645.

Ahmed, R., Coşgel, M., & Miceli, T. (2009). *Law, State Power and Taxation in Islamic History.* Available at: https://www.academia.edu/21412100/Law_state_power_and_taxation_in_Islamic_history?auto=download (accessed 13 January 2022).

Ahram, A. I., & Lust, E. (2016). The Decline and Fall of the Arab State. *Survival, 58*(2), 7–34.

Ahy, M. H. (2018). Networked Communication and the Arab Spring: Linking Broadcast and Social Media. *New Media & Society, 18*(1), 99–116.

Akinwotu, S. A. (2013). A Speech Act Analysis of the Acceptance of Nomination Speeches of Chief Obafemi Awolowo and Chief M.K.O. Abiolo. *English Linguistics Research, 2*(1), 43–51.

Albrecht, S., & Schlumberger, O. (2004). "Waiting for Godot": Regime Change Without Democratization in the Middle East. *International Political Science Review, 25*(4), 371–392.

Alshboul, A., & Oudat, M. A. (2010). "Jordan First": Tribalism, Nationalism and Legitimacy of Power in Jordan. *Intellectual Discourse, 18*(1), 65–96.

Anderson, L. (2011). Demystifying the Arab Spring: Parsing the Differences Between Tunisia, Egypt and Libya. *Foreign Affairs, 90*(3), 1–5.

Ansari, Z. I. (1961). Contemporary Islam and Nationalism: A Case Study of Egypt. *Die Welt Das Islams, 7*(4), 3–38.

Aras, B., & Falk, R. (2015). Authoritarian 'Geopolitics' of Survival in the Arab Spring. *Third World Quarterly, 36*(2), 322–336.

Awdallah, B., & Malik, A. (2013). The Economics of the Arab Spring. *World Development, 45*, 296–313.

Ayoob, M. (2004). Political Islam: Image and Reality. *World Policy Journal, 21*(3), 1–14.

Bank, A., Richter, T., & Sunik, A. (2014). Durable yet Different: Monarchies in the Arab Spring. *Journal of Arabian Studies, 4*(2), 163–179.

Bartold, V. V. (1963). Caliph and Sultan. *Islamic Quarterly, 7*(3), 117–135.

Beetham, D., & Lord, C. (2001). Legitimizing the EU: Is There a 'Post-parliamentary Basis' for Its Legitimation? *Journal of Common Market Studies, 39*(3), 443–462.

Bellin, E. (2004). The Robustness of Authoritarianism in the Middle East: Exceptionalism in Comparative Perspective. *Comparative Politics, 36*(92), 139–157.

Bellin, E. (2012). Reconsidering the Robustness of Authoritarianism in the Middle East: Lessons from the Arab Spring. *Comparative Politics, 44*(2), 127–149.

Bërdufi, N., & Dushi, D. (2015). Social Contract and the Government's Legitimacy. *Mediterranean Journal of Social Sciences, 6*(6 S1), 392–398.

Berman, S. (2013). The Promise of the Arab Spring. In Political Development, No Gain without Pain. *Foreign Affairs, 92*(1), 64–74.

Bjorgvinsson, L. A. (2011). *Speech Act Theory: A Critical Overview*. Available at: https://skemman.is/handle/1946/8360 (accessed 9 January 2022).

Bottoni, R. (2007). The Origins of Secularism in Turkey. *Ecclesiastical Law Journal, 9*(2), 175–186.

Boyle, J. A. (1961). The Death of the Last 'Abbasid Caliph: A Contemporary Muslim Account. *Journal of Semitic Studies, 6*(2), 145–161.

Broers, A. (2009). John Locke on Equality, Toleration and the Atheist Exception. *Inquiries Journal/Student Pulse, 1*(12). Available at: http://www.inquiriesjournal.com/articles/75/john-locke-on-equality-toleration-and-the-atheist-exception (accessed 11 January 2022).

Bruns, A., Burgess, J., & Highfield, T. (2013). The Arab Spring and Social Media Audiences. *American Behavioral Scientist, 57*(7), 871–898.

Bruschi, F., & Maesschalck, M. (2015). Law and Belief: A Pragmatist Interpretation of the Althusserian Conception of Legal Ideology. *Law and Critique, 26*, 281–303.

Bulliet, R. W. (2013). *Religion and the State in Islam: From Medieval Caliphate to the Muslim Brotherhood* (Occasional Paper Series, Paper No. 2). Center for Middle East Series, University of Denver.

Burns, J. H. (2005). Happiness and Utility: Jeremy Bentham's Equation. *Utilitas, 17*(1), 46–61.

Campante, F. R., & Chor, D. (2012). Why Was the Arab World Poised for Revolution? Schooling, Economic Opportunities, and the Arab Spring. *The Journal of Economic Perspectives, 26*(2), 167–187.

Carbonnier, J. (2013). *The Arab Spring and Its Different Outcomes: Explaining the Variation in the State of Democratisation*. Available at: https://lup.lub.lu.se/student-papers/search/publication/4001341 (accessed 24 January 2022).

Cavatorta, F. (2012). *Arab Spring: The Awakening of Civil Society. A General Overview*. Available at: https://www.iemed.org/publication/arab-spring-the-awakening-of-civil-society-a-general-overview/ (accessed 11 January 2022).

Christiano, T. (2003). The Authority of Democracy. *The Journal of Political Philosophy, 11*(2), 1–25.

Culcasi, K. (2016). Warm Nationalism: Mapping and Imagining the Jordanian Nation. *Political Geography, 54*, 7–20.

Devine, J. (2000). The Positive Political Economy of Individualism and Collectivism: Hobbes, Locke, and Rosseau. *Politics & Society, 28*(2), 265–304.

Diamond, L. (2013). What Ever Happened to Bahrain? *Hoover Digest, 2*, 84–89.

Dos Santos, T. (1970). The Concept of Social Classes. *Science & Society, 34*(2), 166–193.

Dunmire, P. L. (2012). Political Discourse Analysis: Exploring the Language of Politics and the Politics of Language. *Language and Linguistics Compass, 6*(11), 735–751.

Epstein, S., & Miller, M. S. (2015). Money, Inflation and the Arab Spring in Bahrain. *European Research Studies, 18*(1), 25–42.

Fadda-Conrey, C. (2011). Arab American Citizenship in Crisis: Destabilizing Representations of Arabs and Muslims in the US After 9/11. *MFS Modern Fiction Studies, 57*(3), 532–555.

Fairclough-Ietcu, I. (2008). Legitimation and Strategic Maneuvering in the Political Field. *Argumentation, 22*, 399–417.

Gallets, B. (2015). Black September and Identity Construction in Jordan. *Journal of Georgetown University-Qatar Middle Eastern Studies Student Association, 12*, 116–124.

Gengler, J., & Lambert, A. L. (2016). Renegotiating the Ruling Bargain: Selling Fiscal Reform in the GCC. *The Middle East Journal, 70*(2), 321–329.

Gillespie, M. (2013). BBC Arabic, Social Media and Citizen Production: An Experiment in Digital Democracy Before the Arab Spring. *Theory, Culture & Society, 30*(4), 92–130.

Gilley, B. (2006). The Meaning and Measure of State Legitimacy: Results for 72 Countries. *European Journal of Political Research, 45*, 499–525.

Greenwood, S. (2003). Jordan, The Al-Aqsa Intifada and America's "War on Terror." *Middle East Policy, X*(3), 90–111.

Grigoryan, N. (2015). The Ruling Bargain: Sovereign Wealth Funds in Elite-Dominated Societies. *Economics of Governance, 17*(2), 165–184.

Grupico, T. (2011). *The Dome in Christian and Islamic Sacred Architecture.* Available at: https://go.gale.com/ps/i.do?id=GALE%7CA317588296&sid=googleScholar&v=2.1&it=r&linkaccess=abs&issn=1556763X&p=AONE&sw=w&userGroupName=anon%7Ef04e77#:~:text=The%20architects%20of%20Christian%20and,more%20directly%20from%20each%20other.&text=In%20the%20Islamic%20as%20much,articulation%20of%20a%20spiritual%20journey (accessed 10 January 2022).

Guriev, S., & Treisman, D. (2015). *How Modern Dictators Survive: An Informational Theory of the New Authoritarianism.* Available at: https://www.eui.eu/Documents/DepartmentsCentres/Economics/Seminarsevents/Guriev-Micro.pdf (accessed 17 January 2022).

Haimerl, M. (2013). *In Search of Legitimacy in Times of Crisis: Governance Transfer by the Gulf Cooperation Council (GCC)* (Berlin Working Paper on European Integration No. 18). Frei Universität Berlin.

Hamdi, H., & Sbia, R. (2013). Dynamic Relationships Between Oil Revenues, Government Spending and Economic Growth in an Oil-Dependent Economy. *Economic Modelling, 35*, 118–125.

Haqqani, H. (2012). Islamists and the "Arab Spring." *Journal of Democracy, 24*(2), 5–14.

Hatina, M. (2003). Historical Legacy and the Challenge of Modernity in the Middle East: The Case of al-Azhar in Egypt. *Muslim World, 93*(1), 51–68.

Hawkins, S. (2011). Who Wears *Hijab* with the President: Constructing a Modern Islam in Tunisia. *Journal of Religion in Africa, 41*, 35–58.

Hays, C. (2013). Political Discourse Analysis: The Dangers of Methodological Absolutism. *Political Studies Review, 11*, 321–327.

Heiss, A. (2012). The Failed Management of a Dying Regime: Hosni Mubarak, Egypt's National Democratic Party, and the January 25 Revolution. *Journal of Third World Studies, XXIX*(1), 155–171.

Herrold, C. E. (2016). NGO Policy in Pre- and Post-Mubarak Egypt: Effects on NGOs' Roles in Democracy Promotion. *Nonprofit Policy Forum, 7*(2), 189–212.

Hertog, S. (2011). Rentier Militaries in the Gulf States: The Price of Coup-Proofing. *International Journal of Middle East Studies, 43*(3), 400–402.

Ibrahim, A. (2006). *Universal Values and Muslim Democracy.* Available at: https://www.journalofdemocracy.org/articles/universal-values-and-muslim-democracy/ (accessed 13 January 2022).

Ilamaran, A. (2016, May 5). *How Republics Fell and Monarchies Survived the Arab Spring.* Available at: http://chicagopolicyreview.org/2016/05/05/how-republics-fell-and-monarchies-survived-the-arab-spring/ (accessed 15 January 2022).

Ismail, R. (2012). The Saudi Ulema and the Shi'a of Saudi Arabia. *Journal of Shi'a Islamic Studies, V*(4), 403–422.

Kamrava, M. (2013a). Introduction. In *The Evolving Ruling Bargain in the Middle East: Summary Report* (p. 1). Georgetown University Center for International and Regional Studies.

Kamrava, M. (2013b). The Rise and Fall of Ruling Bargains in the Middle East. In *The Evolving Ruling Bargain in the Middle East: Summary Report* (pp. 2–3). Georgetown University Center for International and Regional Studies.

Karateke, H. K. (2005). *Legitimizing the Ottoman Sultanate: A Framework for Historical Analysis.* Available at: https://lucian.uchicago.edu/blogs/ottomanturkish/files/2011/01/LEGITIMIZING-THE-OTTOMAN-SULTANATE.pdf (accessed 13 January 2022).

Kechichian, J. A. (1986). The Role of the Ulama in the Politics of an Islamic State: The Case of Saudi Arabia. *International Journal of Middle East Studies, 18*(1), 53–71.

Khair Bani Doumi, M. (2018). Public Freedoms in the Jordanian Constitution: Rhetorics and Realities. *Journal of Mass Communication & Journalism, 8*(4). Available at: https://www.omicsonline.org/open-access/public-freedoms-in-the-jordanian-constitution-rhetorics-and-realities-2165-7912-1000384-104185.html (accessed 2 January 2022).

Khan, S. A. (2007). *The "Caliphate Question": British Views and Policy Toward Pan-Islamic Politics and the End of the Ottoman Caliphate.* Available at: https://www.ajis.org/index.php/ajiss/article/download/427/2158 (accessed 13 January 2022).

King, S. J. (2011). *The Constitutional Monarchy Option in Morocco and Bahrain* (Policy Brief, 33).

Korany, B. (2013). Microcosms of the Arab Spring: Sociology of Tahrir Square. In *The Evolving Ruling Bargain in the Middle East: Summary Report* (pp. 19–20). Georgetown University Center for International and Regional Studies.

Kuran, T. (1998). The Vulnerability of the Arab State: Reflections on the Ayubi Thesis. *The Independent Review, III*(1), 111–123.

Lloyd, S. A. (2014). *Hobbes's Moral and Political Philosophy.* Available at: http://plato.stanford.edu/entries/hobbes-moral/#StaNatStaWar (accessed 18 January 2022).

Liden, G. (2014). Theories of Dictatorships: Sub-Types and Explanations. *Studies of Transition States and Societies, 6*(1), 50–67.

Linz, J. J., Minoves, J. F., & Stepan, A. (2014). Democratic Parliamentary Monarchies. *Journal of Democracy, 25*(2), 35–52.

Liu, Z. (2008). The Relations Between Nationalism and Islam in the Middle East. *Journal of Middle Eastern and Islamic Studies, 2*(1), 69–78.

Lucas, R. E. (2011). Is the King's Dilemma Only for Presidents? Available at: https://carnegieendowment.org/sada/43333 (accessed 24 January 2022).

Maalej, Z. A. (2012). The "Jasmine Revolt" Has Made the Arab Spring: A Critical Discourse Analysis of the Last Three Political Speeches of the Ousted President of Tunisia. *Discourse & Society, 23*(6), 679–700.

Mabon, S. (2013). Aiding Revolution? Wikileaks, Communication and the 'Arab Spring' in Egypt. *Third World Quarterly, 34*(10), 1843–1857.

Markham, T. (2014). Social Media, Protest Cultures and Political Subjectivities of the Arab Spring. *Media, Culture & Society, 36*(1), 89–104.

Maziad, M. E. (2019). *The Language of Collapsing Power: A Cognitive-Linguistic Critical Discourse Analysis of the Arab Spring Speeches of Mubarak.* Available at: https://www.repository.cam.ac.uk/handle/1810/294149 (accessed 23 January 2022).

Miles, W. F. S. (1996). Political Para-Theology: Rethinking Religion, Politics and Democracy. *Third World Quarterly, 17*(3), 525–535.

Milton-Edwards, B. (2017). *Jordan's Troubles in Its Own Backyard.* Available at: https://www.brookings.edu/blog/markaz/2017/02/22/jordans-troubles-in-its-own-backyard/ (accessed 11 January 2022).

Montag, W. (1995). "The Soul Is the Prison of the Body": Althusser and Foucault, 1970–1975. *Yale French Studies, 88*, 53–77.

Muasher, M. (2011). *Jordan's Proposed Constitutional Amendments—A First Step in the Right Direction.* Available at: https://carnegieendowment.org/2011/08/17/jordan-s-proposed-constitutional-amendments-first-step-in-right-direction-pub-45366 (accessed 11 January 2022).

Nagarajan, K. V. (2013). Egypt's Political Economy and the Downfall of the Mubarak Regime. *International Journal of Humanities and Social Science, 3* (10), 22–39.

Nassif, H. B. (2013). Wedded to Mubarak: The Second Careers and Financial Rewards of Egypt's Military Elite, 1981–2011. *Middle East Journal, 67*(4), 509–530.

Nussbaum, M. (2011). Rawls' *Political Liberalism.* A Reassessment. *Ratio Juris, 24* (1), 1–24.

Obaid, N. (2014). *A Saudi Arabian Defense Doctrine: Mapping the Extended Force Structure the Kingdom needs to lead the Arab World, Stabilize the Region, and Meet its Global Responsibilities.* Cambridge, Massachusetts: Belfer Centre for Science and International Affairs. Available at: http://www.belfercenter.org/sites/default/files/legacy/files/Saudi%20Strategic%20Doctrine%20-%20web.pdf (accessed 8 June 2017).

Paust, J. J. (2013). International Law, Dignity, Democracy and the Arab Spring. *Cornell International Law Journal, 46*(1), 1–19.

Peter, F. (2016). *Political Legitimacy.* Available at: http://plato.stanford.edu/entries/legitimacy/ (accessed 18 January 2022).

Pin, A. (2016). *The Arab Road to Dignity: The Goal of the "Arab Spring"* (Working Paper #408). Kellogg Institute for International Studies.

Plant, R. (1982). Jürgen Habermas and the Idea of Legitimation Crisis. *European Journal of Political Research, 10*(4), 341–352.

Quinn, J. J. (2009). When You Can't Find the Perfect Match: Using the Accumulated Most Similar Design in Case Studies. *Journal of Political Science Education, 5*, 250–267.

Ra'ees, W. (2004). *Asabiyyah*, Religion and Regime Types: Re-reading Ibn Khaldun. *Intellectual Discourse, 12*(2), 159–180.

Rangwala, G. (2015). The Creation of Governments In-Waiting: The Arab Uprisings and Legitimacy in the International System. *Geoforum, 66*, 215–223.

Razi, H. (1990). Legitimacy, Religion and Nationalism in the Middle East. *The American Political Science Review, 84*(1), 69–91.

Raz, J. (2006). The Problem of Authority: Revisiting the Service Conception. *Minnesota Law Review, 90*, 1003–1044.

Robinson, G. E. (1998). Defensive Democratization in Jordan. *International Journal of Middle East Studies, 30*(3), 387–410.

Rossi, E. (2014). Legitimacy and Consensus in Rawls' Political Liberalism. *Iride: Filosofia e discussione pubblica, 27*(1), 1–23.

Ryan, C. R. (2004). "Jordan First": Jordan's Inter-Arab Relations and Foreign Policy Under King Abdullah II. *Arab Studies Quarterly, 26*(3), 43–62.

Ryan, C. R., & Schwedler, J. (2004). Return to Democratization or New Hybrid Regime?: The 2003 Elections in Jordan. *Middle East Policy, 11*(2), 138–151.

Sadiki, L. (2002a). Bin Ali's Tunisia: Democracy by Non-democratic Means. *British Journal of Middle East Studies, 29*(1), 57–78.

Sadiki, L. (2002b). The Search for Citizenship in Bin Ali's Tunisia: Democracy Versus Unity. *Political Studies, 50*, 497–513.

Sanauddin, N. (2013). A Most Masculine State: Gender, Politics and Religion in Saudi Arabia by Madawi Al-Rasheed. *The Kelvingrove Review, 12.* Available at: http://www.gla.ac.uk/media/media_298317_en.pdf (accessed 29 January 2022).

Schwedler, J. (2012). *The Politics of Protest in Jordan*. Available at: https://www.files.ethz.ch/isn/170149/1701.201203.schwedler.politicsprotestjordan.pdf (accessed 11 January 2022).

Shaapera, S. A. (2015). Evaluating the Social Contract Theoretical Ideas of Jean Jacques Rousseau: An Analytical Perspective on the State and Relevance to Contemporary Society. *African Journal of Political Science and International Relations, 9*(2), 36–41. Available at: http://academicjournals.org/journal/AJPSIR/article-full-text-pdf/99A103649804 (accessed 11 January 2022).

Shehata, D. (2011). The Fall of the Pharoah: How Hosni Mubarak's Reign Came to an End. *Foreign Affairs, 90*(3), 26–32.

Shryock, A. J. (1995). Popular Genealogical Nationalism: History Writing and Identity Among the Balqa Tribes of Jordan. *Comparative Studies in Society and History, 37*(2), 325–357.

Sika, N. (2013). The Arab State and Social Contestation. In *The Evolving Ruling Bargain in the Middle East: Summary Report* (pp. 6–7). Georgetown University Center for International and Regional Studies.

Snider, E. A., & Faris, D. M. (2011). The Arab Spring: U.S. Democracy Promotion in Egypt. *Middle East Policy, 18*(3), 49–62.

Tobin, S. A. (2012a). 'Jordan's Arab Spring: The Middle Class and Anti-Revolution. *Middle East Policy, 19*(1), 96–109.

Steele, D. A. (1993). *A Comparison of Hobbes and Locke on Natural Law and Social Contract*. The University of Texas at Austin. Available at: https://apps.dtic.mil/sti/citations/ADA270299 (accessed 18 January 2022).

Uzzel, J. (2012, November 7). Biopolitics of the Self-Immolation of Mohamed Bouazizi. *E-International Relations*. Available at: http://www.e-ir.info/2012/11/07/biopolitics-of-the-self-immolation-of-mohamed-bouazizi/ (accessed 18 January 2022).

Vajda, G. (2012). Ahl al-Kitab. Bearman, P. et al., *Encyclopedia of Islam*. Available at: https://referenceworks.brillonline.com/entries/encyclopaedia-of-islam-2/ahl-al-kitab-SIM_0383 (accessed 5 January 2022).

Valbjørn, M. (2019). What's so Sectarian About Sectarian Politics? Identity Politics and Authoritarianism in a New Middle East. *Studies in Ethnicity and Nationalism, 19*(1), 127–149.

Vandewalle, D. (1980). Bourguiba, Charismatic Leadership and the Tunisian One Party System. *Middle East Journal, 34*(2), 149–158.

Van Dijk, T. (2003). Discourse, Ideology and Context. *Folia Linguistica, 35*(1–2), 11–40.

Van Dijk, T. (2006a). Ideology and Discourse Analysis. *Journal of Political Ideologies, 11*(2), 114–140.

Van Dijk, T. (2006b). Discourse and Manipulation. *Discourse and Society, 17*(2), 359–383.

Van Leeuwen, T. (2007). Legitimation in Discourse and Communication. *Discourse and Communication, 1*(1), 91–112.

Vogel, F. E. (2008). *Shari'a as Law and Legal System: Changing Perceptions*, The Department of Near Eastern Languages and Civilisation at the University of Washington. Available at: https://nelc.washington.edu/sites/nelc/files/documents/events/2008sharia-frankvogel.pdf (accessed 17 January 2022).

Ware, L. B. (1988). Ben Ali's Constitutional Coup in Tunisia. *Middle East Journal, 42*(4), 587–601.

Webb, A. K. (2017). Resonance of the Arab Spring: Solidarities and Youth Opinion in the Global South. *International Political Science Review, 39*(2), 290–305.

Wehrey, F. (2013). Bahrain's Decade of Discontent. *Journal of Democracy, 24*(3), 116–126.

Winckler, O. (2015). How Many Qataris Nationals Are There? *The Middle East Quarterly, 22*(2). Available at: http://www.meforum.org/5081/how-many-qataris (accessed 2 June 2017).

Yom, S. L., & Gause, F. G., III. (2012). Resilient Royals: How Arab Monarchies Hang On. *Journal of Democracy, 23*(4), 74–88.

Media Reports

ADHRB. (2017). *Bahrain Dissolves Wa'ad, Last Major Opposition Society*. Available at: https://www.adhrb.org/2017/05/bahrain-dissolves-last-major-opposition-society/ (accessed 04 January 2022).

AFP. (2014). *Fearing Backlash, Jordan Asserts Al-Aqsa Custodianship*. Available at: https://www.dailymail.co.uk/wires/afp/article-2836430/Fearing-backlash-Jordan-asserts-Al-Aqsa-custodianship.html (accessed 08 January 2022).

Al Jazeera. (2011a). *Profile: Hosni Mubarak*. Available at: http://www.aljazeera.com/focus/2009/12/200912693048491779.html (accessed 18 January 2022).

Al Jazeera. (2011b). *Timeline: Egypt's Revolution*. Available at: https://www.aljazeera.com/news/middleeast/2011/01/201112515334871490.html (accessed 5 January 2022).

al-Khalidi, S. (2012, November). *Protests Erupt in Jordan After Fuel Prices Rise*. Available at: https://uk.reuters.com/article/uk-jordan-protests-idUKBRE8AD00F20121114 (accessed 10 January 2022).

Arab News. (2018). *Bahrain Elected Among 18 Countries to Join the Human Rights Council by UN General Assembly*. Available at: http://www.arabnews.com/node/1387296/middle-east (accessed 19 January 2022).

Ayres, I., & Macey, J. (2011, February 18). Egypt's Economy and Mubarak's Fall. *Politico*. Available at: http://www.politico.com/story/2011/02/egypts-economy-and-mubaraks-fall-049736 (accessed 12 January 2022).

Aziz, S. F. (2016, May 20). *Egypt's Unsustainable Military Regime.* Available at: https://www.alaraby.co.uk/english/Comment/2016/5/20/Egypts-unsustainable-military-regime (accessed 21 January 2022).

Bahrain News Agency. (2004, December). *King Hamad's Speech: National Day.* Available at: http://www.bna.bh/portal/en/news/380400 (accessed 29 May 2017, no longer online as of 21 January 2022).

BBC. (2003, September 12). *UN Lifts Libya Sanctions.* Available at: http://news.bbc.co.uk/1/hi/world/africa/3102342.stm (accessed 10 January 2022).

BBC. (2011). *Tunisia: President Zine al-Abidine Ben Ali Forced Out.* Available at: https://www.bbc.co.uk/news/world-africa-12195025 (accessed 5 January 2022).

BBC. (2014a, March 3). *Egypt Police Jailed over 2010 Death of Khaled Said.* Available at: http://www.bbc.co.uk/news/world-middle-east-26416964 (accessed 21 January 2022).

BBC. (2014b, August). *Sandhurst's Sheikhs: Why Do So Many Gulf Royals Receive Military Training in the UK?* Available at: http://www.bbc.co.uk/news/magazine-28896860 (accessed 2 January 2022).

BBC. (2016, September 28). *Oman Country Profile.* Available at: http://www.bbc.co.uk/news/world-middle-east-14654150 (accessed 7 January 2022).

BBC. (2017). *Profile: Hosni Mubarak.* Available at: http://www.bbc.co.uk/news/world-middle-east-12301713 (accessed 12 January 2022).

BBC. (2018a). *Bahrain Country Profile.* Available at: https://www.bbc.co.uk/news/world-middle-east-14540571 (accessed 18 January 2022).

BBC. (2018b). *Bahrain Profile—Timeline.* Available at: https://www.bbc.co.uk/news/world-middle-east-14541322 (accessed 24 January 2022).

BBC. (2018c). *Jordan Profile.* Available at: https://www.bbc.co.uk/news/world-middle-east-14636713 (accessed 24 January 2022).

Birnbaum, M., & Warrick, J. (2011). *As Bahrain Stifles Protest Movement, U.S.* Muted Objection Draws Criticism. Available at: https://www.washingtonpost.com/world/as-bahrain-stifles-protest-movement-uss-muted-objections-draw-criticism/2011/04/14/AFziTofD_story.html?utm_term=.6f058ff44a70 (accessed 23 January 2022).

Black, I. (2007). *Fear of a Shia Full Moon.* Available at: https://www.theguardian.com/world/2007/jan/26/worlddispatch.ianblack (accessed 5 December 2021).

Borgognone, S., & Furlow, R. (2018). *The US Must Tell Bahrain's Rulers: It's Time to Reform.* Available at: https://www.defenseone.com/ideas/2018/06/us-must-tell-bahrains-rulers-reform/148984/ (accessed 11 January 2022).

Bradley, M. (2010, December). Political Protests Widen in Egypt. *Wall Street Journal.* Available at: https://www.wsj.com/articles/SB10001424052748703727804576017523474449448 (accessed 24 January 2022).

British Broadcasting Corporation. (2016). *Egypt Country Profile*. Available at: http://www.bbc.co.uk/news/world-africa-13313370; (accessed 26 January 2022).

Bronner, E. (2011, March). *Bahrain Tears Down Monument as Protestors Seethe*. Available at: http://www.nytimes.com/2011/03/19/world/middleeast/19bahrain.html (accessed 7 January 2022).

Brown, N. J. (2011). *Egypt's Constitutional Ghosts*. Available at: https://www.foreignaffairs.com/articles/north-africa/2011-02-15/egypts-constitutional-ghosts (accessed 11 January 2022).

Butler, W. (2011). *Saudi Arabian Intervention in Bahrain Driven by Visceral Sunni Fear of Shias*. Available at: https://www.theguardian.com/world/2011/mar/20/bahrain-saudi-arabia-rebellion (accessed 19 January 2022).

Cavendish, R. (2007). A Failed Coup in Jordan. *History Today, 57*(4). Available at: http://www.historytoday.com/richard-cavendish/failed-coup-jordan (accessed 08 January 2022).

Daraghi, B. (2014). *Former Tunisia President Changed Business Rules to Family's Benefit*. Available at: https://www.ft.com/content/f90e2ac0-a302-11e3-ba21-00144feab7de (accessed 11 January 2022).

Darwesh, G. (2002, February 15). Bahrain Becomes a Kingdom. *Arab News*. Available at: http://www.arabnews.com/node/218544 (accessed 12 January 2022).

Dickinson, E. (2013). *Bahrain Selected as HQ of Arab Court for Human Rights*. Available at: https://www.thenational.ae/world/mena/bahrain-selected-as-hq-of-arab-court-for-human-rights-1.330101 (accessed 19 January 2022).

Driesbach, T., & Joyce, R. (2014, March 27). Revealing Tunisia's Corruption Under Ben Ali. *Al Jazeera*. Available at: http://www.aljazeera.com/indepth/features/2014/03/revealing-tunisia-corruption-under-ben-ali-201432785825560542.html (accessed 03 January 2022).

Due-Gundersen, N. (2020, June 15). Playing Tourist: Impressions of Riyadh, Saudi Arabia During the Coronavirus. *International Policy Digest*. Available at: https://intpolicydigest.org/playing-tourist-impressions-of-riyadh-saudi-arabia-during-the-coronavirus/ (accessed 20 January 2022).

Elmasry, M. (2015, July 3). *Morsi Myths: Re-examining Justifications for Egypt's Coup*. Available at: http://www.middleeasteye.net/columns/myths-about-morsi-examining-justifications-egypt-s-2013-cou-1248467631 (accessed 21 January 2022).

El Masry, S. (2012, October 30). *Egypt's Constitutional Experience*. Available at: https://dailynewsegypt.com/2012/10/30/egypts-constitutional-experience-2/ (accessed 3 January 2022).

Fahim, K. (2011, January 21). Slap to a Man's Pride Set Off Tumult in Tunisia. *The New York Times.* Available at: http://www.nytimes.com/2011/01/22/world/africa/22sidi.html?_r=3&pagewanted=2&src=twrhp (accessed 12 January 2022).

Fahim, K. (2013). Loyalists to Dominate Jordan's New Parliament. Available at: https://www.nytimes.com/2013/01/25/world/middleeast/jordan-elections-favor-government-loyalists.html (accessed 04 January 2022).

Fakkar, G. (2015, January 27). Story Behind the King's Title. *Arab News.* Available at: http://www.arabnews.com/saudi-arabia/news/695351 (accessed 12 January 2022).

Farrell, W. (1981, October 7). *Sadat Assassinated at Army Parade as Men amid Ranks Fire into Stands; Vice President Affirms 'All Treaties'.* Available at: https://www.nytimes.com/1981/10/07/world/sadat-assassinated-army-parade-men-amid-ranks-fire-into-stands-vice-president-041355.html (accessed 09 September 2022).

Farrell, W. (1981a, October 15). *Mubarak, in Tears at Swearing In, Tells Egyptians, "This Is My Fate".* Available at: http://www.nytimes.com/1981/10/15/world/mubarak-in-tears-at-swearing-in-tells-egyptians-this-is-my-fate.html (accessed 12 January 2022).

Farrell, W. (1981b, November 9). *Mubarak Pledges to Improve Living for All Egyptians.* Available at: http://www.nytimes.com/1981/11/09/world/mubarak-pledges-to-improve-living-for-all-egyptians.html (accessed 12 January 2022).

Fukuyama, F. (2012, January 12). The Drive for Dignity. *Foreign Policy.* Available at: http://foreignpolicy.com/2012/01/12/the-drive-for-dignity/ (accessed 17 January 2022).

Gambrell, J. (2018). *Kuwait, Saudi Arabia and UAE Pledge $10B for Bahrain.* Available at: https://www.apnews.com/211c7399b9d843a6a808364fe5fd50d6 (accessed 19 January 2022).

Gavlak, D. (2011, February). *Middle East Protests: Jordan Sees Biggest Reform Rally.* Available at: http://www.bbc.co.uk/news/world-middle-east-12582869 (accessed 10 January 2022).

Ghazal, M. (2016, January) *Population Stands at Around 9.5 Million, Including 2.9 Million Guests.* Available at: http://www.jordantimes.com/news/local/population-stands-around-95-million-including-29-million-guests (accessed 11 January 2022).

Glusac, E. (2009, November 22). A Night, and Day, in Tunisia at a New Resort. *The New York Times.* Available at: http://query.nytimes.com/gst/fullpage.html?res=9F0DE4D81538F931A15752C1A96F9C8B63 (accessed 12 January 2022).

Goldberg, J. (2013, April). *The Modern King in the Arab Spring*. Available at: https://www.theatlantic.com/magazine/archive/2013/04/monarch-in-the-middle/309270/ (accessed 24 January 2022).

Greene, R. L. (2011, February 21). *Saif Qaddafi Pulls a Ben Ali?* Available at: https://www.economist.com/blogs/johnson/2011/02/arabic_dialect (accessed 08 January 2022).

Greenfield, D. (2013). *Optimism After Jordan's Election*. Available at: https://foreignpolicy.com/2013/01/25/optimism-after-jordans-election/ (accessed 15 January 2022).

Global Security. (2016). *Council of Senior Ulema*. Available at: http://www.globalsecurity.org/military/world/gulf/sa-ulama.htm (accessed 13 January 2022).

Haaretz. (2011). *Jordan's King Abdullah Approves Constitutional Reforms*. Available at: https://www.haaretz.com/1.5184945 (accessed 11 January 2022).

Hall, E. (2012). *Year After Arab Spring, Digital, Social Media Shape Region's Rebirth*. Available at: https://adage.com/article/global-news/year-arab-spring-digital-social-media-shape-region-s-rebirth/235259/ (accessed 24 January 2022).

Hartlaub, H. (2014, February). *The Dying Tide of Protests in Jordan*. Available at: http://muftah.org/dying-tide-of-protests-in-jordan/#.WRMmHdLyuM8 (accessed 10 January 2022).

Hiro, D. (2013, August 23). *Analysis: What Do Egypt's Generals Want?* Available at: http://america.aljazeera.com/articles/2013/8/23/what-do-egypt-s-generalswant.html (accessed 21 January 2022).

Jehl, D. (1999). *The King and the "Cabby" Inspect Jordan Incognito*. Available at: https://www.nytimes.com/1999/08/09/world/the-king-and-the-cabby-inspect-jordan-incognito.html (accessed 1 January 2022).

Jordan Times. (2018). Jordan Marks 72nd Independence Anniversary. Available at: http://www.jordantimes.com/news/local/jordan-marks-72nd-independence-anniversary (accessed 11 January 2022).

Kingdom of Bahrain. (2012). *Bahrain Disburses $2.6 Million from Victim's Compensation Fund in First 17 Cases*. Available at: https://www.prnewswire.com/news-releases/bahrain-disburses-26-million-from-victims-compensation-fund-in-first-17-cases-160404545.html (accessed 19 January 2022).

Knell, Y. (2013). *The Complicated Legacy of Egypt's Hosni Mubarak*. Available at: https://www.bbc.co.uk/news/world-middle-east-21201364 (accessed 04 January 2022).

Lower, M. (2013). *Abdullah Appears Not to Have Taken to the Crown the Way His Father Did*. Available at: https://yourmiddleeast.com/2013/08/01/abdullah-appears-not-to-have-taken-to-the-crown-the-way-his-father-did/ (accessed 9 January 2022).

Luck, T., & Warrick, J. (2012). Jordan Hit with More Protests, Work Stoppages Over Fuel Price Hikes. *Washington Post*. Available online at: https://www.washingtonpost.com/world/middle_east/jordan-hit-with-more-protests-work-stoppages-over-fuel-price-hikes/2012/11/14/7adc28ce-2e63-11e2-beb2-4b4cf5087636_story.html (accessed 9 September 2022).

McClatchy Newspapers. (2011). *Tunisian President Ben Ali Flees Country as Thousands Protest*. Available at: https://www.mcclatchydc.com/news/special-reports/article24607879.html (accessed 10 January 2022).

McEvers, K. (2012, January). *Bahrain: The Revolution That Wasn't*. Available at: http://www.npr.org/2012/01/05/144637499/bahrain-the-revolution-that-wasnt (accessed 8 January 2022).

McGreal, C., & Shenker, J. (2011). *Hosni Mubarak Resigns—And Egypt Celebrates a New Dawn*. Available at: https://www.theguardian.com/world/2011/feb/11/hosni-mubarak-resigns-egypt-cairo (accessed 04 January 2022).

Meky, S. (2014, January 25). *Remembering Khaled Saeed, Whose Death Sparked Egypt's Revolution*. Available at: http://english.alarabiya.net/en/perspective/features/2014/01/25/Khaled-Saeed-Egypt-s-Jan-25-icon-remembered-unlike-before.html (accessed 21 January 2022).

Middle East Eye. (2017, May). *Bahrain Heading for 'Total Suppression' with Secular Group Ban*. Available at: http://www.middleeasteye.net/news/secular-bahrain-opposition-group-says-it-has-been-dissolved-566223564 (accessed 8 January 2022).

Miller, E. (2013, March 19). *King Abdullah Chides Atlantic Interviewer*. Available at: http://www.timesofisrael.com/king-abdullah-chides-atlantic-interviewer/ (accessed 05 January 2022).

Murad, N. (2014, February). *Here Is How Jordan Escaped the Arab Spring*. Available at: https://www.aljazeera.com/opinions/2014/2/9/here-is-how-jordan-escaped-the-arab-spring (accessed 10 January 2022).

Nafaa, H. (2010, May 10). *An Alternative Mubarak May Day Speech*. Available at: http://www.egyptindependent.com/opinion/alternative-mubarak-may-day-speech (accessed 19 January 2022).

Nazer, F. (2013). "Saudi Code" Prevents Arab Spring in Kingdom. *Al-Monitor*. Available at: https://www.al-monitor.com/originals/2013/02/saudi-arabia-arab-spring-king-abdullah-saudi-code.html (accessed 09 September 2021).

News, A. (2002, March 20). Despite 11/9, Tourism Up in Morocco and Tunisia. *Afrol News*. Available at: http://www.afrol.com/News2002/mor004_tun_tourism.htm (accessed 12 January 2022).

New York Times. (2014, May 21). Hosni Mubarak's Path from Presidency to Prison and Beyond. Available at: https://www.nytimes.com/interactive/2013/08/21/world/middleeast/Mubarak_timeline.html (accessed 10 January 2022).

Press TV Doc. (2016). *Ben Ali: The Black Books* [film]. Available at: https://www.youtube.com/watch?v=xG50BvGQX9g (last accessed 30 January 2022).

Regencia, T. (2018). *Clashes Mark Anniversary of Bahrain's 2011 Uprising.* Available at: https://www.aljazeera.com/news/2018/02/clashes-mark-anniversary-bahrain-2011-uprising-180214075612644.html (accessed 23 January 2022).

Reuters. (2011). *Bahrain Announces Fund to Pay Crackdown Victims.* Available at: https://english.ahram.org.eg/NewsContentP/2/21922/World/Bahrain-announces-fund-to-pay-crackdown-victims.aspx (accessed 19 January 2022).

Royal Hashemite Court. (2001a). *The Great Arab Revolt.* Available at: http://www.kinghussein.gov.jo/his_arabrevolt.html (accessed 05 January 2022).

Royal Hashemite Court. (2001b). *The Making of Transjordan.* Available at: http://www.kinghussein.gov.jo/his_transjordan.html (accessed 05 January 2022).

Ryan, Y. (2011, January 20). The Tragic Life of a Street Vendor. *Al Jazeera.* Available at: http://www.aljazeera.com/indepth/features/2011/01/2011 11684242518839.html (accessed 12 January 2022).

Saab, B. Y. (2018). *Relocating the Fifth Fleet?* Available at: https://www.the-american-interest.com/2018/08/22/relocating-the-fifth-fleet/ (accessed 18 January 2022).

Said, E. (2001). *Islam and the West Are Inadequate Banners.* Available at: https://www.theguardian.com/world/2001/sep/16/september11.terrorism3 (accessed 26 January 2022).

Said, W. M. (2018). *Jordan's Role Over Holy Sites in East Jerusalem Legal and Sovereignty Related.* Available at: http://www.jordantimes.com/opinion/walid-m-sadi/jordans-role-over-holy-sites-east-jerusalem-legal%C2%A0and-sovereignty-related (accessed 08 January 2022).

Schaer, C. (2021). How Stable is Jordan Really? *DW News.* Available at: https://www.dw.com/en/how-stable-is-jordan-really/a-57106768 (accessed 9 September 2022).

Shah, D. (2011, December 26). *Arab Spring: "It Was the First Time I Felt I Belonged".* BBC. Available at: http://www.bbc.co.uk/news/world-middle-east-16275176 (accessed 12 January 2022).

Shehabi, A. (2013). *Bahrain's Sovereign Hypocrisy.* Available at: https://foreignpolicy.com/2013/08/14/bahrains-sovereign-hypocrisy/ (accessed 3 January 2022).

Stead, R. (2018). *Jordan Has a Duty to Defend Jerusalem and Al-Aqsa.* Available at: https://www.middleeastmonitor.com/20180714-jordan-has-a-duty-to-defend-jerusalem-and-al-aqsa/ (accessed 08 January 2022).

Thames TV. (1972). *King Hussein of Jordan—Interview* [film]. Available at: https://www.youtube.com/watch?v=rCYJchah3kY (accessed 08 January 2022).

The Economist. (2003, April). Jordan's Secret Police: Behave, or Else. Available at: http://www.economist.com/node/1682805 (accessed 08 January 2022).

The Economist. (2016). The Arab Revolt. Available at: https://www.economist.com/the-economist-explains/2016/06/03/the-arab-revolt (accessed 08 January 2022).

Trade Arabia. (2012). *Bahrain Creates $26.5 Billion Fund for Unrest Victims*. Available at: http://www.tradearabia.com/news/law_214192.html (accessed 19 January 2022).

United Press International. (1985, May). *Car Bomber Fails in Attempt to Kill Leader of Kuwait*. Available at: https://www.nytimes.com/1985/05/26/world/car-bomber-fails-in-attempt-to-kill-leader-of-kuwait.html (accessed 23 January 2022).

Voice of America. (2011, August). *Facebook Becomes Divisive in Bahrain*. Available at: https://www.voanews.com/a/facebook-becomes-divisive-in-bahrain-127958073/143943.html (accessed 7 January 2022).

Warren, J. (2012). *Jordanian Protestors, Police Scuffle as Amman Demonstrations Continue*. Available at: https://www.washingtonpost.com/world/middle_east/jordanian-protesters-police-scuffle-as-amman-demonstrations-continue/2012/11/16/b8d93532-2ff7-11e2-a30e-5ca76eeec857_story.html?noredirect=on&utm_term=.6b0d18e3b4ab (accessed 15 January 2022).

Whitaker, B. (2011). *Bahrainis Cannot Be Subdued Forever*. Available at: https://www.theguardian.com/commentisfree/2011/mar/17/bahrain-saudi-intervention-sectarian-conflict-protests (accessed 3 January 2022).

Williams, S. E. (2017, February). *Jordan Austerity: Despite Rising Prices and Anger, Protests Limited*. Available at: http://www.middleeasteye.net/news/jordan-austerity-rally-amman-1693526432 (accessed 10 January 2022).

Zurayk, R. (2011, July 17). *Use Your Loaf: Why Food Prices Were Crucial in the Arab Spring*. Available at: https://www.theguardian.com/lifeandstyle/2011/jul/17/bread-food-arab-spring (accessed 06 January 2022).

Printed/Online Books

Arneson, R. J. (2004). Democracy Is Not Intrinsically Just. In K. Dowding, R. E. Goodin, & C. Pateman (Eds.), *Justice and Democracy* (pp. 40–59). Cambridge University Press.

Austin, J. L. (1962). *How to Do Things with Words: The William James Lectures Delivered at Harvard University in 1955*. Oxford University Press.

Brown, L. C. (2000). *Religion and State: The Muslim Approach to Politics*. Columbia University Press.

Brown, N. J. (2001). *Constitutions in a Nonconstitutional World: Arab Basic Laws and the Prospects for Accountable Government*. SUNY Series in Middle Eastern Studies. State University of New York Press.

Chorin, E. (2012). *Exit the Colonel: The Hidden History of the Libyan Revolution*. Public Affairs.

Coicaud, J. M. (2002). *Legitimacy and Politics: A Contribution to the Study of Political Right and Responsibility*. Cambridge University Press.

El-Haj, A. M., Grote, R., & Röder, T. J. (Eds.). (2016). *Constitutionalism, Human Rights and Islam After the Arab Spring*. Oxford University Press.

Freer, C. (2018). *Rentier Islamism: The Influence of the Muslim Brotherhood in Gulf Monarchies*. Oxford University Press.

Fotion, N. (2000). *John Searle*. Acumen Publishing Limited.

Gaddafi, M. (1999). *Escape to Hell and Other Stories*. Blake Publishing.

Gaddafi, M. (2016). *Other Books by Muammar Al Gaddafi—The Escape to Hell*. Available at: http://algaddafi.org/booksbymuammaralgaddafi/books-by-muammar-al-gaddafi—the-escape-to-hell (accessed 12 January 2022).

Gee, J. P. (2005). *An Introduction to Discourse Analysis: Theory and Method* (2nd ed.). Routledge.

Hobbes, T. (2014). A Secular Defense of Absolutism. In M. Perry (Ed.), *Sources of the Western Tradition* (Vol. II, pp. 20–23). Wadsworth.

Korany, B. (2014). A Microcosm of the Arab Spring: Sociology of Tahrir Square. In B. Korany (Ed.), *Beyond the Arab Spring: The Evolving Ruling Bargain in the Middle East* (pp. 249–276). Oxford University Press.

Menshawy, M. (2017). *State, Memory, and Egypt's Victory in the 1973 War: Ruling by Discourse*. Palgrave Macmillan.

Peter, F. (2009). Democratic Legitimacy Without Collective Rationality. In B. de Bruin & C. F. Zurn (Eds.), *New Waves in Political Philosophy* (pp. 143–158). Palgrave Macmillan.

Peter, F. (2012). Authority and Legitimacy. In G. Gaus & F. D'Agostino (Eds.), *Routledge Companion to Social and Political Philosophy* (pp. 596–608). Routledge.

Raz, J. (2009). *Between Authority and Interpretation: On the Theory of Law and Practical Reason*. Oxford University Press.

Reich, B. (1990). *Political Leaders of the Contemporary Middle East and North Africa: A Biographical Dictionary*. Greenwood Press Inc.

Searle, J. (1965). What Is a Speech Act? In M. Black (Ed.), *Philosophy in America* (pp. 221–239). Allen and Unwin.

Shahrur, M. (2009). Chapter One: Al-Islam and Al-Iman. In D. F. Eickelman (Ed.), *The Qur'an, Morality and Critical Reason: The Essential Muhammad Shahrur* (pp. 21–71). Brill.

Sultany, N. (2017). *Law and Revolution: Legitimacy and Constitutionalism After the Arab Spring*. Oxford Constitutional Theory. Oxford University Press.

Weber, M., & Gerth, H. H. (Eds.). (2009). *From Max Weber: Essays in Sociology*. Routledge Classics in Sociology. Routledge.

Whrey, F. (2014). Bahrain's Decade of Discontent. In L. Diamond & M. F. Plattner (Eds.), *Democratization and Authoritarianism in the Arab World* (pp.315–326, p. 322). Johns Hopkins University Press.

International Organization Reports

2015. *Apart in Their Own Land: Government Discrimination Against Shia in Bahrain-Volume I: Violence, Political Disclusion, and Attacks on the Shia Religious Establishment*. Americans for Democracy and Human Rights in Bahrain (ADHRB).

Amnesty International. (2016, March). *Bahrain: Alarming Spike in Expulsion of Citizens Arbitrarily Stripped of Their Nationality*. Available at: https://www.amnesty.org/en/latest/news/2016/03/bahrain-alarming-spike-in-expulsion-of-citizens-arbitrarily-stripped-of-their-nationality/ (accessed 8 January 2022).

Amnesty International. (2020). *Bahrain 2020*. Available at: https://www.amnesty.org/en/countries/middle-east-and-north-africa/bahrain/report-bahrain/ (accessed 19 January 2022).

Arieff, A. (2011). *Political Transition in Tunisia*. Congressional Research Service.

Besch, S., et al. (2016). *Europe After Brexit: Unleashed or Undone?* Centre for European Reform. Available at: https://www.cer.org.uk/sites/default/files/pb_euafterBrexit_15april16.pdf (accessed 16 January 2022).

Brumberg, D. (2005). *Democratization Versus Liberalization in the Arab World: Dilemmas and Challenges for U.S. Foreign Policy*. The Strategic Studies Institute.

Brumberg, D. (2012). Sustaining Mechanics of Arab Autocracies. *Arab Uprisings: The Arab Monarchy Debate* (POMEPS Briefings, 16).

Central Intelligence Agency. (2017). *Egypt*. Available at: https://www.cia.gov/library/publications/the-world-factbook/geos/eg.html (accessed 30 January 2022).

CIA World Factbook. (2017). *Middle East: Bahrain*. Available at: https://www.cia.gov/library/publications/resources/the-world-factbook/geos/print_ba.html (accessed 2 January 2022).

Crisis Group. (2018). *On the Politics Behind Tunisia's Protests*. Available at: https://www.crisisgroup.org/middle-east-north-africa/north-africa/tunisia/politics-behind-tunisias-protests (accessed 10 January 2022).

El-Sherif, A. (2014). *Egypt's Post-Mubarak Predicament*. Available at: https://carnegieendowment.org/files/post_mubarak_predicament.pdf (accessed 6 January 2022).

Freedom House. (2021). *Bahrain*. Available online at: https://freedomhouse.org/country/bahrain/freedom-world/2021 (accessed 9 September 2022).

Freedom House. (2022). *Bahrain*. Available at: https://freedomhouse.org/country/bahrain/freedom-world/2021 (accessed 11 January 2022).

Glynos, J., et al. (2009). *Discourse Analysis: Varieties and Methods.* ESCRC National Centre for Research Methods Review Paper. ESRC National Centre for Research Methods.

Grewal, S. (2016). *A Quiet Revolution: The Military After Ben Ali.* Carnegie Middle East Center.

Hawthorne, E. (2016). *The Strangely Stable Kingdom of Jordan.* Available at: https://worldview.stratfor.com/article/strangely-stable-kingdom-jordan (accessed 15 January 2022).

Henderson, S. (2017). *Beyond Islamists and Autocrats: Bahrain's Stalled Reforms and the Future U.S. Role.* Available at: https://www.washingtoninstitute.org/policy-analysis/bahrains-stalled-reforms-and-future-us-role (accessed 1 January 2022).

Human Rights Watch/Middle East. (1997). *Jordan: Clamping Down on Critics-Human Rights Violations in Advance of the Parliamentary Elections.* Available at: https://www.hrw.org/reports/1997/jordan/JORDAN97.pdf (accessed 08 January 2022).

Kartveit, K., & Jumbert, M. G. (2014). *Civil-Military Relations in the Middle East: A Literature Review* (Chr. Michelsen Institute Working Paper 5).

Khalaf, A. (2008). *Bahrain's Parliament: The Quest for a Role.* Available at: https://carnegieendowment.org/sada/21282 (accessed 11 January 2022).

Mabon, S. (2012). *The Battle for Bahrain: Iranian-Saudi Rivalry.* Available at: http://www.mepc.org/battle-bahrain-iranian-saudi-rivalry (accessed 8 January 2022).

Magen, A. (2013). *The Crisis of Governance in the Middle East: Implications for Democracy, Development and Security.* International Institute for Counter-Terrorism (ICT).

Mattelaer, A., & Severs, E. (2014). *A Crisis of Democratic Legitimacy? It's About Legitimation, Stupid!* (European Policy Brief, 14). Egmont Royal Institute for International Relations.

Oxford Business Group. (2017). *Qatar Remains a Leading Player in Oil and Gas.* Available at: https://www.oxfordbusinessgroup.com/overview/market-share-matters-despite-global-price-volatility-country-remains-leading-player-oil-and-gas (accessed 2 January 2022).

Raphaeli, N. (2003). The Grooming of Gamal Husni Mubarak. *Inquiry & Analysis, 141.* Available at: https://www.memri.org/reports/grooming-gamal-husni-mubarak (accessed 29 January 2022).

Stratfor, LLC. (2017). *Bahrain's Importance to the United States.* Available at: https://www.stratfor.com/image/bahrains-importance-united-states (accessed 2 June 2017, offline as of 20 January 2022).

Thaler, D. (2004). The Middle East: The Cradle of the Muslim World. In *The Muslim World After 9/11* (pp. 69–144). RAND Corporation.

The Carter Center. (2014). *The Constitution-Making Process in Tunisia*. Available at: https://www.cartercenter.org/resources/pdfs/news/peace_publications/democracy/tunisia-constitution-making-process.pdf (accessed 11 January 2022).

Tobin, S. A. (2012). *Jordan's Arab Spring: The Middle Class and Anti-revolution*. Available at: http://www.mepc.org/jordans-arab-spring-middle-class-and-anti-revolution (accessed 11 January 2022).

UNHCR. (1999). Freedom in the World 1999 – Bahrain. *Refworld*. Available at: https://www.refworld.org/category,COI,FREEHOU,,BHR,5278c8e3b,0.html (accessed 9 September 2022).

UNHCR. (2007). *Iraqis in Jordan: Their Number and Characteristics*. Available at: https://www.unhcr.org/455443a80.pdf (accessed 11 January 2022).

U.S. Energy Information Administration. (2016a). *Bahrain*. Available at: https://www.eia.gov/beta/international/country.cfm?iso=BHR (accessed 2 January 2022).

U.S. Energy Information Administration. (2016b). *Kuwait*. Available at: https://www.eia.gov/beta/international/country.cfm?iso=KWT (accessed 2 January 2022).

Wahba, M. M. (2017). *GCC: A Force for Regional Stability*. Available at: https://agsiw.org/gcc-force-regional-stability/ (accessed 18 January 2022).

World Bank. (2015). *Population, Total*. Available at: http://data.worldbank.org/indicator/SP.POP.TOTL?locations=KW-BH-QA (accessed 2 January 2022).

Social Media

Facebook. (2017). *We Are All Khaled Said*. Available at: https://www.facebook.com/elshaheeed.co.uk?filter=3 (accessed 08 April 2022).

Index

A

activists, 45, 51, 62, 64–67, 69, 128, 165
'adl
  religion, 25, 155, 171
Aid, 47, 50, 52, 55, 62, 75, 80, 87, 90, 100, 101, 115, 138, 139, 167
al-Khalifas
  monarchies, 60, 64–66, 69, 70, 99, 100, 124, 125, 137, 162, 191
Al-Sabah
  monarchies, 5, 6
Armed Forces, 23, 44, 46, 71–74, 77, 84, 85, 87, 89, 93, 101, 122, 123, 168, 201
'asabiyya, 39, 40, 99
austerity, 47, 48, 52
Ayoob
  religion, 26, 118, 161

B

Barrakat Essahel Affair, 45, 89, 92, 93
Beneficial Consequences, 10, 11, 13–15, 18, 59, 73, 96, 115, 121, 122, 129, 131, 132, 134, 135, 139, 151, 158, 163, 170, 172, 175, 179, 189, 195
Black September, 43–45
Bouazizi, Mohamed, 20, 51, 68, 83, 93
Brown, L.C., 21, 22, 28, 117, 151, 166
Brown, N.J., 26, 94, 165
Bulliet, R.W., 14, 16, 18, 23, 27, 118, 130, 149, 161, 167

C

Caliph
  religion, 17, 24
constitutions, 7, 29, 94, 111, 142, 156, 176, 182, 190–192

D

democracy, 10, 12, 30, 38, 47, 90, 91, 93, 95, 101, 170, 171

E

East Bank, 42, 45, 48, 99, 100, 113, 151
employment
  Arab Spring, 15, 45, 52, 171, 174, 180

F

fitna, 3, 26, 27, 117, 118, 139, 150, 151, 154, 156, 179–181, 190, 199

N. Due-Gundersen, *Non-Democratic Legitimacy During the Arab Spring*, https://doi.org/10.1007/978-3-031-11882-1

G

Gaddafi, Muammar, 19–21, 29, 31, 87, 90
GCC
  Gulf, 16, 58, 59, 65, 68, 101, 121, 122, 124, 126, 158, 160, 162, 163, 178

I

Ikhwan, 43, 46, 76–79, 83
imam
  religion, 9
International Monetary Fund (IMF), 47, 48, 51, 52, 80–82, 90
invasion of Iraq, 49, 51, 57
Iran, 3, 57, 66, 67, 69, 122, 123, 126, 127, 137, 157, 164, 206
Iranian, 3, 64, 66, 67, 69, 70, 100, 126, 206
Islamic law
  religion, 10, 14, 17, 18, 22, 24, 25, 27, 29, 80, 130, 149, 155, 161, 167, 170
Islamist(s)
  religion, 29, 31, 47, 49, 61, 63, 76, 78–81, 84, 88, 91, 93, 99
Israel, 42, 43, 47, 49, 72, 113

K

King Hussein
  monarchies, 40, 42–45, 52, 58, 113
Kuwait, 2, 5, 58, 67, 127

L

Libya, 4, 6, 19–21, 52, 87, 90

M

majlis, 13, 61, 64, 114, 159, 180
MBS
  Saudi Arabia, 1
Mecca, 17, 39, 42
monarchies, 1, 6, 7, 12, 13, 38, 55, 70, 71, 93–101, 114, 126, 127, 137–142, 158, 159, 179, 180, 183, 190, 191, 194
Muhammad bin Salman
  Saudi Arabia, 1
mukhabarat, 38, 44–46, 48, 49, 53, 93, 101, 115, 116, 148, 149
Muslim Brotherhood, 29, 43, 46, 47, 49, 61, 62, 75–79, 81, 83, 91, 131, 151, 165

N

nationalism, 39–43, 45, 46, 50, 76, 77, 79, 85, 140, 170
9/11, 30, 49, 50, 52, 79, 91

O

oil, 3, 6, 11, 20, 21, 30, 38, 50, 52, 54–60, 65, 68, 70, 71, 95, 96, 98, 115, 122, 125, 128, 142, 152, 159, 161, 163, 164, 179, 182, 190, 191
Oman, 58
Ottoman, 28, 39

P

Palestinian Liberation Organization (PLO), 43
Palestinians, 42, 44, 45, 49, 62, 99, 113, 114, 150

parliament, 12, 13, 40, 46–48, 50, 60–64, 70, 77, 94, 99, 100, 114, 139, 159
paternalism
  non-democratic, 10, 15, 92, 113, 117, 120, 128–133, 136, 137, 165, 177, 180
patronage, 3, 40, 47, 50, 52, 54, 97, 100, 113, 153
Peninsula Shield Force
  Gulf, 4, 70, 101, 123, 125–127, 138, 158, 162, 163, 178, 205
Peter, Fabienne, 10–16, 18, 19, 30, 114, 117, 119, 121, 123, 124, 126–131, 133–135, 138, 148, 152, 153, 157, 159, 163, 167, 170, 171, 173, 178
political persuasion, 4, 5, 7
Political Quietism
  religion, 26–29, 117, 166
Popular Front for the Liberation of Palestine (PFLP), 44
Prophet Muhammad
  religion, 25, 26, 39, 40, 55, 98–100, 117–119, 139, 141, 149, 164, 179

R

reforms, 3, 4, 20, 55, 60, 63, 64, 70, 80, 93, 97, 101, 118, 119, 121, 122, 125, 127, 129, 130, 135–142, 155, 167, 171, 173, 175
religion, 1, 6, 7, 9, 14, 16, 18, 19, 21, 23, 26–28, 38–40, 55, 73, 76, 77, 86, 91, 97–100, 112, 113, 124, 128, 130, 133, 136, 137, 139, 140, 142, 149, 155, 156, 161, 163, 164, 167, 179, 181, 189–191
Religious Legitimacy
  religion, 7, 14, 16, 18, 19, 39, 40, 55, 56, 67, 73, 85, 96, 97, 100, 111, 113, 114, 116–120, 128, 136, 140, 142, 156, 179, 181, 189–192, 194
rentier
  oil, 11, 40, 47, 54, 55, 97, 101
'resilient royals'
  monarchies, 6
ruling bargain, 6, 7, 10, 11, 13, 15, 21, 25–30, 37, 38, 47, 50, 52, 54–56, 59, 60, 68, 71–73, 85, 92, 95–98, 100, 111–115, 177–183, 189–191, 194, 195

S

Sandhurst, 58
Saudi Arabia, 1, 2, 21, 23, 41, 42, 58, 60, 66, 67, 69, 95, 101, 118, 123, 127, 135, 141
Sectarianism, 10, 56, 61, 63, 64, 101, 127, 164, 189
security
  ruling bargain, 3, 5, 6, 14, 21, 30, 39, 40, 45, 48, 50, 53–56, 65, 68–71, 85, 87, 89, 93, 95, 100, 101, 115, 118–124, 126–131, 134, 136, 137, 139–141, 150, 157–160, 162, 163, 170, 175, 178, 179, 189–191
September 11th, 20, 30, 49, 79, 90
Shari'a
  religion, 25
Shia'a, 4, 57, 60–63, 66–70, 98–100, 124, 126, 127, 137, 162, 191
social contract
  ruling bargain, 11, 12, 14, 15, 25, 27, 30, 38, 40, 42, 47, 48, 72, 74, 77, 78, 80, 82, 83, 95, 113, 115, 117, 122, 125, 137, 140, 149–151, 153, 170, 175, 177, 191
social media, 2, 65, 66

socio-economic benefits
ruling bargain, 7, 25, 42, 47, 115, 125, 190
sons and daughters
paternalism, 3, 11, 15, 20, 113, 128, 137, 202, 206
Speech Acts, 4, 111, 133, 139, 147
subsidies, 6, 13, 40, 47, 51, 59, 60, 68, 72, 75, 79, 80, 83, 85, 97, 115, 119, 131, 134, 136, 152, 161, 164, 166, 173, 175, 176, 182, 189, 191, 199
Sultan
religion, 18, 24, 58
Sunni, 4, 22, 23, 60–64, 66–68, 98, 99, 101, 124, 126, 127, 137, 158, 160, 162, 178, 191
Syria, 51, 52, 113, 118, 191
Syrians, 52, 54

T
traditionalism
monarchies, 6, 13, 37, 39, 55, 71, 73, 96, 139, 140, 142, 180, 182, 183, 191, 194
tribalism, 39–41, 45, 48, 115, 141
tribe(s), 28, 38, 40–42, 54, 55, 99, 101

U
ulema
religion, 22–25
utilitarian
non-democratic, 10, 11, 19, 121, 152, 159, 175, 177, 179

V
Victims Compensation Fund
bahrain, 4, 122, 125, 127, 160, 161, 163, 164, 179, 189, 190, 204
Visions, 3

W
War on Terror, 31, 49, 79, 91
Weber, M., 13, 96, 141, 148, 154, 157, 164, 166–168, 172, 173, 176, 179, 181, 182
welfare, 4, 6, 7, 11, 13, 16, 43, 51, 55, 59, 68, 70, 72, 75, 76, 78, 80, 83, 95, 96, 123, 125, 137, 142, 159–161, 163, 164, 166, 179, 180, 182, 189–191
West Bank, 42, 50, 98, 99, 151

Ingram Content Group UK Ltd.
Milton Keynes UK
UKHW012100050723
424591UK00001B/49

9 783031 118838